WORLD HISTORY

This edition published by Parragon in 2011
Parragon
Queen Street House
4 Queen Street
Bath BA1 1HE, UK
www.parragon.com

Authors: Anita Ganeri, Hazel Mary Martell, Brian Williams
Consultant: Andrew Robertshaw
This edition produced by Tall Tree Ltd, London

ISBN 978-1-4454-4648-6
Printed in China

WORLD HISTORY

Parragon

Bath • New York • Singapore • Hong Kong • Cologne • Delhi
Melbourne • Amsterdam • Johannesburg • Auckland • Shenzhen

Contents

The History of the World

What is history? In its broadest sense, history is the story of people – the study of our past. Some historians look at important events, such as wars, revolutions and governments, while others are interested in ordinary people's lives. Our lives today are shaped by decisions and actions made decades, centuries or even thousands of years ago. By understanding the past, we may be able to gain a more balanced view of the present.

The basic aims of history are to record and explain our past. Historians study a range of written and oral (spoken) evidence. Combined with archaeology (the study of things people have left behind them, such as buildings and objects), historians interpret the facts to build up a picture of the past.

The first people to study history seriously were the ancient Greeks. In the 5th century BC, the Greek historian Herodotus (known as 'the Father of History') set out to write a true and systematic record of the wars between the Greeks and the Persians. He hoped to preserve the memory of past events and show how two peoples came into conflict with one another.

The scientific study of archaeology only really began in the 18th century. Archaeologists today investigate the tiniest fragments to help create a more complete picture of the past.

Interpreting the evidence is the most fascinating part of an historian's or archaeologist's job. But historians must always be aware of bias or prejudice in the things that they read or write. Bias means being influenced by a particular point of view, while prejudice means 'judging before' – before you have all the facts.

Historians are also influenced by the times in which they live. Modern historians try to avoid applying the values of the present to their interpretations of the past.

History is not just concerned with the distant past. It is the story of our lives – what is news today will be history tomorrow. Change can be sudden and dramatic, and long-held ideas may be overturned.

The Ancient World

p12 A stone hand axe with chips removed to sharpen it.

p21 A clay tablet shows an early form of writing called cuneiform.

p24 A stone statue found in the ruins of Mohenjo Daro.

p36 Socrates was one of the most influential philosophers.

p43 Christianity became Rome's official religion in AD 391.

p22 Hieroglyphics was the system of picture-writing used in ancient Egypt.

The vast period of time from 2.5 million years ago to AD 500 saw the appearance of the first human beings and the creation of the first civilizations. Our earliest ancestors appeared in Africa some 2.5 million years ago, having evolved from man-apes who came down from the trees and learned to walk upright on two legs.

Over thousands of years, people learned how to make fire to keep themselves warm and to cook their food, how to hunt and how to make tools. The first-ever metal tools and weapons were made in the Middle East about 7,000 years ago.

Throughout the world, early people lived by hunting animals and gathering wild fruit, roots and nuts to eat. By 10,000 years ago, however, an extraordinary change was taking place. People learned how to grow their own crops on patches of land and to raise their own animals for food. For the first time in history, people began to build permanent homes, followed by towns and cities.

p42 Julius Caesar was a brilliant Roman general who defeated his rivals in Rome and became dictator.

By about 5000 BC, the world's first civilizations began to emerge along the banks of rivers where the land was extremely rich for farming. The Sumerians, Assyrians and Babylonians built magnificent cities and temples on the fertile plains between the Tigris and Euphrates rivers. The ancient Egyptians flourished along the river Nile. By about 500 BC, important civilizations had also appeared in India, China, Persia and in North and South America.

The great age of ancient Greece and Rome is known as the Classical period. These two mighty civilizations played a major role in shaping the modern world. From Greece came discoveries in politics, philosophy and science. These were spread farther afield by the Greek conqueror Alexander the Great, and by the Romans, who were great admirers of Greek culture and knowledge.

The Romans added achievements of their own and, by the 1st century AD, they ruled over the most powerful empire ever seen. However, by AD 500 their empire had fallen and the Middle Ages had begun.

p29 The Chinese philosopher Confucius was born in about 551 BC, at a time when wars were frequent. He dedicated his life to teaching people how to live in peace. His teachings formed the basis of the Chinese civil service up to the beginning of the 20th century.

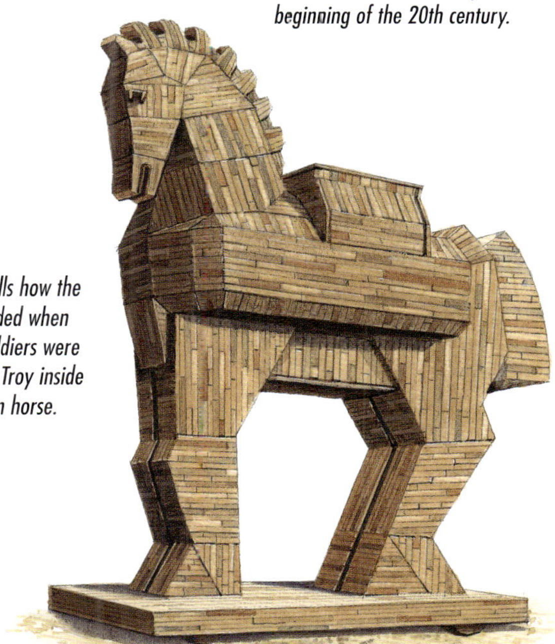

p27 Legend tells how the Trojan War ended when Mycenaean soldiers were smuggled into Troy inside a huge wooden horse.

p22 Egyptian farmers at work in their fields. The farmers' year was governed by the flooding of the river Nile. When the flood made farmwork impossible, farmers were sent to work on the royal buildings.

c. 4 million years ago
Australopithecus (meaning 'southern ape') appear in Africa. They walk upright on two legs instead of on all fours.

c. 2.5–1.5 million years ago
Homo habilis ('handy man') appear in Africa. They are the first people to make and use tools.

c. 1.5 million years ago
Homo erectus ('upright man') appear in Africa. They are the first people to spread out of Africa.

c. 120,000 years ago
The Neanderthals, a sub-species of *Homo sapiens* ('wise man'), appear in Africa, Asia and Europe. They are the first humans to bury their dead.

c. 35,000 years ago
Homo sapiens sapiens (modern humans) are living in many parts of the world, including Australia.

c. 30,000 years ago
The Neanderthals die out as modern humans appear in Asia and Europe.

c. 20,000 years ago
Modern humans have crossed from Asia into the Americas.

The First Humans

There has been life on Earth for some 4 billion years, but the first human-like creatures appeared about 7 million years ago. These 'man-apes' came down from the trees in which they had lived, like other primates. They walked on two legs and learned how to use tools.

A set of Australopithecine footprints *was found by Mary Leakey in 1978, preserved in volcanic ash at Laetoli, Tanzania. It showed that early hominids walked upright on two legs.*

The Toumai skull found in Chad, in Africa, in 2002 may be from the oldest human-like creature known. Some scientists think it is 7 million years old. The oldest fossil dates from about 4 million years ago, when the Australopithecines lived in Africa. The most complete skeleton of an *Australopithecus* was found in Ethiopia in 1974. The individual, nicknamed 'Lucy', died about 3 million years ago, aged about 40. She was as tall as a 10-year-old human.

As early people evolved, *they gradually became less like apes and more like humans. They developed larger brains, and bodies designed for walking upright, with longer legs than arms. Standing upright left their hands free for using tools and weapons.*

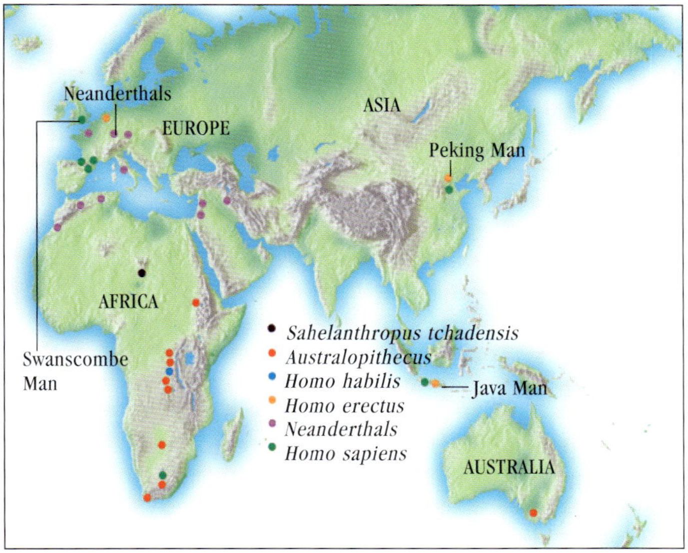

This map shows *the location of important fossil remains of early hominids and humans.* Homo erectus *was the first great colonizer, spreading out of Africa. Scientists still argue whether* Homo sapiens *first appeared in Africa or developed in other parts of the world.*

FIRE

People first made fire by striking two flints together. Fire gave them protection from wild animals, allowed them to cook food, and provided heat and light.

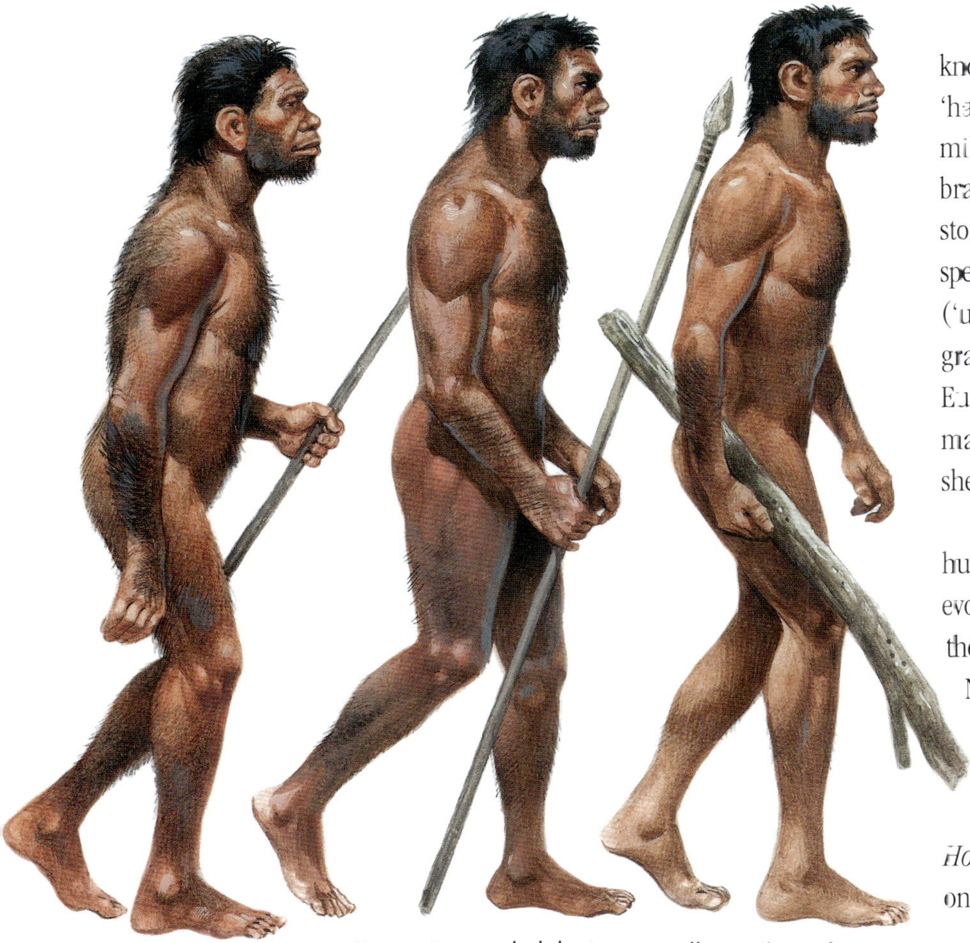

Homo erectus   Homo sapiens neanderthalensis   Homo sapiens sapiens

The first true human beings, known as *Homo habilis* (Latin for 'handy man'), appeared about 2.5 million years ago. They had bigger brains and made tools from sticks and stones. A million years later another species, known as *Homo erectus* ('upright man') had appeared and gradually spread out of Africa into Europe and Asia. These early humans made better tools (for hunting), built shelters and also used fire.

Many scientists believe that modern humans, *Homo sapiens* ('wise man'), evolved from these hominids. Two of these human species lived side by side: Neanderthal people and modern people. However, by about 20,000 years ago the Neanderthals had died out, and modern humans, *Homo sapiens sapiens*, were living on all of the continents.

Making Tools

c. 2 million–12,000 years ago The Old Stone (Palaeolithic) Age. First stone tools made.
From 12,000 years ago The Middle Stone (Mesolithic) Age. Greater variety of stone tools made.
From 10,000 years ago The New Stone (Neolithic) Age. Stone sickles and hoes.
c. 7,000 years ago The Copper Age begins in the Middle East. First metal tools are made.
5,500 years ago The Bronze Age begins in the Middle East. Copper is first used in Europe.
3,000 years ago The Iron Age begins in Europe. (Iron is used from c. 700 BC in the Middle East and Africa.)

The first known tools were made by *Homo habilis* more than 2 million years ago. These were very simple tools made from pebbles. Gradually tools became more advanced. People soon discovered that flint was one of the best tool-making materials. Not only was it very hard, but it could also be chipped into many different shapes and sizes.

Using a pebble, a hard stick or an antler as a hammer, early people shaped flints into sharp-edged hand axes, knives, scrapers and choppers. When blunt, the edges were resharpened with further chipping. Hand axes are among the oldest-known tools, with some dating from about 2 million years ago. They were used for cutting plants, meat and skins.

Flint, bone and antler were also used for making weapons. Bows and arrows were first used about 15,000 years ago. About 7,000 years ago, people in the Middle East learned how to make metal tools from copper. By 3000 BC they were using a stronger alloy of copper – the Bronze Age had begun.

Antler spearhead

Flint cutter

Flint fire lighter

Hand axe

Stone lamp

***Stone Age tools** included lamps, cutters and spearheads. For 98 per cent of the time that people have lived on Earth, their tools have been made from stone, bone, wood, ivory and antler.*

Flint scraper

***Stone Age people** used flint blades to skin animals and scrape them clean. The hides were used for making clothes, tents and bags. Pieces were sewn together using needles made of antler or bone.*

Cave Art

The earliest works of art were created some 40,000 years ago. During the last Ice Age, early artists painted pictures of the animals they hunted – bulls, reindeer and bison – on the walls of the caves they sheltered in.

c. 40,000 years ago Rock engravings in Australia – may be the oldest known artworks.
c. 29,000 years ago Mammoth hunters make clay figures of people.
c. 26,000 years ago Cave paintings drawn in Namibia, Africa.
c. 24,000 years ago Venus of Willendorf is carved in Austria.
c. 17,000–12,000 years ago Animals are painted on cave walls at Lascaux, France.

***A bison carved** from antler about 29,000 years ago. Its detail shows that the artist must have closely observed real bison.*

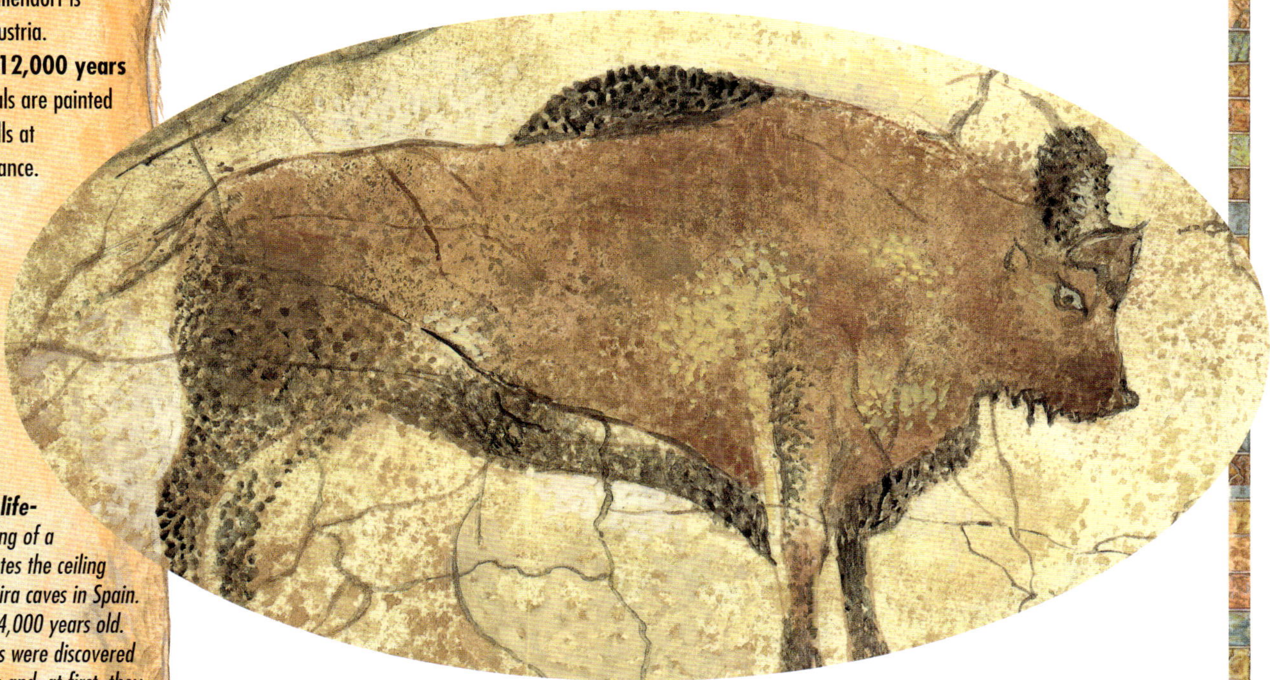

***An almost life-sized** painting of a bison decorates the ceiling of the Altamira caves in Spain. It is about 14,000 years old. The paintings were discovered in the 1870s and, at first, they were thought to be modern forgeries. It was not until the first decade of the 20th century that they were proved to be thousands of years old.*

Paints were made from minerals such as clay, lime and charcoal. These were ground into a powder and mixed with water or animal fat. They were applied with brushes made from fur, feathers, moss or frayed twigs. The paintings were not done simply for decoration and they may have had a religious or magical meaning. Perhaps the painters thought they would bring good luck for hunting.

Cave paintings have been found in Europe, Africa, Asia and Australia. Europe's most famous paintings cover the walls of the Altamira caves (Spain) and Lascaux caves (France). Painted between 17,000 and 12,000 years ago, they include bison, horses, mammoths, reindeer and four huge white bulls. The Lascaux caves were discovered in 1940 by four schoolboys, who were looking for their dog. The caves are now closed to the public, but full-sized copies of the prehistoric masterpieces have been made for people to see.

Life in the Ice Ages

During long periods of Earth's history, large areas of land were covered by ice. As temperatures fell, sheets of ice up to 200 metres thick spread across land and sea. The last of these ice ages had a dramatic effect on human and animal life.

c. 2 million years ago
The Quaternary Ice Age begins. It consists of 17 glacials (cold periods) separated by 17 interglacials (warmer periods).

c. 24,000 years ago
The Ice Age enters its latest glacial. Ice covers about a third of the Earth. Sea levels fall by over 100 m.

c. 22,000 years ago
Hunter-gatherers cross from Asia into North America via a 'land bridge' across the Bering Strait.

c. 18,000 years ago
The last Ice Age reaches its coldest point. People living at Mezhirich in the Ukraine build huts from mammoth bones and tusks.

c. 14,000 years ago
The Bering Strait floods over again as the ice melts and sea levels rise.

c. 12,000 years ago
In Europe, glaciers retreat and the Ice Age ends.

c. 8,000 years ago
Rising sea level separates Britain from the continent of Europe.

The earliest Ice Age occurred some 2.3 billion years ago. Geological evidence shows that succeeding Ice Ages lasted between 20 and 50 million years. As the climate cooled, glaciers formed at the North and South poles. The ice advanced and retreated in waves, known as glaciations.

The most recent Ice Age entered its coldest period about 22,000 years ago, when ice sheets covered much of North America and northern Europe and Asia. As the seas froze, the sea level fell by over 100 metres in places, exposing 'bridges' of land between land masses. The Bering Strait between Siberia and Alaska, for example, became dry land, allowing animals, such as mammoths, to move between Asia and North America.

HOW ANIMALS ADAPTED
This baby mammoth was found, perfectly preserved, in the frozen ground of Siberia, Russia. Animals had to adapt to survive the Ice Age. Over time, some animals, such as the mammoth and the woolly rhinoceros, grew larger, because a larger body conserves heat better.

Chasing after these animals came human hunters – the first humans to colonize North America. Camels, deer and horses moved from the Americas into Asia. When the climate warmed, the ice melted, sea levels rose, and this and other land bridges disappeared.

Conditions were extremely harsh for the people who lived near the ice sheets. Woolly mammoths were a valuable source of meat, skin (for clothes) and bones (for weapons and carvings). Men hunted in groups, driving the mammoths up against cliff-faces so that they could close in for the kill. They attacked with sharp spears made of flint and wood, and large stones. One mammoth provided enough meat to last many months. Leftovers were stored in holes dug in the frozen ground. Bones and tusks made a framework for huts, covered with hides and turf.

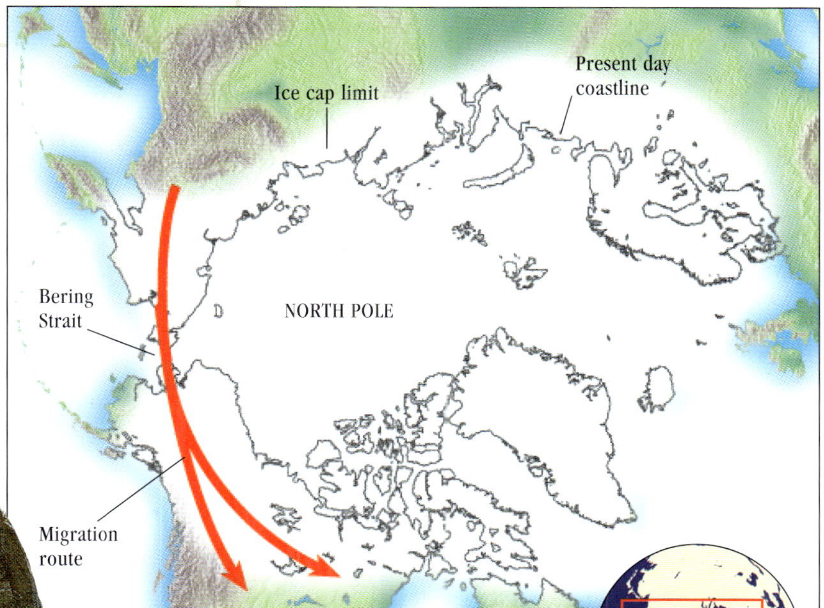

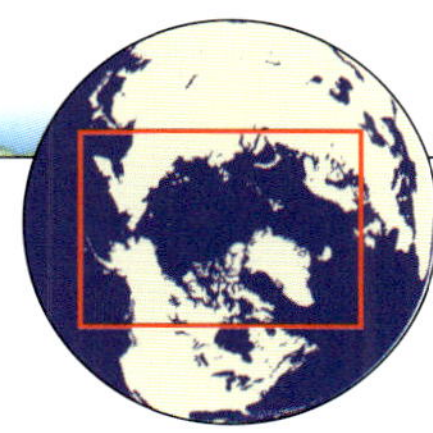

This map shows *the extent of the ice cover in the Northern Hemisphere during the last Ice Age. 'Land bridges' exposed by the drop in sea level allowed people and animals to migrate between Asia and North America.*

Men hunted mammoths *in groups. They would either corner one of the huge beasts against a cliff-face or trap it in a pit dug across its migration route. Then they killed it with spears and stones, and removed the skin, tusks and meat.*

c. 10,500 BC The first clay pots are made in Japan.

c. 8000 BC Farming begins in the Middle East in an area known as the Fertile Crescent, and in Southeast Asia. Sheep are domesticated in Iraq.

c. 7000 BC Farming develops in Central and South America. Clay pots for storing grain and water are made in the Middle East and Africa.

c. 6500 BC The oldest-known textiles are woven at Çatal Hüyük in Turkey.

c. 6000 BC Beer, made from grain, is brewed in the Middle East.

c. 5000 BC Farming is adopted in China and Egypt and spreads to Europe. It also begins in India, along the Indus and Ganges river valleys.

c. 4400 BC Horses are domesticated in Eastern Europe and used for riding for the first time.

c. 4000 BC The first ploughs, made of sharp, forked sticks, are used in the Middle East. The earliest plough marks discovered are in Mesopotamia.

The First Farmers

For most of human history, people found food by hunting wild animals and gathering berries, nuts and roots. They lived as nomads, following the herds of animals they hunted. Then, about 10,000 years ago in 8000 BC, a huge change took place. People learned how to grow crops and rear animals for food.

Instead of having to roam farther and farther afield to find food to eat, people found they could grow enough for their families on a small patch of land. This meant that they had to settle in one place all year round and build permanent homes. These people were the first farmers. Their farming settlements grew to become the first villages, which in turn grew to become the first towns. Plants and animals that are grown or raised by people are known as 'domesticated'. The first domesticated plants and animals were developed from those that were found in the wild. Wheat and barley, which had grown wild in parts of the Middle East for thousands of years, were two of the first crops to be domesticated. People collected seeds from these wild plants and sowed them in ground dug over with deer antlers.

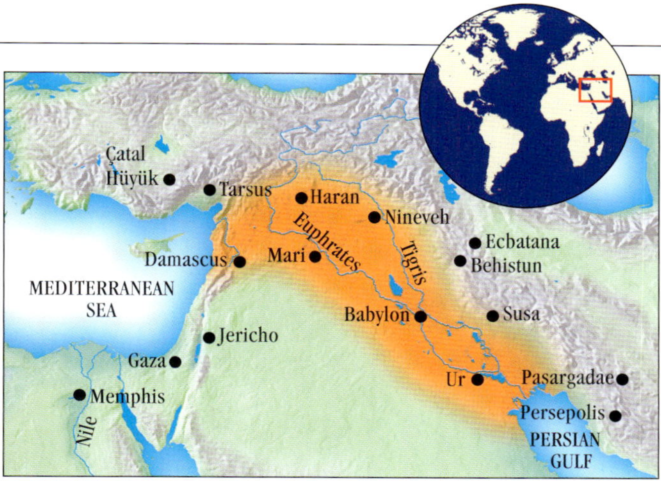

The first farms *developed in the Near East and Europe in a region known as the Fertile Crescent (orange area). Farming spread throughout Europe and western Asia, but it developed independently in the rest of Asia and in the Americas.*

Ploughs were not invented until about 6,000 years ago in 4000 BC. After the seeds had been planted, the crop was harvested and the grain ground into flour to make bread, which was baked on hot stones. Farmers also learned how to tame wild sheep, goats and pigs and how to breed them, so that they no longer had to go hunting for their meat.

DESERT ROCK ART

Cave paintings in Algeria dating from 10,000 years ago show people hunting giraffe, hippos and elephant. Later paintings show farmers tending herds of cattle. After about 3000 BC, when the Sahara's climate became drier, the rock art shows desert animals, such as camels.

On farms in Europe *in about 3000 BC, people made clay pots, which they fired in kilns and used for storing grain and water. They used stone axes to fell trees and clear land, and stone sickles to harvest crops. They also spun wool and wove it into cloth on looms (far left).*

c. 9000 BC A shrine stands on the site of ancient Jericho in the Middle East.
c. 8000 BC Jericho, built on the west bank of the river Jordan, thrives – some 2,000 people live there. The first bricks are made by Jericho's people.
c. 7000 BC Jericho is destroyed by an earthquake (the town is later rebuilt). Çatal Hüyük is founded. Evidence exists of terraced roofs and wall paintings of a bull and a woman. A trade in obsidian dates from this period.
c. 6500 BC Some 5,000 people live in Çatal Hüyük. Linen, made from flax, is woven into cloth for clothes – the oldest known textiles.
c. 6200 BC The Samarra culture is founded in northern Iraq.

The First Towns

Once people began to farm and to settle in permanent villages, the world's population grew rapidly. Towns grew up with a more complex way of life. More houses were built, services such as roads, drainage systems and shops were established, and trade between towns flourished.

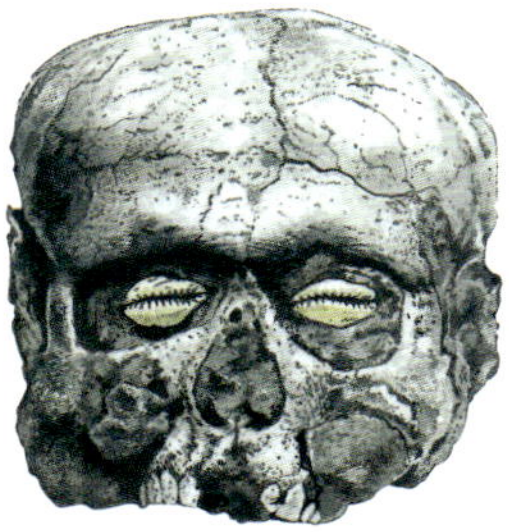

This skull *of a young woman was found in Jericho. It may have been used in religious rituals of ancestor worship.*

Little is known about the first towns, but the ruins of two ancient towns – Jericho in Jordan and Çatal Hüyük in Turkey – have given archaeologists a fascinating glimpse into the past.

Jericho dates from about 8000 BC, and is one of the oldest towns to have been excavated. It was built near a natural spring that was used by farmers to water their fields. Wheat and barley were grown, and sheep and goats raised. Jericho stood on an important trade route and quickly grew wealthy. Among the goods traded were obsidian (a volcanic, glassy rock), shells and semi-precious stones. Massive stone walls, some 3 metres thick and more than 5 metres high, were built to keep out enemies.

A lookout was kept from a 9-metre tall circular watchtower. Inside the walls were small, circular houses made of mud bricks. At one time up to 2,000 people lived there. Jericho's walls were destroyed many times, but not by invading enemies: they were toppled by a series of earthquakes.

Çatal Hüyük was built on a fertile river plain. Its people grew wheat, barley and vegetables, bred cattle and traded in obsidian. By 6500 BC, some 5,000 people lived there. They lived in rectangular houses, interconnected with no outside doors. People entered through holes in the roofs, reached by ladders. If the town was attacked, the ladders were drawn up, leaving no obvious means of entry.

__The town of__ Çatal Hüyük in about 6000 BC. Rooms were painted with vultures and headless men, and contained plaster bulls' heads and statuettes of mother goddesses. The men shown dressed as vultures (in the centre) are priests. It is thought that the dead were put on platforms for vultures to pick clean.

__People have lived__ in the ancient town of Jericho continuously since about 8000 BC. In the 8th century AD, the Arabic ruler Caliph Hisham ibn Abd al-Malik started to build a palace there, for use as a royal hunting lodge. Hisham's Palace was never completed, but its ruins are still standing.

c. 5000 BC Early Sumerians begin to farm in Ubaid, southern Mesopotamia (Iraq).
c. 4000 BC The start of the Uruk Period. The Sumerians learn how to smelt metal. They use sailing boats to navigate the Tigris and Euphrates rivers.
c. 3500 BC The Sumerians invent writing and the wheel. They discover how to make bronze from copper and tin.
c. 2900–2400 BC The Early Dynastic Period. Kings are established in the main Sumerian cities.
c. 2400–2100 BC Sumer is conquered by the Akkadians, then by the Gutians.
c. 2300 BC The Sumerian city of Agade dominates the region.
c. 2100 BC The city of Ur reaches the height of its power under King Ur-Nammu.
c. 2000 BC The epic of Gilgamesh is first written down. The city of Ur is destroyed by the Elamites. Sumerian civilization comes to an end.

***The Sumerians** made splendid jewellery from gold and silver inlaid with semi-precious stones. Craftworkers also made furniture, wine cups and musical instruments. Such treasures were found in the Royal Tombs at Ur when they were excavated.*

Mesopotamia and Sumer

One of the world's earliest civilizations grew up on the fertile plains between the rivers Tigris and Euphrates, in what is now Iraq. The area became known as Mesopotamia, 'the land between the two rivers'. About 5000 BC, the Sumerians settled in southern Mesopotamia.

The fertile land of Mesopotamia was ideal for growing crops. Farmers soon learned how to build irrigation canals to bring water from the rivers to their fields. As more food was grown, the population increased, and by about 3500 BC some villages had grown into thriving towns. The towns of Ur and Uruk grew to become cities, and then independent city-states.

The cities were ruled by Councils of Elders, who appointed lugals (generals) to lead the armies in times of war. As wars between rival cities became more frequent, the lugals' powers grew, and from about 2900 BC the lugals were kings, ruling for life.

In the centre of each city stood a temple to the city's patron god or goddess. The Sumerians believed the gods controlled every aspect of nature and everyday life. It was vital to keep the gods happy with daily offerings, or they might send wars, floods or disease to punish the people.

The Sumerians were expert mathematicians. They had two systems of counting. One was decimal, using units of 10 like the system we use today; the other used units of 60 – the Sumerians were the first to divide an hour into 60 minutes. They also devised a calendar, a complex legal system, and used the wheel for pot-making and on carts. But their most important invention was writing.

***Writing was invented** in Sumer in about 3500 BC, as a way of keeping temple records and merchants' accounts. This Sumerian clay tablet shows the cuneiform ('wedge shaped') symbols used to represent words.*

***The Sumerians** may have built reed houses similar to those of the Marsh Arabs, who live on the banks of the river Tigris in southern Iraq today.*

***A great ziggurat,** or stepped temple, was built in the city of Ur by King Ur-Nammu in about 2100 BC.*

GILGAMESH

The epic of King Gilgamesh and his quest to find the secret of eternal life is the most famous of the Sumerians' many myths and legends. He learns that a plant that gives immortality grows at the bottom of the sea, but the plant is stolen by a snake before he can use it.

- **c. 5000–3100 BC** Predynastic Period in Egypt.
- **c. 3200 BC** Early hieroglyphs are used in Egypt.
- **c. 3100 BC** King Menes unites Egypt.
- **c. 3100–2686 BC** Archaic Period (Dynasties 1 and 2).
- **c. 2686–2150 BC** Old Kingdom (Dynasties 3 to 6).
- **c. 2589–2566 BC** Reign of King Khufu (Dynasty 4).
- **c. 2580 BC** The Great Pyramid at Giza is built.
- **c. 2246–2150 BC** Reign of King Pepi II (Dynasty 6), the longest reign in history.
- **c. 2150–2040 BC** First Intermediate Period (Dynasties 7 to 10).
- **c. 2040–1640 BC** Middle Kingdom (Dynasties 11 to 13). King Mentuhotep II reunites Egypt.
- **c. 1640–1552 BC** Second Intermediate Period (Dynasties 14 to 17). The Hyksos people from Asia overrun Egypt.
- **c. 1552–1085 BC** The New Kingdom in Egypt (Dynasties 18 to 20).
- **c. 1085–664 BC** Third Intermediate Period (Dynasties 21 to 25).
- **c. 664–332 BC** The Late Period (Dynasties 26 to 30).
- **332 BC** Alexander the Great takes control of Egypt.
- **323–30 BC** Rule by the Ptolemies until Cleopatra kills herself in 30 BC. Egypt then becomes a province of the Roman empire.

Ancient Egypt

***Hieroglyphics** was the system of picture writing used in ancient Egypt. Each picture, or hieroglyph, stood for an idea or a sound. Hieroglyphs were written on walls as well as on sheets of papyrus.*

Without the life-giving waters of the river Nile, ancient Egypt would have been a barren desert, too dry for farming. The river gave the ancient Egyptians drinking water, as well as water for irrigation. It also deposited rich soil along its banks each year when it flooded.

***When a body was mummified,** the dead person's liver, lungs, stomach and intestines were removed, wrapped and stored in containers called canopic jars.*

Along the Nile's banks, farmers grew wheat and barley, flax, fruit and vegetables. They also raised cattle, sheep and goats. So vital was the river that the Greek historian Herodotus described ancient Egypt as the 'gift of the Nile'.

The first villages of ancient Egypt appeared some 7,000 years ago. In time, these small settlements increased in size and two kingdoms were created – Lower Egypt in the Nile delta and Upper Egypt along the river valley. In about 3100 BC, King Menes, the ruler of Upper Egypt, united the two kingdoms and built his capital at Memphis.

The king was the most powerful person in ancient Egypt. He was worshipped as the god Horus. From about 1554 BC, the king was given the title 'pharaoh', from the Egyptian words 'per aa', meaning 'great house'. Two officials, called viziers, helped him govern and collect taxes. Officials also ran the major state departments – the Treasury, the Royal Works (which supervised the building of pyramids and tombs), the Granaries, Cattle and Foreign Affairs. Every aspect of Egyptian life was under the pharaoh's control.

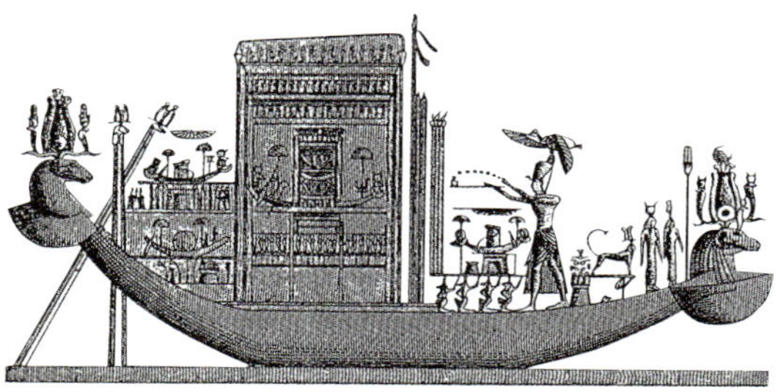

***Boats were the main form of transport,** used for fishing, hunting and carrying cargo and passengers. When a pharaoh died, his body was taken by barge to his tomb.*

***Farmers at work in Egypt.** The farmers' year was split into three parts: the Inundation (July to November) when the Nile flooded, the Growing Season (December to March) and Harvest (March to July). When the flood made farmwork impossible, farmers were sent to work on the royal buildings.*

The Great Temple at Abu Simbel *was built by King Rameses II. Four gigantic seated statues of the king guard the entrance.*

PYRAMID CONSTRUCTION

No one knows exactly how the pyramids were built. It is thought that stone blocks, some as heavy as cars, were pulled to the site on wooden sledges dragged by teams of workers. These were hauled up a series of spiral mud and brick ramps into place. Layer by layer the pyramid grew. Finally, the capstone at the top was added and the whole structure covered in white limestone casing blocks. Then the ramps were dismantled.

The Egyptians believed that for a person's soul to prosper in the next world, the body had to be preserved. This is why they made mummies. Dead bodies were embalmed and dried, then wrapped in linen strips and placed in coffins. The finest tombs were those of the kings. Some were buried in pyramids, but later rulers of Egypt were laid to rest in rock tombs, in the Valley of the Kings near Luxor. Most tombs were ransacked by robbers, but one survived largely intact. It was discovered and opened in 1922 by British archaeologist Howard Carter. The tomb belonged to the boy-king Tutankhamun, and inside were priceless treasures of a vanished world.

c. 7000 BC The oldest village in the Indus Valley, Mehgarh, is founded.
c. 5500 BC Evidence of use of pottery.
c. 3000 BC Farming settlements grow up along the river Indus.
c. 2500 BC The Indus Valley civilization is at its height.
c. 2300–2000 BC Evidence of trade and cultural exchange between Indus Valley and Mesopotamian civilizations.
c. 1800 BC Evidence of a decline in Indus Valley culture. People start to leave cities and those left behind have little food to eat.
c. 1700 BC Many Indus Valley cities are abandoned.
c. 1500 BC The region is taken over by the Aryans – Indo-Europeans from western Asia. Their religious beliefs mix with those of the people from Indus cities to form the basis of the religion of Hinduism.

Indus Valley

About 3000 BC, a great civilization grew up along the river Indus in the Indian subcontinent (in what is now Pakistan). It is known as the Indus Valley civilization. About 2500 BC, it reached the height of its power.

This stone statue, *found among the ruins of Mohenjo Daro, may be of a priest or king.*

The streets of Mohenjo Daro *were laid out in a grid and had a drainage system for the houses. Important buildings included the hilltop citadel and the Great Bath, used for religious rituals.*

The Indus Valley civilization was larger than either Sumer or ancient Egypt. Its two great cities were Harappa and Mohenjo Daro, each with a population of some 40,000 people.

The civilization had a highly organized system of trade. Merchants traded grain and other agricultural produce, grown on the fertile river plains. Artefacts and jewellery were also traded for precious metals and cloth. From about 2000 BC, however, this mighty civilization began to decline, possibly because terrible floods destroyed the crops, or because the river Indus changed course and the fertile farmland dried up. Another theory is that over-grazing left the land too dry and poor to support crops.

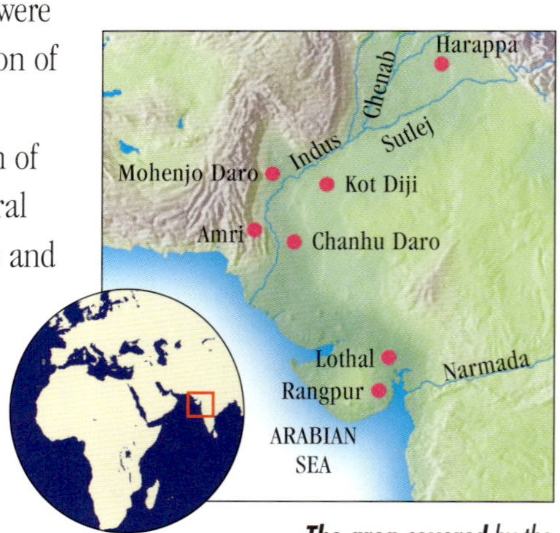

The area covered *by the Indus Valley civilization (in what is now Pakistan) and its main cities.*

c. **4500 BC** People start building megaliths throughout western Europe.
c. **4000 BC** The first passage graves are built at Carnac, France.
c. **3200 BC** Newgrange grave is built in Ireland.
c. **2800–2000 BC** Stonehenge is built in England.
c. **2750–2000 BC** Megalithic temples are built in Malta.

Megalithic Europe

From about 4500 BC, people throughout Europe began building monuments such as stone circles, using massive standing stones called megaliths. They also erected dolmens – two upright stones topped by a horizontal one – that were used as tombs.

This clay mother-goddess figure *was found at the Hypogeum, a megalithic underground monument on the island of Malta.*

Stone circles were laid out carefully, according to strict mathematical rules, but no one is sure what they were used for. They may have been used for studying the Sun, Moon and stars, or they may have been temples, where religious ceremonies were held. Experts think that sacrifices, both human and animal, may have taken place inside these intriguing circles of stone.

Megalithic builders also constructed stone monuments over the graves of their dead. Often these were long, passage-like chambers lined with megaliths and buried under a mound of earth, a structure known as a barrow.

One tomb contained over 40 skeletons, possibly several generations of the same family. The bodies were not put immediately into the grave, but were exposed until most of the flesh had rotted away. Offerings of food and drink, pots and tools were left at the tomb entrance for the dead to use in the next world.

Stonehenge *in England was built in three stages from about 2800 BC. Some of the stones align with the Sun on Midsummer's Day; others with the phases of the Moon.*

c. 6000 BC The first farmers settle in Crete.

c. 3000–1000 BC People on Crete and mainland Greece learn how to make bronze.

c. 2000 BC The first palaces are built on Crete.

c. 1700 BC The palaces are destroyed by earthquakes, but are later rebuilt.

c. 1600 BC The Mycenaeans first reach Crete.

c. 1450 BC A volcanic eruption destroys all the palaces on Crete, Knossos included.

Minoans

The Minoan civilization was the first major civilization in Europe. It began on the island of Crete and was named after its legendary ruler, King Minos. It was at the height of its power from about 2000 BC.

The Minoans had a rich culture, with a highly organized society and a flourishing economy. Merchants travelled throughout the Mediterranean, trading wine, grain and olive oil from Crete for amber, ivory and precious metals.

Towns were built around huge palaces. These weren't just royal residences; they also contained workshops, shrines and storage for goods. By 1450 BC, most of the palaces had been destroyed, probably by earthquakes or volcanic eruptions, and Crete was taken over by the Mycenaeans.

Legend tells of a monster *(half-man, half-bull) that lived in a labyrinth (maze) under the palace of Knossos. It was called the Minotaur. According to the stories, it was killed by Theseus, an Athenian prince. Bulls may have been sacred to the Minoans.*

Many huge clay jars, *used for storing oil, wine and grain, were discovered at Knossos.*

Knossos *was the largest Minoan palace. Built around a central courtyard used for religious ceremonies, it had 1,300 rooms. The walls of the royal apartments were decorated with frescos. The ruins of Knossos were found by Sir Arthur Evans in 1894.*

Mycenaeans

c. 1600–1100 BC Mycenaeans dominate mainland Greece.
c. 1450 BC Mycenaeans become rulers of Crete.
c. 1300 BC Existing palace at Mycenae is built.
c. 1250 BC Traditional date of the fall of Troy.
c. 1200 BC Mycenaean culture begins to decline, possibly due to crop failure and a weak economy. People begin to abandon the great cities.
c. 1100 BC Ancient city of Mycenae is destroyed by fire, possibly lit by invading Dorians.
c. 1100–800 BC The Dark Ages in Greece.
479 BC Mycenae sends 400 men to fight against the Persians at the battle of Thermopylae.
468 BC Neighbouring state of Argos besieges and destroys the city of Mycenae.

From about 1600 BC to 1100 BC, the Mycenaeans dominated mainland Greece. They lived in separate, small kingdoms, although they shared the same language and beliefs. They were named after their greatest city, Mycenae.

A gold death mask, *once believed to have covered the face of Agamemnon, the legendary king of Mycenae and hero of the Trojan War. Scholars now think the grave it came from dated from 300 years before his time.*

The Mycenaeans built their great palaces on hilltops surrounded by massive stone walls. This type of fortified city was easy to defend from attack, and was called an acropolis, which means 'high city' in Greek. The Mycenaeans were farmers and traders. They founded colonies on other Greek islands such as Rhodes and Cyprus. They also seem to have been successful warriors.

Many pieces of armour and weapons have been found in Mycenaean graves. In 1876, a group of five shaft graves were discovered, containing 16 members of the royal family. Five of them had exquisite gold death masks over their faces, and with them was buried a priceless hoard of golden treasure.

The Trojan War *began when Agamemnon led an army to bring back his sister-in-law, Helen, after she had eloped with a Trojan prince, Paris. Legend tells how the Mycenaean soldiers were smuggled into Troy inside a huge wooden horse.*

The Lion Gate *was the main gateway into Mycenae. The two carved lions may have been symbols of the Mycenaean royal family. The gate was built in about 1250 BC.*

Ancient China

c. 1766–1027 BC The Shang dynasty rules China.
1027–256 BC The Zhou dynasty rules China.
c. 551 BC Birth of the great teacher, Confucius.
481–221 BC The Warring States Period, when most of China is in a state of civil war.
221 BC Shi Huangdi unites China and founds the Qin dynasty. He becomes China's first emperor.
212 BC The Burning of the Books by Shi Huangdi – his suppression of ideas that did not match his own.
210 BC Death of Shi Huangdi.
206 BC The Qin dynasty collapses and the Han dynasty rules China until AD 9.

Early copper 'coins' were shaped like tools, and were different in each state. Under Shi Huangdi, all coins were made round with a hole in them, so that they could be strung together.

The earliest civilizations in China grew up along the banks of three major rivers – the Chang Jiang, Xi Jiang and Huang He. Farmers used the water to irrigate their crops, but often suffered bad floods.

From about 2205 BC, China was ruled by a series of dynasties (ruling families). Evidence shows that the first was the Shang dynasty, which began in about 1766 BC. The Shang ruled for more than 400 years, until they were conquered by the Zhou. Zhou rule lasted until 221 BC. During this time many wars were fought between the rival kingdoms that made up the Zhou lands. But it was also a period of economic growth, with foreign trade in Chinese silk, jade and porcelain.

By 221 BC, the kingdoms of China had been at war for more than 250 years. Gradually, the Qin (or Ch'in), a war-like dynasty from the northwest, united the country and established the empire that gives China its name. The first emperor of the united China, Shi Huangdi, reorganized government and standardized money, weights and measures. A road and canal network was built to link up various parts of the country, and the Great Wall of China was built across the northern border to keep out the hostile Hsung Nu (the Huns). Shi Huangdi was a brilliant but ruthless general and politician, putting scholars to death if their ideas did not match his own. The Qin dynasty was overthrown in 206 BC, four years after Shi Huangdi's death.

***A terracotta soldier** from the enormous underground tomb of Shi Huangdi, who was buried in 210 BC with all that he needed to survive the afterlife. This included a vast army, 10,000 strong, of life-sized, individual clay soldiers.*

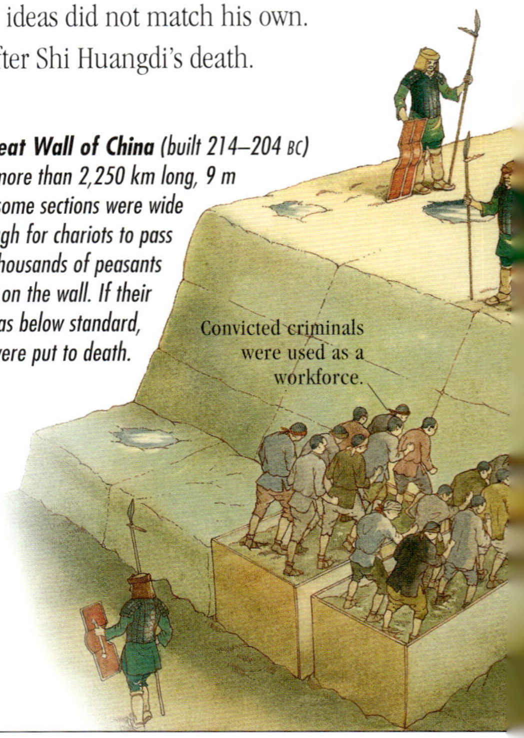

***The Great Wall of China** (built 214–204 BC) was more than 2,250 km long, 9 m high and some sections were wide enough for chariots to pass along. Thousands of peasants worked on the wall. If their work was below standard, they were put to death.*

CONFUCIUS

The philosopher Confucius was born in about 551 BC, at a time when wars were frequent. He dedicated his life to teaching people how to live in peace. His teachings formed the basis of the Chinese civil service up to the beginning of the 20th century.

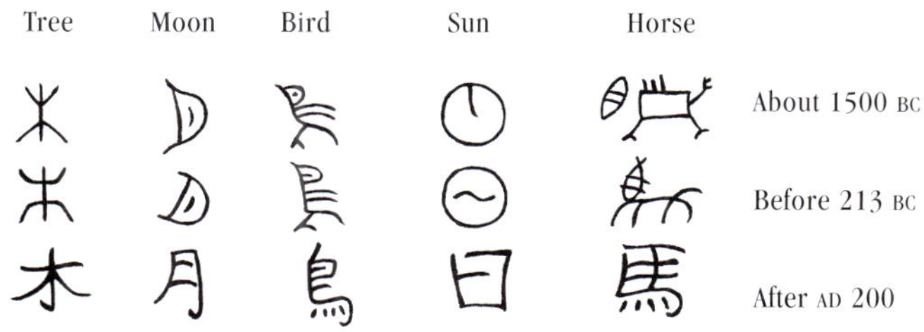

The earliest Chinese writing *from the Shang dynasty was made up of picture symbols showing the objects that they represented. Over time, these picture symbols became more abstract in form.*

c. 2750 BC Founding of the Phoenician city of Tyre.
c. 1500 BC Phoenician cities flourish.
c. 1500 BC Phoenicians settle on island of Cyprus.
c. 1300 BC Phoenicians make commercial agreements with ancient Egypt.
c. 1140 BC Phoenicians set up the colony of Utica in North Africa.
c. 1100 BC Phoenicians independent of foreign rule.
c. 1000 BC The Phoenician alphabet is well developed.
c. 814 BC The city of Carthage is founded in North Africa.
729 BC The Assyrian king, Shalmaneser V, invades Phoenicia.
c. 727 BC The Greeks adopt the Phoenician alphabet.
725 BC Phoenician navy defeats the Assyrians in the first recorded naval battle.
536 BC Carthaginians drive the Greeks out of Corsica.
480 BC Phoenician ships under Persian command are defeated by the Greeks at battle of Salamis.
332 BC Alexander the Great conquers Phoenicia.

Phoenicians

The Phoenicians were the greatest traders and seafarers of the ancient world. Their cities of Tyre and Sidon became centres of a vast trade network. They also set up colonies around the Mediterranean Sea. One was Carthage, which became a great power and Rome's rival.

***The Phoenicians** were famous for their craft skills. They were particularly skilled in glass-making and glass-blowing. This funeral mask is made from coloured glass.*

The Phoenicians lived along the eastern coast of the Mediterranean (in what is now part of Syria, Lebanon and Israel). In large ships made of cedar wood, they ventured as far west as Britain and down the African coast. Phoenician potters, ivory carvers, metal workers and carpenters made goods for everyday use and for export. Goods traded included glassware, timber, cedar oil and ivory. But their most famous export was a purple-red dye made from a kind of shellfish. They were such expert navigators that, about 600 BC, the Egyptian king Necho II hired Phoenician sailors to sail around Africa. The expedition is said to have taken three years.

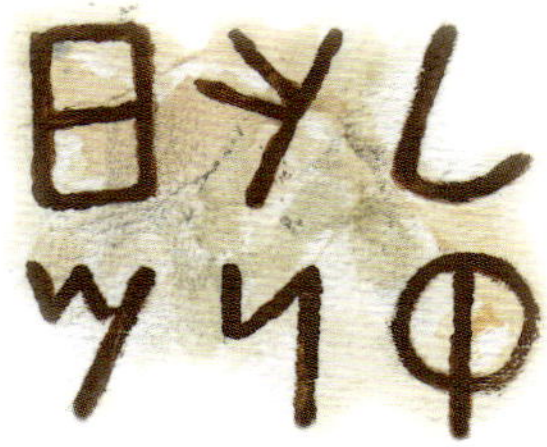

***By about 1000 BC,** the Phoenicians had developed an alphabet of 22 letters. Vowels were later added by the Greeks. In time, the Greek version was adapted by the Romans, and this forms the basis of today's alphabet.*

***Phoenician cargo ships** had square sails and oars. A lookout kept watch for pirates. On arrival in Carthage, on the North African coast, merchant ships used one port and the navy another.*

c. 1850 BC Abraham leads his people from Ur in Mesopotamia to Canaan (Palestine).
c. 1200 BC Moses leads the Hebrews out of Egypt.
c. 1020 BC Saul becomes the first king of Israel.
c. 1000 BC David succeeds Saul as second king of Israel and makes Jerusalem his capital city.
c. 960 BC Solomon builds the Temple in Jerusalem.
c. 922 BC Solomon dies; his kingdom is divided.
c. 722 BC The Assyrians conquer Israel.
c. 587 BC The Babylonians conquer Judah and destroy the first temple of Jerusalem.
c. 538 BC King Cyrus of Persia allows the Jews to return to Jerusalem.
332 BC The region is conquered by Alexander the Great.
c. 63 BC The Romans conquer Judah, which they call Judea.

Hebrews

The Hebrews were the ancestors of the Jews. They lived in the land of Canaan (later called Palestine) and their belief in one God gave rise to the religion of Judaism. The Hebrews became known as Israelites.

***The Bible tells how God** gave Moses the Ten Commandments (holy laws for a good life) written on slabs of stone.*

Canaan was a crossroads on trade routes. According to the Bible, a shepherd named Abraham led his people to Canaan from southern Mesopotamia. His grandson Jacob had 12 sons, after whom the 12 Hebrew tribes or Israelites were named. The Bible tells how the Hebrews were enslaved in Egypt, but were led to freedom around 1200 BC by Moses, whose successor Joshua took them back to Canaan.

From about 1029 BC, the Hebrews united to fight their enemies under a strong king, Saul. Saul's successor, David, formed the kingdom of Israel and made Jerusalem his capital. In Jerusalem, King Solomon built the first Temple. After Solomon died, his kingdom split into Israel and Judah. Both kingdoms fell to invaders from Assyria, Babylonia and Persia. Many Israelites became slaves or went into exile. In 167 BC, the Jews rebelled and set up an independent kingdom, named Judah, but in 63 BC the Romans conquered Judah, and later drove out most of the Jews.

***The Tower of Babel** in Babylon, where many Jews were made captive in the 500s BC. The Bible tells how God, angry at this attempt to build a tower to reach heaven, made the workers speak different languages, so the tower was never finished.*

c. 1200–300 BC The Olmec civilization flourishes on the coast of Mexico.

c. 1200–200 BC The Chavin civilization flourishes on the coast of northern Peru.

c. 1100 BC The Olmecs build a great ceremonial centre at San Lorenzo.

c. 1000 BC The Olmec city of La Venta becomes a major centre for fishing, farming and trade.

c. 850–200 BC Chavin de Huantar in the Peruvian Andes is at the height of its power.

c. 700 BC Olmecs abandon San Lorenzo.

c. 400–300 BC La Venta is abandoned and destroyed.

Ancient America

Over 3,000 years ago, two great civilizations grew up in ancient America – the Olmecs in western Mexico and the Chavin along the coast of northern Peru. Their ancestors had come from Asia across the Bering Strait 'land bridge' thousands of years before. At first, they lived as nomadic hunter-gatherers, but later they settled in farming communities.

A Chavin stone vessel *carved in the shape of an animal. Chavin craft workers produced large quantities of clay pots and sculptures, which they traded with their neighbours.*

The Olmec civilization is thought to have been the first to develop in North America. It started as a small group of villages dotted around the Gulf of Mexico. Gradually these villages merged to form towns, and by around 1200 BC the civilization was flourishing. One of the main centres of Olmec culture was the city of La Venta on an island off the Mexican coast. The people who lived there were fishermen and farmers. The Olmecs built huge earth pyramids where religious ceremonies were held.

The Olmecs carved massive stone heads. *Some stood almost 3 metres high. These may have depicted rulers, gods or famous players of a ball game, played as part of religious worship.*

The Olmecs made hundreds of sculptures *from stone, jade and clay. These tiny jade and serpentine figures were part of a group found buried at La Venta, Mexico, in 1955.*

Many of their sculptures and carved masks depict a half-human, half-jaguar creature, possibly a powerful god. The system of writing developed by the Olmecs influenced many later cultures, such as the Maya.

The Chavin civilization began in Peru in about 1200 BC and lasted for about 1,000 years. It is named after the great religious site of Chavin de Huantar which was built in around 850 BC. It consisted of a huge stone temple surrounded by a maze of rooms. At the heart of the temple was a great statue of the Smiling God, with a human body and a snarling face. The Chavin also worshipped jaguar spirits, eagles and snakes.

This map shows the locations *of the Olmec and Chavin civilizations. The Chavin was the most widespread of the early cultures in the Andes region. It was followed by the Nazca and the Moche civilizations.*

The Olmecs built huge stepped pyramids *made of earth. Here they worshipped and performed religious ceremonies. The pyramid at La Venta was 34 metres high. Around it were several squares, paved to look like jaguar masks.*

c. 2000–1450 BC The Old Assyrian empire.
1813–1781 BC Reign of King Shamshi-Adad, a great warrior and empire builder.
c. 1894 BC The Amorite people establish the minor kingdom of Babylon in Mesopotamia.
c. 1792–1750 BC Reign of King Hammurabi. Babylon first rises to power.
c. 1595 BC Babylon is plundered by the Hittites, then falls to the Kassites.
c. 1595–1155 BC The Kassites rule Babylon.
c. 1126–1105 BC Nebuchadnezzar I reigns.
c. 626–529 BC Babylon re-emerges as a major power in the Middle East.
c. 626–605 BC King Nabopolassar defeats the Assyrians and rules Babylon. Babylonian army, under Nebuchadnezzar, defeats Egypt to win Syria.
612 BC Assyria is invaded and conquered by the Medes and Babylonians.
c. 605–562 BC Nabopolassar's son Nebuchadnezzar II rules Babylon.
c. 597 BC Nebuchadnezzar conquers Judah (southern Palestine) and puts down three rebellions there.
586 BC Nebuchadnezzar destroys Jerusalem and exiles its people to Babylon.
c. 539 BC Babylon is conquered by the Persians and becomes part of the mighty Persian empire.

Assyrians, Hittites and Babylonians

King Ashurbanipal *(668–627 BC) was the last great Assyrian ruler. He was a ruthless military leader, but is also remembered for his splendid palace at Nineveh.*

The Assyrians and Hittites were two of the most warlike peoples of the ancient world. The Assyrians eventually conquered the Hittites and founded an empire that lasted from about 1000 to 612 BC. Babylon first grew powerful under the rule of King Hammurabi (c. 1792–1750 BC). He extended Babylon's frontiers to include Sumer and Akkad, and rebuilt the city of Babylon, making it his capital.

From their fast war chariots, *Hittite archers fired arrows and spearmen hurled spears into the enemy ranks.*

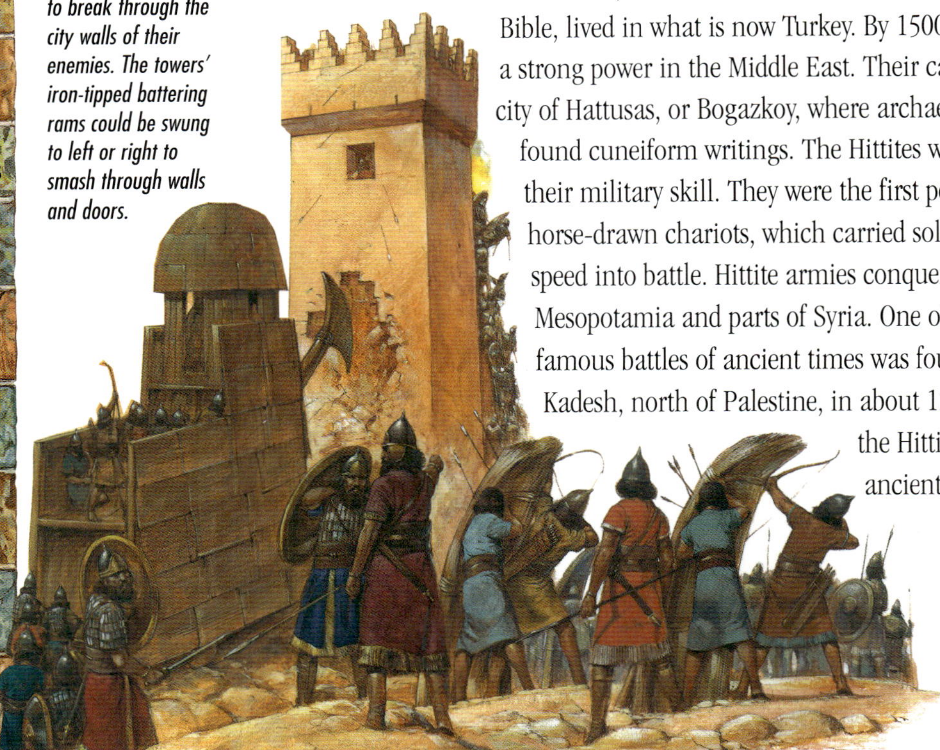

The Assyrian army *used fearsome assault towers mounted on wheels to break through the city walls of their enemies. The towers' iron-tipped battering rams could be swung to left or right to smash through walls and doors.*

The Hittites, who are mentioned several times in the Bible, lived in what is now Turkey. By 1500 BC they were a strong power in the Middle East. Their capital was the city of Hattusas, or Bogazkoy, where archaeologists have found cuneiform writings. The Hittites were feared for their military skill. They were the first people to use horse-drawn chariots, which carried soldiers at high speed into battle. Hittite armies conquered Babylon, Mesopotamia and parts of Syria. One of the most famous battles of ancient times was fought at Kadesh, north of Palestine, in about 1285 BC between the Hittites and the ancient Egyptians.

Legend says *that the Hanging Gardens of Babylon were built for Nebuchadnezzar's Persian wife, Amytis, because she missed the green hills of her homeland. The gardens were one of the Seven Wonders of the ancient world.*

After about 1190 BC, Hittite power was weakened. In 717 BC their eastern city of Carchemish was captured by the Assyrian king Sargon II. The Hittites then became part of the new Assyrian empire.

The Assyrians came from what is now Iraq. They were ruled by soldier-kings, who led huge, well-trained, well-equipped armies. The Assyrians were ruthless against enemy cities. They demanded yearly tributes from conquered peoples; anyone who defied them risked torture and death.

The last great ruler of Assyria, Ashurbanipal, made Nineveh his capital and collected a huge library there. Soon after his death in 627 BC the Assyrian empire ended. It had become too large and ungovernable, and fell to the invading Medes and Babylonians. Hammurabi, the Babylonian king, was a just and diplomatic ruler. He is famous for his code of law, the oldest surviving in the world. After his death, Babylon was invaded by the Hittites, Kassites, Chaldeans and Assyrians. The Assyrian king Sennacherib destroyed the city in 689 BC. But Babylon regained its former glory during the 6th century BC under King Nebuchadnezzar II. The king conquered a huge empire and made the city perhaps the grandest in the ancient world.

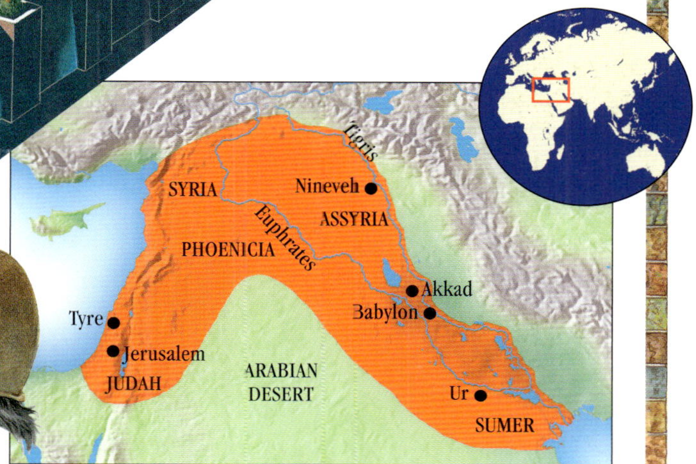

This map shows *the extent of the Babylonian empire under Nebuchadnezzar II. His army defeated the Egyptians to take Syria.*

King Nebuchadnezzar II *(ruled c. 605–562 BC) captured Syria and Palestine, and forced many of the people of Jerusalem to live in captivity in Babylon.*

The blue-tiled Ishtar Gate *was the northern entrance to Babylon. It was named after the goddess of love and war. Bulls and dragons, symbols of the god Marduk, decorated the gate.*

c. 900 BC The state of Sparta is founded by the Dorians.
c. 800–500 BC The Archaic Period. Greece revives after a period of decline called the Dark Ages.
776 BC The first Olympic Games are held at Olympia.
c. 750–550 BC Many Greek colonies are set up around the Mediterranean.
c. 700 BC The Greek poet Homer composes the *Iliad* and the *Odyssey*.
c. 508 BC Democracy is introduced in Athens.
c. 500–336 BC The Classical Period. Greek culture reaches its height.
490–449 BC The Persian Wars. The Greeks are victorious.
479–431 BC The Golden Age of Athens, a time of great prosperity and achievement for the city.
447–438 BC Parthenon temple is built in Athens.
431–404 BC Athens and Sparta fight the Peloponnesian Wars. Sparta wins with Persian help.
430 BC Plague devastates Athens.
371 BC Sparta is defeated by the Greek city-state of Thebes.
362 BC The Thebans are defeated at the battle of Mantinea by the Spartans and Athenians.
338 BC The Greeks are defeated by the Macedonians at the battle of Chaeronea. This spells the end of Greek independence.

Ancient Greece

***Pericles** was leader of Athens from 443–429 BC. The most famous and popular politician of the 'Golden Age', he ordered the rebuilding of Athens after its destruction by the Persians.*

By about 800 BC, Greece saw the rise of a new civilization that transformed the ancient world. Its influence has lasted to the present day. Ancient Greece was divided into small, independent city-states, each with its own government and laws. The two most important were mighty Athens and Sparta.

Most city-states were ruled by a group of wealthy nobles (an oligarchy). Resentment led to revolts, and absolute rulers (tyrants) were appointed to restore law and order. Then, in about 508 BC, a new type of government was introduced in Athens. It was called democracy, meaning 'rule by the people', and gave every free man a say in how the city should be run. Many countries today are democracies, but with votes for all.

The Classical Period (when Greek culture was at its height) lasted from about 500 BC to 336 BC. During that time, Greece was involved in two long-running wars. In 490 BC the Persians invaded. The Greek city-states joined forces and eventually defeated them in 449 BC. One of the most famous battles took place at Marathon in 490 BC. A messenger named Pheidippides ran the 40 kilometres back to Athens carrying news of the Greek victory. His run is immortalized in the modern marathon race.

***Socrates** (c. 469–399 BC), the son of an Athenian sculptor, was one of the most influential of all ancient Greek philosophers. He taught people to think about good and evil. Some people did not approve of his ideas, however, and he was forced to commit suicide.*

***Greek warships** had sails and several banks of oars on either side, which made them very fast and easy to manoeuvre.*

Greek actors *were all men. They wore different masks and costumes for characters that were happy, sad, male, female, old or young. The Greeks were the first to build theatres; the largest could hold an audience of 18,000 people.*

But peace did not last. In 431 BC war broke out between Athens and Sparta (the Peloponnesian Wars). After laying siege to Athens, the Spartans starved the Athenians into submission. In 404 BC, Athens was forced to surrender.

The ancient Greeks were great scholars, thinkers and teachers. At first, they answered questions about life and nature with stories about the gods. Later, they started to look for practical and scientific ways of making sense of the world about them. Their scholars were called philosophers, which means 'lovers of knowledge'. They included Socrates, Plato and Aristotle.

Drama and sport played a very important part in the lives of the ancient Greeks. Greek theatre grew from the performance of songs and dances at an annual festival dedicated to Dionysus, the god of wine. These performances were acted out by a group of men called a chorus.

Sport was important not only as a form of entertainment, but also as a way of keeping men fit and healthy for war. There were many competitions for athletes. The oldest and most famous was the Olympic Games, held every four years at Olympia. For the five days of the games, a truce was called between the city-states to allow the athletes safe passage to Olympia. Athletes trained hard for months before the games. The prize for the winners was a simple olive crown cut from a sacred tree, and a hero's welcome, fame and fortune when they arrived back home.

The Greek army *depended on its hoplites, or foot soldiers. Hoplites carried heavy round shields and long spears for stabbing the enemy. The split, skirt-like tunics allowed easy movement.*

The phalanx advanced in formation, spearpoints bristling, scattering the enemy foot soldiers.

In battle, *Greek hoplites formed a phalanx – a block of soldiers eight or more ranks deep.*

549 BC Cyrus the Great of Persia conquers Lydia.
539 BC Persians conquer Babylon.
526 BC Cambyses of Persia conquers Egypt.
521–486 BC Reign of Darius I, Persia's 'king of kings'.
499–479 BC Persians led by Darius I and Xerxes try, but fail, to conquer Greece.
356 BC Alexander is born; becomes king in 336 BC after Philip II is murdered.
334 BC Alexander's army invades the Persian empire.
333 BC Alexander defeats Darius III's huge Persian army at the Battle of Issus.
332 BC Alexander conquers Egypt.
331 BC Alexander defeats the Persians at the battle of Gaugamela.
327 BC Alexander reaches India. He is forced to turn back in 324 BC.
323 BC Alexander dies in Babylon. War breaks out between his generals and his empire is divided.

Alexander and the Persians

After the squabbles following the Persian Wars, Macedonia became the dominant force in Greece. Its young king, Alexander, led his armies on an epic march of conquest, crushing the Greeks' traditional enemies, the Persians.

The Persian homeland was in what is now Iran. The Persians had come to rule an empire that stretched eastward to India and as far west as Turkey. Powerful Persian kings, such as Cyrus the Great, commanded huge and efficient armies. Darius I (521–486 BC) built fine roads for carrying messages quickly across the empire, which he reorganized into provinces called satrapies. From 499 BC, Persia turned against the Greeks, but in 480 BC its invasion fleet was defeated at the Battle of Salamis.

Power then swung towards Greece. In 338 BC, Macedonia's warrior king Philip II gained control of all the Greek states by victory at Chaeronea. When Philip was murdered in 336 BC, his son Alexander became king, aged 20. It took Alexander just 13 years to conquer the largest empire in the ancient world, spreading Greek (and Persian) culture far and wide.

***Alexander** on his great warhorse, Bucephalus.*

***This mosaic** from the Roman city of Pompeii shows Darius III (right) fleeing from Alexander, whose head is visible on the left.*

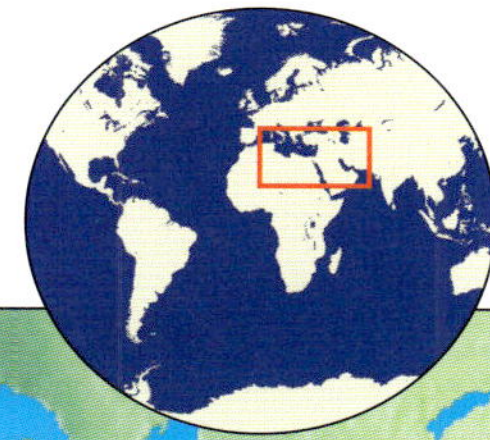

In 334 BC, Alexander led his army against the Persians. He wanted not only to conquer their lands, but also to replenish his royal treasuries. In 333 BC, he defeated the Persian king Darius III at the battle of Issus, and by 331 BC had conquered the whole of Persia and become its king. To strengthen the ties between the two peoples, Alexander included Persians in his government. He also wore Persian clothes and married a Persian princess, Roxane. He went on to invade India, defeating King Porus at the battle of the river Hydaspes. It was to be his final expedition. His exhausted army refused to go on, and Alexander was forced to retreat to Babylon. He died there of a fever in 323 BC, aged 32. After his death, the empire was divided among his leading generals.

***The map shows** the extent of Alexander's empire and the route he took to conquer the east.*

***The city of Persepolis,** built by Darius I, was the magnificent capital of the Persian kings. The ruins of the city lie near Shiraz in modern-day Iran. When Alexander captured Persepolis in 331 BC, he burned the grand royal palace to the ground.*

c. 600–500 BC Celtic culture develops in Austria and later in France.
c. 500 BC Evidence of trade between the Celts and the Etruscans. Celts arrive in Ireland from Spain.
c. 400 BC The Celts build farms and hill-forts in southern and western Europe.
390 BC The Gauls (French Celts) sack the city of Rome.
225 BC The Romans defeat the Gauls at the battle of Telamon in Italy.
58–50 BC Julius Caesar conquers all of Gaul (France).
52 BC Vercingetorix leads a revolt against the Romans in Gaul, but is defeated by Juilius Caesar.
AD 43 Roman Emperor Claudius invades Britain and defeats Celtic leader Caratacus.
AD 61 Boudicca is defeated in a revolt she leads against the Romans in Britain.

The Celts

Celtic peoples spread westward across Europe from about 800 BC. They lived in tribal groups, settling in hillforts and farms. The Celts were unable to unite against a common enemy – the formidable Roman legions.

The Celts were brave and fearless warriors, but they were equally skilled at metal-working, making beautifully decorated weapons, jewellery and drinking cups. They were also gifted storytellers, passing down stories of their gods and history by word of mouth. Later, Roman writers recorded many details of Celtic life and culture. They reported that the Celts worshipped many different gods and goddesses, and offered sacrifices in their honour. Religious rituals and ceremonies were performed by priests, called druids. In charge of each of the Celtic tribes was a chieftain. One of the most famous of these was Vercingetorix, a chieftain of the Arveni, a Celtic tribe that lived in central Gaul (France). In 52 BC, he led a rebellion against the Romans that was successful initially. However, he was later defeated by Julius Caesar's well-trained army.

***Celtic craftworkers** made beautiful metal objects, such as this silver horse harness. Many highly decorated Celtic artefacts have survived.*

***Maiden Castle** was one of the strongest Iron Age hill-forts in Britain. Approaching invaders could be seen a long way off, and the fort's concentric earthworks made it difficult to capture.*

Many Celtic tribes built huge hilltop forts surrounded by massive protective earthworks, where they lived safe from attack. Victory in battle was celebrated with feasts that could last for several days, drinking and the recital of long poems telling of the deeds of Celtic heroes and gods. Their greatest god was Daghdha, the 'Good God', who controlled the weather and the harvest and brought victory in battle.

Celtic warriors were famed and feared for their bravery in battle. Wars frequently broke out between rival Celtic tribes – a weakness that helped the Romans to overwhelm them more easily.

BOUDICCA

The Roman emperor Claudius invaded Britain in AD 43. Some Celts fought back fiercely. In AD 60, Boudicca (or Boadicea), queen of the Iceni, a Celtic tribe in eastern Britain, led a revolt against the Romans. The Celts burned London and killed some 70,000 Romans and townspeople. But her army was defeated in AD 61, and Boudicca killed herself by drinking poison.

Safe within a hillfort, *families lived with their animals in circular wooden huts. The huts were thatched and had walls of mud-plastered sticks. A huge iron cooking pot hung over the fire in the centre.*

753 BC The traditional date for the founding of Rome.
c. 509 BC The founding of the Roman Republic.
264–146 BC The Punic Wars between Rome and Carthage in North Africa. Carthage is destroyed.
49 BC Julius Caesar seizes power. In 44 BC, he is assassinated.
31 BC Octavian defeats Antony and Cleopatra at the Battle of Actium.
27 BC End of the Republic, start of the Roman empire.
27 BC–AD 14 Octavian takes the title Augustus and rules as the first Roman emperor.
c. AD 80 In Rome, the Colosseum is completed.
AD 98–117 The empire reaches its greatest extent.
AD 117–138 Hadrian rules.
AD 180 End of the *Pax Romana* (Roman Peace), a time of stability.
AD 286 Emperor Diocletian divides the Roman empire into west and east.
AD 410 Rome is captured by Alaric the Visigoth.
AD 451 Attila the Hun invades Roman Gaul.
AD 476 The last western emperor, Romulus Augustulus, is deposed. The eastern empire continues as the Byzantine empire.

***Roman coins** bore the head of the emperor and were used in trade all over the empire. Peaceful trading was one of the benefits of Roman rule.*

The Romans

According to legend, the city of Rome was founded in 753 BC by the twin brothers Romulus and Remus. The boys were abandoned by their uncle to die on the banks of the river Tiber in central Italy. But they were rescued by a she-wolf, and later found and raised by a shepherd.

To repay the she-wolf, Romulus and Remus vowed to build a city in her honour on the Palatine Hill where she had found them. In a quarrel about the city boundaries, Remus was killed and Romulus became the first king of Rome. From humble beginnings as a small group of villages, Rome grew to become the capital of the most powerful empire the western world had ever seen.

At first, Rome was ruled by kings, but, in about 509 BC, King Tarquin the Proud was expelled from Rome, and for almost the next 500 years Rome was run as a republic. Power passed to the Senate, a law-making body made up of nobles and headed by two officials, called consuls. The consuls were elected each year to manage the affairs of the Senate and the army. By about 50 BC, Rome had conquered most of the lands around the Mediterranean. But rivalry between army generals plunged Rome into civil war. In 27 BC, Octavian, the adopted son of Julius Caesar, became the first Roman emperor. He was charged with restoring peace.

***Julius Caesar,** a brilliant Roman general, defeated his rivals in Rome to seize power as dictator in 49 BC. He was assassinated on 15 March, 44 BC.*

***The Colosseum** is one of the most impressive Roman remains in Rome. It was built to stage gladiator fights, a popular form of entertainment. Gladiators were trained slaves or prisoners, who fought each other or wild animals. The Colosseum held up to 45,000 spectators.*

Roman soldiers *were well trained and well organized. Wearing heavy armour and plumed bronze or iron helmets, they were capable of marching 30 km a day carrying weapons, food and camping kit.*

HANNIBAL

From 264 to 146 BC, Rome waged a series of wars, called the Punic Wars, against the Phoenician city of Carthage in North Africa, to gain control of the Mediterranean. In 218 BC, the Carthaginian general Hannibal led a surprise attack on the Romans. He marched over the Alps into Italy with 35,000 men and 37 elephants. Carthage was eventually defeated.

CHRISTIANITY AND ROME

The Romans worshipped many gods and often adopted new religions from the people they conquered. Jesus Christ was born (probably in 4 BC) in Palestine, which was then a Roman province. His teachings attracted fervent followers, but upset local Jewish leaders, and he was crucified by the Romans. Christ's followers, among them the apostle Paul, spread the new religion of Christianity throughout the Roman world. Despite persecution, the faith grew and, in AD 391, it became the official religion of Rome.

Under the emperors, Rome gained control of much of Europe, North Africa and the Middle East.

The Roman army was originally formed to protect the city of Rome. It was made up largely of volunteer soldiers. General Marius (155–86 BC) reorganized the army into a more efficient force. Soldiers were paid wages and joined up for 20 to 25 years. Ordinary soldiers were grouped into units called legions, each made up of about 5,000 men. The legions, in turn, were made up of smaller units, called centuries, of 80 men. These were commanded by soldiers called centurions.

Roman society was divided into citizens and non-citizens. There were three classes of citizens – patricians, the richest aristocrats; equites, the wealthy merchants; and plebeians, the ordinary citizens. All citizens were allowed to vote in elections and to serve in the army. They were also allowed to wear togas.

Building, mining and all hard manual labour was done by the vast workforce of slaves. Many slaves were treated cruelly, but some were paid a wage and could eventually buy their freedom.

African Cultures

From 2000 BC The kingdom of Kush begins in Nubia.
c. 900 BC Kush gains independence from Egypt.
c. 600 BC The Nok culture begins in northern Nigeria.
AD 100s The kingdom of Axum (in what is now Ethiopia) rises to power.
c. AD 200 The Nok culture comes to an end, but has a lasting effect on the artistic styles of Africa.
AD 320–350 King Ezana rules Axum and converts to Christianity.
c. AD 350 Axum overruns the city of Meroe and brings the Kushite kingdom to an end.
AD 500s Axum rules part of western Arabia.
c. AD 1000 The kingdom of Axum collapses as Islam expands.

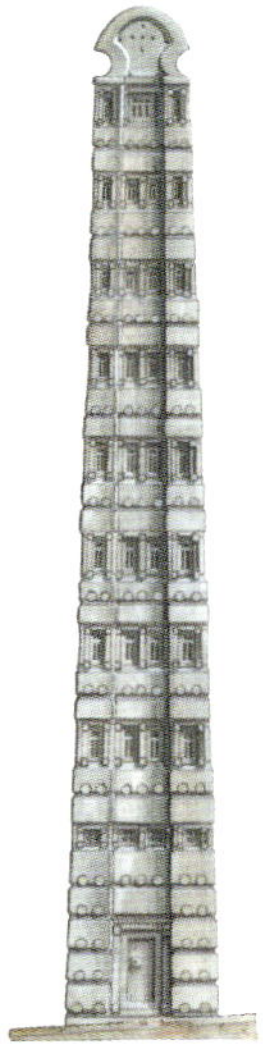

***The people of Axum** built huge obelisks, up to 30 m tall. Carved from single stone slabs, they may have been symbols of power or burial monuments for the royal family.*

One of the great early African civilizations grew up in Nubia (now northern Sudan) in about 2000 BC. Called the kingdom of Kush, it was conquered by Egypt in 1500 BC. Kush, in turn, defeated Egypt in about 728 BC and ruled it for 100 years.

In the 3rd century BC, the capital of Kush moved to Meroe, on the banks of the river Nile. The city became an important centre of iron-working. Another early centre of iron-working developed in what is now northern Nigeria (in West Africa) about in 600 BC. The people of the region were known as the Nok. Their culture flourished until about AD 200. The Nok mined iron and smelted it in clay furnaces. They used the iron to make tools such as hoes and axes that were used to clear the land for crops.

***Life in a Nok village** centred around farming and iron-working. To extract iron from iron ore (a metal-bearing rock), the ore was put into a furnace. Potters used furnaces, too, to fire the terracotta heads that they made.*

The Nok also made iron arrowheads, spears and knives, as well as stone tools and distinctive clay figures.

The kingdom of Axum rose to power in the 2nd century AD. Located in what is now northern Ethiopia, Axum lay on an important trade route and grew rich from buying and selling spices, incense and ivory. Its major trading partners were Arabia, Egypt and Persia. In about AD 320, Axum's King Ezana converted to Christianity. In the 6th century AD Axum conquered part of western Arabia. By AD 1000, however, it had collapsed as a new Islamic empire from Arabia expanded its influence.

***A wall painting** from an ancient Egyptian tomb showing Nubians bringing gifts for Egypt's pharaoh. Egyptian expeditions to Nubia brought back gold, cattle and slaves.*

***The map** shows the kingdoms of Kush, Axum and Nok. The Nok were named after the village where clay figures, like this head (right), were found.*

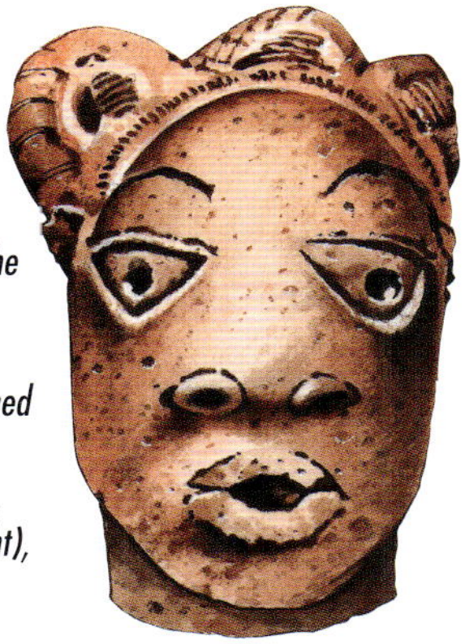

c. 563 BC Birth of the Buddha in Lumbini, Nepal.
c. 483 BC Death of the Buddha in Kushinagara, India.
c. 321 BC Chandragupta seizes power and founds the Mauryan dynasty.
269–232 BC Reign of Ashoka Maurya, thought by some to be the greatest ruler of ancient India.
260 BC Ashoka converts to Buddhism after the Battle of Kalinga.
c. AD 320 The beginnings of Gupta power emerge in the Ganges valley.
c. AD 350 Axum overruns the city of Meroe and brings the Kushite kingdom to an end.
c. AD 350–550 The Gupta empire brings a Golden Age of Hinduism to India.
AD 380–415 The reign of Chandra Gupta II, greatest of the Gupta kings.
c. AD 550 Hun invasions weaken Gupta power. The empire splits into smaller kingdoms.

In early Buddhist art, *Buddha was shown by a symbol such as a footprint, a wheel, a lotus flower or a sacred tree.*

Empires of India

In about 321 BC, a young prince, Chandragupta Maurya, founded an empire that stretched across northern India from the Hindu Kush in the west to Bengal in the east. This was the first Indian empire.

Exquisite wall paintings *cover the Buddhist cave temples at Ajanta in western India. The paintings date from the time of the Gupta empire. Some show scenes from the life of the Buddha.*

Chandragupta's grandson, Ashoka, came to the throne in 269 BC. He extended the empire until most of India came under Mauryan rule. In 260 BC, Ashoka's army fought a bloody battle against the people of Kalinga in eastern India. Sickened by the bloodshed, Ashoka was filled with remorse. He converted to Buddhism and vowed to follow its religious teachings of peace and non-violence.

Ashoka travelled far and wide throughout his empire, listening to people's views and complaints and trying to improve their lot. He had edicts carved on pillars for people to see, and sent out special officers to explain his policy of religious tolerance, respect for others and peace.

After the collapse of the Mauryan empire in about 185 BC, India was divided into small, independent kingdoms.

HINDUISM

The Hindu religion began more than 4,000 years ago as ideas from the Indus Valley civilization mingled with those of invading peoples. Under Ashoka, Buddhism became the major religion of India. Hinduism enjoyed a revival under the Guptas. Today, more than three-quarters of Indians are Hindu. The main symbol of Hinduism is the word 'Om' (shown right).

In AD 320, Chandra Gupta I, ruler of the kingdom of Magadha in the Ganges valley, enlarged his kingdom. The Gupta empire ruled northern India for the next 200 years. Chandra Gupta's son, Samudra, extended the empire and increased its trading links. He was succeeded by Chandra Gupta II. During his reign, India enjoyed a golden age.

Under the Guptas, arts and literature flourished, as did science, medicine and mathematics. Great poets and artists were invited to the splendid royal court. Hinduism replaced Buddhism as the major religion of the empire, and many new temples and shrines were built. Sanskrit, the sacred, classical language of India, became the language of the court.

The gateway *to the great stupa (Buddhist shrine) of Sanchi, which was built during Ashoka's reign. The first stupas contained relics of the Buddha. Ashoka had stupas built throughout his empire.*

Emperor Ashoka Maurya. *In Sarnath, where the Buddha first taught, Ashoka erected a tall pillar topped with four lions and four wheels (symbols of Buddhism).*

BUDDHISM

Buddhism was founded by an Indian prince, Siddharta Gautama (c. 563–483 BC), who gave up his comfortable life to seek enlightenment. He found enlightenment while sitting and meditating under a Bo tree. He spent the rest of his life travelling and teaching. Buddhism teaches that people, like all living things, are part of an endless round of birth, change, death and rebirth. Buddhism spread from India to other parts of Asia, and beyond.

The Middle Ages

The period from about 500 to 1400 in Europe is known as the Middle Ages, or the medieval period. It began with the fall of the Roman empire and ended with the Renaissance, when a revival of art and learning swept through Europe.

The medieval period was an age of wars and conquests. Some wars were fought to gain more territory, while others were wars of religion, fought between people of differing faiths in an age when religion dominated most people's lives. At this time, China's civilization was far in advance of the rest of the world. Africa and America saw the emergence of strong, well-organized empires based on trade, while the spread of Islam from Arabia across the Middle East and into North Africa and Spain brought a new way of life to a vast area.

p65 The Domesday Book was created in 1085.

p52 A Frankish stone monument, possibly a gravestone. The carving shows a warrior with a long broadsword, a favourite weapon of the Franks.

p55 A Muslim star chart of a constellation.

p74 The Mongol ruler, Genghis Khan, was a ruthless leader.

p56 A massive stone figure found at Tiahuanaco in Bolivia.

p57 A Mayan calendar, with 18 months of 20 days each.

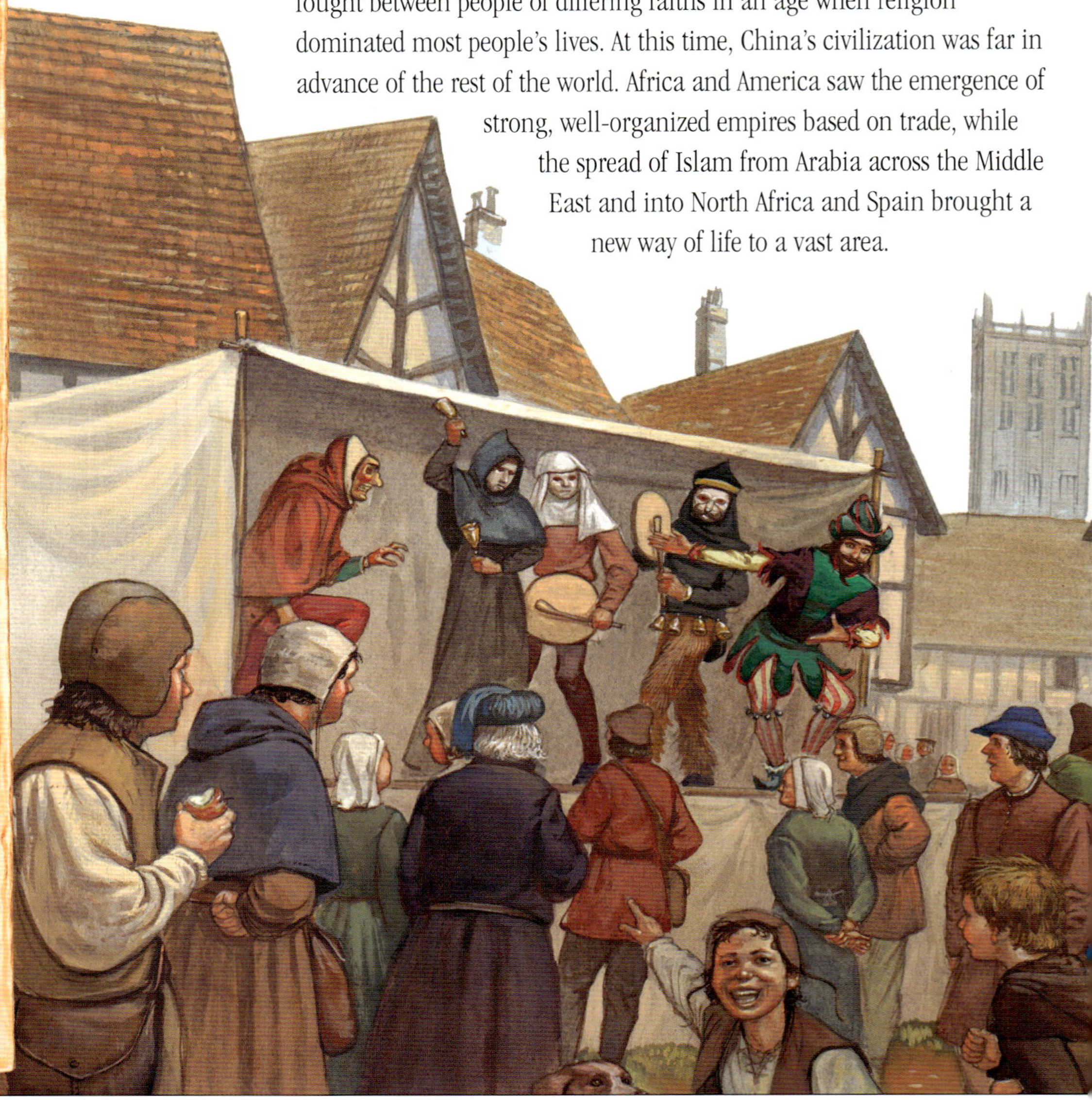

p76 A procession of penitents whipping themselves in the streets during the outbreak of the Black Death in the 14th century.

p80 A Japanese Samurai warrior wore a steel horned helmet and fought with bow, sword and lance. His body armour was made in pieces from leather or lacquered iron strips, and so was very flexible.

During the Middle Ages, ordinary people lived simply, as farmers in villages or as craftworkers in towns. Many built their own houses, made their own clothes and grew their own food. Poor people obeyed local landowners or lords, who in turn served a more powerful king or emperor. The rulers ordered castles and palaces, temples and cathedrals to be built. These huge stone buildings often took many years, and even centuries, to construct.

Few people travelled far from their homes. Those who did venture into foreign lands included merchants, soldiers and a few bold explorers who wrote accounts of their travels. Few people could read or write, and learning was passed down by word of mouth. In Europe, the monasteries were centres of learning, while in Asia the Chinese and Arabs led the way in the studies of science and technology, medicine and astronomy.

p72 Market day in a medieval European town. People brought in farm produce to sell, visited stalls and shops, gossiped and drank at the alehouse. Acrobats, actors and dancing bears amused the crowds.

330 Constantinople is founded.
408 Emperor Theodosius begins building a great wall to protect Constantinople.
445 Attila the Hun attacks. He is paid to go away.
476 Fall of the Western Roman empire.
c. 501 A long series of wars with Persia begins.
527–565 Reign of Justinian I.
678 An Arab siege of Constantinople is defeated.
900s Second Golden Age. The Balkans and Russia come under Byzantine influence.
1054 The Christian Church in Constantinople breaks with the Church in Rome.
1081 Alexius I Comnenus seizes power and reforms government.
1200 The Byzantine empire begins to break up under attacks from Turks and Bulgarians.
1204 Constantinople is sacked by Crusaders.
1341–54 Civil war in the Byzantine empire.
1453 Turks capture Constantinople – end of the Byzantine empire.

Byzantium

For over 500 years, the Roman empire brought a unique way of life to a vast area of land. But in 476 the western half of the empire collapsed, overrun by invading German tribes. In the east, Roman rule continued to flourish under what is called the Byzantine empire.

Constantine the Great *(275–337) was the first Christian emperor of Rome. He moved the empire's capital from Rome to Byzantium and renamed the city Constantinople.*

The old Greek city-port of Byzantium (modern-day Istanbul in Turkey) was the centre of the Byzantine (eastern Roman) empire. Renamed Constantinople after the first Byzantine emperor, Constantine, it became the seat of the Byzantine emperors and the centre of the eastern Christian Church. Within the Byzantine empire, Greek and Roman arts and learning were preserved. Byzantine churches, such as Hagia Sophia, contained detailed frescoes and mosaic pictures that were made from hundreds of pieces of glass or stone.

The Byzantine empire reached its peak in the 500s, under the emperor Justinian and his general Belisarius. It included Italy, Greece, Turkey, parts of Spain, North Africa and Egypt. Justinian's powerful wife, Theodora, helped him govern.

This map shows the Byzantine *(eastern Roman) empire at its height in the 500s. It extended from the eastern Mediterranean to Spain in the west.*

Justinian issued a code of laws on which the legal systems of many European countries were later based. Constantinople was a busy port and meeting place for traders from as far away as Spain, China and Russia. But invaders from the east – Avars, Slavs and Bulgars – threatened this last Roman empire. After Justinian's death in 565, Byzantium was weakened by many wars and eventually fell to the Turks in 1453.

The magnificent church of Hagia Sophia *in Istanbul was completed in 537. It took only six years to build. The minarets were added later when it became a mosque. It is now a museum.*

Chariot races *mixed thrills with politics. Howling mobs in the Hippodrome cheered for the Blues or the Greens, in support of one or other of the rival political factions.*

241 First mention of Franks, fighting the future Roman emperor Aurelian in Mainz.
350 Franks are brought under Roman rule.
428 Salian Franks (living in the Netherlands and lower Rhineland) throw off Roman rule and invade Gaul, led by King Chlodio.
451 Franks join with Romans to defeat Attila the Hun at the Battle of Châlons.
c. 466 Clovis is born. In 481, he becomes king of the Franks.
486 Franks defeat the last great Roman army in the West, at the Battle of Soissons.
496 Clovis defeats the Alemanni near the River Seine.
506 Franks defeat the Visigoths.
511 Clovis dies.
540 Franks control most of Gaul and lands in what is now Germany.
687 After the Battle of Tertry, Pepin of Herstal becomes the most powerful Frankish leader.
732 Charles Martel defeats a Muslim army at the Battle of Poitiers.
751 Last Merovingian king, Childeric III, is overthrown. Pepin the Short (Charlemagne's father) becomes king.

The Franks

The Franks were the strongest of all the western European peoples who struggled for land and power after the end of the Roman empire in 476.

***An ivory carving** shows Gregory the Great, pope from 590 to 604. From the time of Clovis, the Franks were Christian.*

Under their first great leader, Clovis, the Franks spread out from their homeland around the river Rhine (in what is now Germany). They fought their neighbours, such as the Visigoths and Burgundians, until by 540 they had conquered most of the old Roman province of Gaul (modern France, which is named after the Franks).

Clovis defeated rival chieftains to bring all the Frankish tribes under his control. His family became known as the Merovingian dynasty, after his grandfather Merovich. Clovis became a Christian and ruled from Paris, governing his lands through bishops and nobles. The nobles or lords held estates known as manors, which were ploughed and farmed by peasants.

Frankish leaders were always ready to defend their estates and conquer new territories.

***A Frankish stone** monument, possibly a gravestone. The carving shows a warrior with a long broadsword, a favourite weapon of the Franks.*

***Tough Frankish warriors** rode into battle with shaven heads and topknots, wearing light mail armour. They were formidable cavalry fighters, whose loyalty was rewarded with booty. Frankish armies defeated the Romans, Gauls and Visigoths who tried to halt their expansion.*

Their eagerness to ride into battle meant they needed servants for military service. In return, the servants were granted land. This was the beginning of feudalism. Leading families jockeyed for the king's favour. In the 600s, two rival clans fought for power. The Austrasians ousted the Neustrians, and their chief, Pepin of Herstal, founded a new ruling family. Pepin's son, Charles Martel (known as 'the Hammer'), won an historic battle at Poitiers against Muslim invaders in 732. This defeat checked the advance of Islam into central Europe. Martel's son, Pepin the Short, was the first Frankish king anointed by the pope, in 754. But the greatest of the Frankish rulers was Pepin's son, Charlemagne.

The Franks were farmers. *They tilled their fields in strips using wheeled ploughs pulled by oxen. Oxen were slower than horses, but stronger.*

An example of fine metalwork *from the Frankish period. This gold and enamel buckle dates from the 6th to 7th centuries and would have been worn by a rich noble.*

570 Probable birth date of Muhammad.
610 Muhammad begins preaching in Mecca.
622 Muhammad's flight to Yathrib (now Medina).
625 Muhammad's teachings are written down in the Koran.
630 Muhammad leads an army into Mecca.
632 Muhammad dies. Abu Bakr becomes the first caliph.
634 Omar succeeds Abu Bakr.
644 Othman (head of the Ummayads) succeeds Omar.
656 The Shiite leader Ali becomes caliph.
661 The Islamic capital is moved from Mecca to Damascus.
732 Abd-al-Rahman, ruler of Spain, invades France. He is defeated by a Frankish army led by Charles Martel.
750 Abbasid dynasty is founded by Abu al-Abbas.
756 Last Ummayad ruler flees from Damascus to Cordoba, Spain.

The Rise of Islam

The new faith preached by the prophet Muhammad in the 600s changed the course of history. Muhammad's followers spread their religion, Islam, by preaching and conquest. By the 700s, Muslims (followers of Islam) ruled most of the Middle East and North Africa.

Before Muhammad, the Arab peoples were not united in any way. Different groups worshipped different gods. Muhammad was a merchant of Mecca, in Arabia. At the age of about 40, he began to preach of belief in one God, after a dream in which an angel told him he was the prophet of Allah (God). The new religion became Islam, which means 'submission to the will of Allah'.

Muhammad had to leave Mecca when some townspeople objected to his new teaching. His journey in 622 to Yathrib (now Medina) is commemorated still as the *Hegira*, which begins the Muslim calendar. In Medina, Muhammad and his followers built the first mosque. His teachings and revelations were written down in what became the Koran, the holy book of Islam.

***Harun al-Rashid** (766–806) was caliph from 786. The power of the Abbasid dynasty of caliphs peaked during his reign.*

***The Alhambra** is a large Moorish fortress and palace in Granada, Spain. Granada was the last Islamic stronghold in Spain before the expulsion of the Moors in 1492.*

The Dome of the Rock *in Jerusalem. Muslims believe Muhammad ascended to heaven from the rock to speak with God, before returning to Earth to spread Islam.*

A Muslim star chart *of a constellation. Muslim astronomers studied the stars and preserved many older Greek ideas about the universe.*

In 630, Muhammad's followers captured Mecca, and Islam became the new religion of Arabia.

When Muhammad died in 632, his father-in-law, Abu Bakr, was chosen as first caliph (successor). A group called the Shiites thought only the descendants of Muhammad's daughter Fatima could lead Islam. Others, known as Sunnis, thought any Muslim could do so. This split continues today.

By 644, the Arabs had conquered most of Syria, Palestine and Persia. After 661, the Ummayad family controlled the growing empire from their capital, Damascus, in Syria. Islam's advance into Europe was halted by the Frankish army of Charles Martel in 732. In 762, the new Abbasid dynasty moved the empire's capital to Baghdad (in what is now Iraq). This city became the centre of the Islamic world.

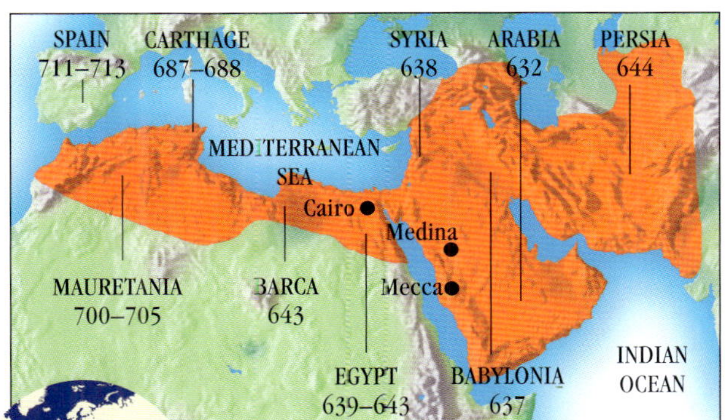

This map shows *how rapidly the new religion of Islam spread from Arabia as far west as Spain.*

3372 BC First date in the Mayan calendar.
400 BC The Maya have built several large pyramid-temples, like those at Tikal in Guatemala.
AD 250 Start of the classic period of the Mayan civilization.
600 Teotihuacan (Mexico) is at its most powerful.
700 Anasazi culture develops in southwestern USA.
750 Teotihuacan is destroyed.
c. 900 Decline of Mayan civilization. People move to the highlands of Mexico and Guatemala.
900 Rise of Toltecs.
968 Toltecs set up their capital at Tula.
1000 Mississippian culture at its height.
1100 Rise of the Chimu kingdom in Peru.
Late 1100s End of the Toltec state.
1200s The Cliff Palace is built at Mesa Verde (in what is now Colorado, USA).
c. 1250 Mayan culture revives: Mayapán is the chief city.
1440 Rebellion against Mayapán rulers.
1517 Start of Spanish conquest of Mayan lands.

American Civilizations

***As people moved south** across the Americas, rich civilizations developed in areas where the land was best suited for farming and settlement.*

Many impressive civilizations flourished in North, Central and South America. The Native Americans who created these civilizations built cliff-top palaces, huge earth mounds and pyramid temples. A few fragments of their civilizations' achievements survive today.

***A massive stone figure,** one of many found at Tiahuanaco in Bolivia. Tiahuanaco was the first planned city in the Andes.*

The Anasazi people lived in what is now the southwestern USA. They grew corn and built amazing cliff houses called pueblos, in which as many as 5,000 people lived.

To the east, the Mississippian people built well-planned towns of single-family houses.

Around AD 700, the largest city in America was in central Mexico. Teotihuacan was home to more than 100,000 people and was at the height of its power from about AD 350 to 750. From then on it was overshadowed by a new power, the Toltecs, who built their own temple-city at Tula.

GREAT SERPENT MOUND

This snake-shaped earthwork was made in about AD 1000 by Native Americans in what is now Ohio, USA. It is about 400 metres long. The mound was a sacred burial place. The snake grew bigger as more burials were added. Similar mounds were built by other peoples, including the Hopewell (c. 300 BC to AD 200).

***Ruins of Uxmal**, a Mayan city in the Yucatan Peninsula, Mexico. In the background, rising above the surrounding jungle, are the ruins of a typical Mayan pyramid-temple.*

In South America, high in the Andes, was the city of Tiahuanaco, which flourished between AD 500 and 1000. Here, people used llamas as pack animals and paddled reed boats on Lake Titicaca. Other city-states of the Andes, such as Huari in Peru, were greatly influenced by Tiahuanaco.

The Maya were at their most powerful from about AD 200 to 900, although their culture lasted until the early 1500s. They lived in well-organized city-states, each with its own ruler. The largest Mayan city was Tikal, in what is now Guatemala, with a population of 60,000. Crowds filled the large squares to watch ceremonies conducted by priests. Religion was important to the Maya. They made sacrifices to please their gods. Mostly, they sacrificed animals, but they also threw human victims into sacred wells. The Maya invented the first writing in America. They wrote codexes (folding books) on pages of tree bark. They also set up tall carved stones to commemorate dates and important events.

***A Mayan calendar.** The Mayan number system was based on 20. The farmers' calendar had 18 months, each with 20 days.*

***A Mayan ruler enters his city.** Each ruler was thought of as a god. Everyone worshipped him and offered tribute in the form of goods, food or work.*

742 Probable birth date of Charlemagne.
768 Pepin the Short (Charlemagne's father) dies.
771 Charlemagne becomes ruler of the Franks.
772 Charlemagne starts war with the Saxons and converts them to Christianity.
774 Charlemagne makes Lombardy (Italy) part of his empire.
778 Charlemagne fights the Muslims in Spain. His army is attacked by the Basques at the Battle of Roncesvalles.
788 Wars with Lombards, Bavarians, Avars, Bretons and others.
800 Charlemagne is crowned Holy Roman Emperor by Pope Leo III.
804 Last of 18 battles against the Saxons.
808 Charlemagne fights the Danes.
814 Charlemagne dies. His son Louis the Pious succeeds him.
817 The Holy Roman empire is split between Louis's sons.

Charlemagne

Charles I, king of the Franks, was known as 'Charlemagne', meaning Charles the Great. He founded the Holy Roman empire in Europe and was long regarded by many people as the 'ideal ruler'.

***Despite Charlemagne's success** in uniting much of Christian Europe, he failed in his attempt to conquer Spain. The Saxons also remained a thorn in his side. Between 772 and 804, he had to face them 18 times in battle.*

Charlemagne was born in 742. His father was King Pepin, who was son of the famous soldier Charles Martel and the founder of the new Frankish ruling family. This family was later called the Carolingian dynasty, after the Latin name for Charlemagne. In 768, Pepin died, leaving his kingdom to his sons Carloman and Charlemagne. Carloman soon died, and Charlemagne was left in sole control.

A very tall man convinced of his own destiny, Charlemagne had learned much from his ruthless warrior father. He led his armies out of the Frankish homeland of France into what are now the Netherlands, Germany and Italy. Wherever he conquered non-Christians, such as the Saxons of Germany and the Avars of Hungary, Charlemagne forced them to become Christians and to take part in mass baptisms.

There was more to Charlemagne than simply waging wars of conquest. He learned to read Latin and greatly admired scholarship. His capital at Aachen was the glittering centre of his empire, with a splendid palace and a heated swimming pool.

***Charlemagne's empire** grew from the lands of Austrasia (France and Germany) that he inherited from his father Pepin in 768 and his brother in 771 (in orange on the map). The Frankish empire was at its biggest extent soon after (orange and red).*

***The iron lance** of the Holy Roman emperors was a holy relic as well as a symbol of power. Around the spearpoint is a gold sheath stretched over a nail reputedly from Christ's cross.*

However, the emperor himself dressed and lived simply. He had books read aloud to him and invited famous scholars to his court, such as Alcuin of York.

Charlemagne's position as Europe's strongest leader was recognized in 800 when the pope crowned him Holy Roman Emperor. After he died in 814, the Holy Roman empire, weakened by attacks, was soon split between his three grandsons. It survived in one form or another until 1806.

After Charlemagne's death, many stories were written about him. A skirmish during his Spanish campaign of 778 became the subject of the medieval epic poem *The Song of Roland*.

The tomb of Charlemagne *at the imperial capital, Aachen, dates from 1215. It is decorated with gold and precious stones. Artists working 400 years after Charlemagne's death were able to refer to written descriptions of his appearance, but had no likeness of him to copy.*

802 King Jayavarman I founds the Khmer empire.
900 Early stages of building the city of Angkor Thom (then called Yasodharapura).
1113–50 Construction of the temple of Angkor Wat in modern Cambodia.
1181 Start of reign of King Jayavarman VII (to 1220).
1300s The Khmer empire is weakened by costly building plans, quarrels within the royal family and wars with the Thais.
1431 Thai army captures Angkor, marking the end of the Khmer empire. A smaller Khmer kingdom lasts until 1863, when the French take control of Cambodia and Angkor Wat is rediscovered.

The Khmer Empire

Between the 9th and 15th centuries, the Khmer empire of Cambodia dominated Southeast Asia. The Khmers were highly skilled builders and engineers. They constructed cities with massive temple complexes, palaces, lakes and canals.

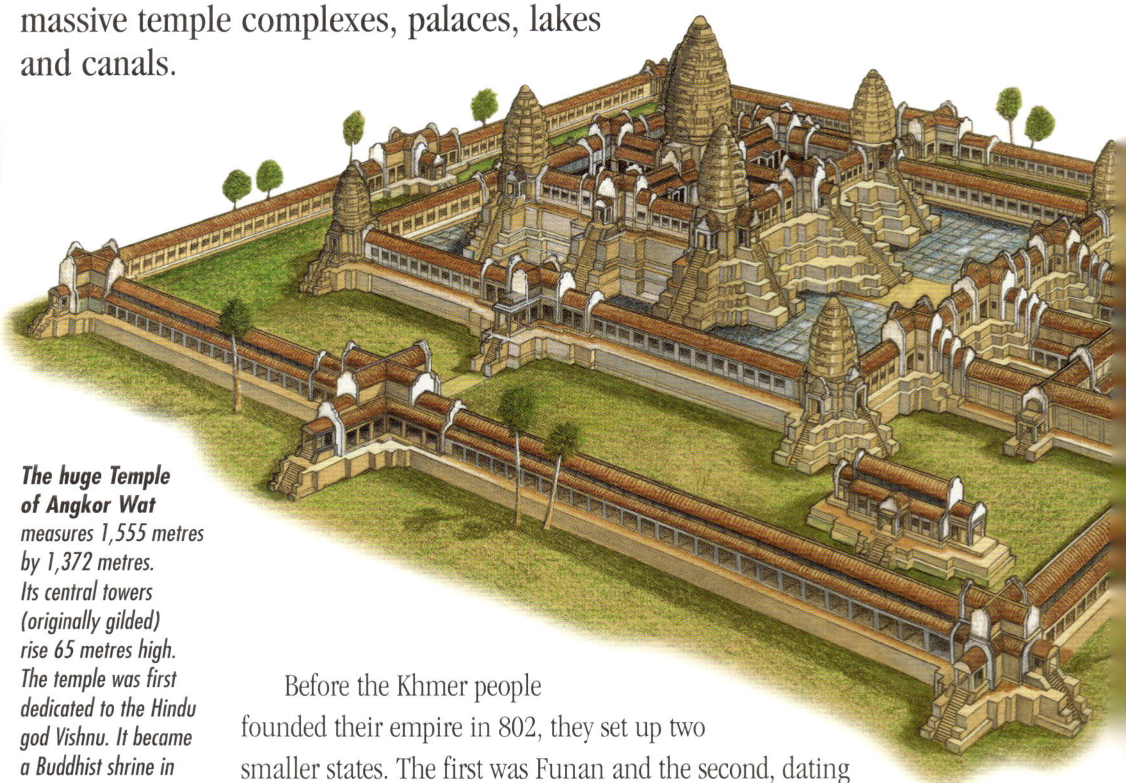

The huge Temple of Angkor Wat *measures 1,555 metres by 1,372 metres. Its central towers (originally gilded) rise 65 metres high. The temple was first dedicated to the Hindu god Vishnu. It became a Buddhist shrine in the 1500s.*

Before the Khmer people founded their empire in 802, they set up two smaller states. The first was Funan and the second, dating from 600, was Chenla. The Khmer empire was created by a strong king named Jayavarman I, who united people living in what are now parts of Cambodia, Thailand, Laos and Vietnam. He and his successors were worshipped as gods.

The ancient books of the Khmers have long since been destroyed, so what we know about them comes mostly from Chinese writings – the Chinese traded with the Khmers, buying spices and rhinoceros horns from them.

The many stone carvings in the ruins of the Khmers' greatest buildings – in the temple of Angkor Wat and in the city of Angkor Thom – also provide a valuable picture of everyday life, as well as recording sacred stories and victories in battle.

At the height of their power *the Khmers controlled much of what are now Cambodia, Thailand and Vietnam.*

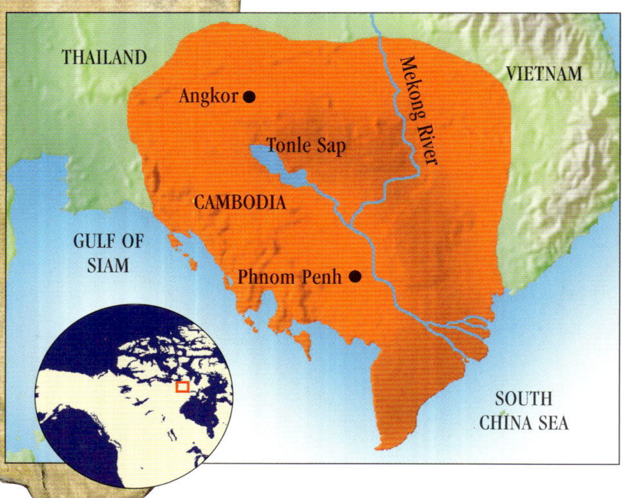

The Khmers built their wealth on rice. They dug irrigation ditches to water their rice fields and grew three crops a year. Never living far from water, they built houses on stilts beside rivers and on the shores of the lake named Tonle Sap.

Surayavarman II, leader of the Khmers from 1113 to about 1150, built Angkor Wat. A successful war leader, he fought in Thailand and Vietnam. The Khmer empire reached its height in the reign of Jayavarman VII (1181–1220). He built roads, hospitals and temples. Like all Khmer kings, he was a Hindu, although most of the people in the empire were Buddhists. The Khmers were fierce warriors, but in the 1400s they were overrun by the Thais. The great city and temple at Angkor were abandoned, and became overgrown by jungle.

Traditional houses in Cambodia *are built on stilts to protect them from flooding. Around Tonle Sap (Great Lake), the largest freshwater lake in Southeast Asia, people still live by fishing and trading from boats.*

Khmer archers *rode into battle on great war elephants. Bells and gongs added to the noise as they attacked. The Khmers held on to their conquests until they were themselves conquered by invaders from Thailand.*

787 First reported Viking raids on English coast.
795 Vikings begin attacks on Ireland.
841 Vikings found Dublin on Ireland's east coast.
c. 860 Vikings settle around the Baltic.
c. 861 Ingolf is the first Viking to reach Iceland.
862 The Slavs and Finns invite the Vikings to rule.
865 A great army of Vikings lands in England.
874 First Viking settlers reach Iceland.
878 Vikings are defeated by King Alfred of England. England is divided between Vikings and English.
886 Vikings are paid a huge sum to end siege of Paris.
900s Viking traders visit Constantinople, which they call 'Miklagaard'.
960 King Harald Bluetooth of Denmark becomes a Christian.
982 Erik the Red reaches Greenland.
c. 1000 Erik's son Leif Eriksson reaches Vinland (North America).
1014 Irish victory at the Battle of Clontarf. Viking dominance of Ireland ends.
1030 By King Olaf the Holy's reign, Norway is Christian.
1066 Last big Viking attack on England, by Harold Hardrada of Norway. His army is defeated at the Battle of Stamford Bridge.
1100s The Swedes are the last Vikings to convert to Christianity.

Wooden bucket

Pottery dish

Iron knife

Leather shoe

***Viking farmers** made tools, clothes, furniture and things to sell at market. Wood, ivory, deer antler, leather, clay, bone and iron were common materials used.*

The Vikings

The Vikings were great explorers. They set sail from Scandinavia (Norway, Sweden and Denmark) looking for new lands, and reached Greenland, Britain, and the Mediterranean and Black seas. Not all came as raiders; many were peaceful farmers and traders.

Scandinavia, the home of the Vikings, was covered in mountains and forests, and had little good farmland. Most Vikings lived close to the sea, tending small fields where they grew rye, barley, wheat, oats and vegetables. They kept cattle and sheep and caught fish. Traders travelled on horseback or by boat to market towns to exchange furs, reindeer antlers and walrus ivory for weapons, jewels and pottery.

Viking families lived in houses made of wood, stone or turf.

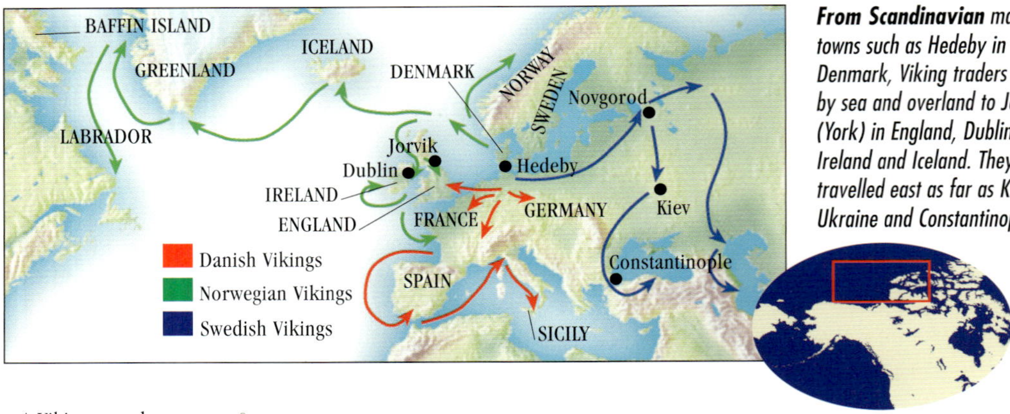

***From Scandinavian** market towns such as Hedeby in Denmark, Viking traders went by sea and overland to Jorvik (York) in England, Dublin in Ireland and Iceland. They travelled east as far as Kiev in Ukraine and Constantinople.*

A Viking sword was heavy and was swung in a wide arc.

The axe was a fearsome weapon at close quarters.

Viking warriors wore chain-mail tunics or, more commonly, leather jerkins.

WEIGHING COINS

Vikings valued coins by weight. Many traders carried balance scales to check that a customer's money was good and to show another merchant that he wasn't being cheated. Little lead weights such as those below were used to check coins. Small scales for weighing silver have been found at Viking settlements.

Many Vikings lived on small farms, *often near to rivers or the sea. They planted cereals and vegetables and kept pigs, cows, goats and sheep. Women wore linen dresses with wool tunics on top, fastened by brooches.*

Smoke from the cooking fire found its way out through a hole in the roof. Around the fire, people sat at benches and tables to eat hearty meals, play dice games and tell stories. The Vikings loved stories, especially those about their heroes and gods. Physical sports such as wrestling, horse fights and ice skating were also popular.

Viking farmers often had thralls (slaves) to help with the work, but most men were karls (freemen). A rich jarl, or landowner, was expected to share his wealth with his followers. As the population increased, farmland became increasingly scarce. From the late 700s, the Vikings began to search for better farmland and greater riches.

Viking longships were fast and strong enough to cross oceans. From the late 700s, bands of Vikings landed on the coasts of western Europe. Attacks on England began in 787. Word quickly spread that they were fierce fighters, and the sight of a Viking sail approaching caused panic. Wielding iron swords and axes, the Vikings raided monasteries and towns, carrying off slaves and booty.

The Vikings also came to seize land. By 865, Vikings from Denmark had begun to settle in eastern England, the islands of Scotland and in Ireland. They attacked what is now France, but were bought off with a gift of land in 911. Sailing west into the Atlantic, Norwegian Vikings settled in Iceland (874) and Greenland (982), and landed in North America (c. 1000). Swedish Vikings travelled east as far as the Black Sea, trading with Greeks and Arabs, who called them the 'Rus' (from which the name 'Russia' comes). Goods from Baghdad and Constantinople found their way back to Viking settlements in eastern England.

THE THING

The Viking law court was called the 'Thing'. Every year, local people came together for several days, and any freeman who had a complaint or an argument to settle could raise the matter. His neighbours would listen and give a judgement. A person refusing to obey the Thing's verdict became an outlaw, to be killed on sight.

Raiders rush from *longships after rowing up a river. Danish Vikings settled much of eastern England, and even after their defeat by King Alfred the Great, the Viking influence on English life remained.*

Feudal Europe

Late 400s Fall of the Roman empire leads to a breakdown in law and order across western Europe.
700s Feudal system starts among the Franks, based on arrangements for landholding and defence.
1066 Normans use the feudal system in England to strengthen their grip on the land after the conquest.
1100 It is now usual for a lord's oldest son to inherit his landholding or fief. (The word 'feudal' comes from a Latin name for fief.)
1200s Feudalism becomes more complex, with layers of vassal-lord relationships, from the king downwards.
1215 King John signs the Magna Carta, limiting the powers of the king of England.
1265 Simon de Montfort, a baron, calls citizens to a meeting with barons and churchmen – the first real Parliament in England. De Montfort's rebellion against King Henry III fails, but royal power in England is never the same again.
1300s Crossbows and cannon render knights less effective. The new technology of war speeds the end of feudalism.

A medieval king *had enormous power to govern. William the Conqueror kept a quarter of England's land for himself and granted the rest to his followers, in return for military service. Every landholder had to swear allegiance (loyalty) to the king.*

In feudal Europe, *the king held most land and power. Next came the lords, bishops and knights, followed by merchants and town craftworkers. Foot soldiers and peasants were the poorest.*

In western Europe, land was distributed by the king to his subjects in return for service. This arrangement, known as feudalism, lasted from the 700s to the 1300s.

In the feudal 'system', the king was at the top of the chain and the poor were at the bottom. In the middle were lords, churchmen, merchants and craftworkers in towns. The king and the noblemen (lords and barons) granted land to people lower down the feudal chain who, in turn, worked and fought for them. The people who worked and fought for their lord were called vassals. In return, the lord protected his vassals against attack from other countries or lords from another region.

Vassals had to supply soldiers to their lord or king on a certain number of days. This was usually for 40 days each year. The vassals also had to pay taxes, which could be in the form of money, farm produce or goods. Any vassal who refused to pay these taxes would have his land taken from him.

Bishop Scribe Lady Lord Falconer Knight

Feudalism first developed among the Franks. It was based on the traditional idea that a strong leader should protect and reward followers for their loyalty. Alongside this military arrangement was the farming system based around the manor.

Poor peasant farmers worked on manors, which were large areas of land held by a lord or knight. Peasants could own a small plot of land, but in return for this, they also had to work the lord's land.

During the early part of the Middle Ages, feudalism strengthened as kings granted more land to their knights, the warriors on whose loyalty and fighting skills they depended. However, the system began to fall apart in the 1200s, when people began using money more, and preferred to pay rent for land rather than be bound by service. The importance of knights and their castles began to lessen in the 1300s, when gunpowder changed the nature of warfare. New cannons could destroy a castle's defences easily. In the meantime, other new weapons, such as the crossbow, could pierce a knight's armour, diminishing his importance on the battlefield.

The disaster of the Black Death further weakened the system. The loss of so many peasant workers to the disease meant that those who survived were in great demand for their work. They could bargain for better conditions, knowing that the lords could not afford to lose their service.

Peasants at work on their lord's land *around his castle. In return for a small piece of land to farm, the peasants paid rent to the lord in the form of money, farm produce or military service.*

Merchant Archer Peasant Beggar

DOMESDAY BOOK

The Domesday (Doomsday) Book was a survey of England made on the orders of William the Conqueror in 1085. Commissioners took details of who owned what land and how many people lived in each village. Most old English villages and towns are listed.

Late 400s Early, simple monasteries are founded in Ireland.
c. 480–550 Life of St Benedict of Nursia, who founds his order of monks in 529.
500s St Columba founds a monastery on Iona, Scotland.
529 Abbey at Monte Cassino in Italy is founded. The Benedictine rule is formulated.
597 St Augustine founds the first English Benedictine monastery at Canterbury.
910 Cluniac order is founded.
966 Mont St Michel in France is built by the Benedictines.
1042 Edward the Confessor founds Westminster Abbey, in London.
1084 Order of Carthusians is founded.
1098 Cistercian order of monks is founded.
1100 Knights of St John (the Hospitallers) found a monastery 'hospital' for pilgrims journeying to the Holy Land.
1119 Order of Knights Templar founded.
1181–1226 Life of St Francis of Assisi, founder of the Franciscan friars.
Late 1100s University of Paris is founded. Monastery libraries help start Europe's universities.
1225–1274 Life of St Thomas Aquinas.

An illuminated manuscript page. *Some monks made the parchment. Others, called scribes, wrote the words, decorating them with paint and gold.*

Church and Monastery

In medieval Europe, thousands of men and women devoted their lives to the Christian Church, working, praying and studying in monasteries and nunneries. Monasteries became centres of learning.

Men and women who became monks or nuns obeyed rules originally set down in the 500s by, among others, St Benedict of Nursia. He taught that a monk or nun should be poor, unmarried and obedient. Monks wore simple robes, shaved their heads and lived together in communities known as monasteries. The head of the monastery was the abbot. Some later abbots managed large estates and even commanded knights. The head of a nunnery, a religious house for women, was called an abbess.

Monks and nuns followed a daily programme of prayer and worship, attending up to eight services every day. Monks ate together in a dining hall, called the refectory, and worked in the fields or in workshops. Later, lay brothers (workers who were not monks) did the heaviest work. Monks cared for the sick in the monastery's infirmary, gave food and shelter to travellers, and carefully copied books, creating brilliantly coloured letters and pictures, called illuminations. These books were kept in the large monastery libraries, so preserving ancient knowledge.

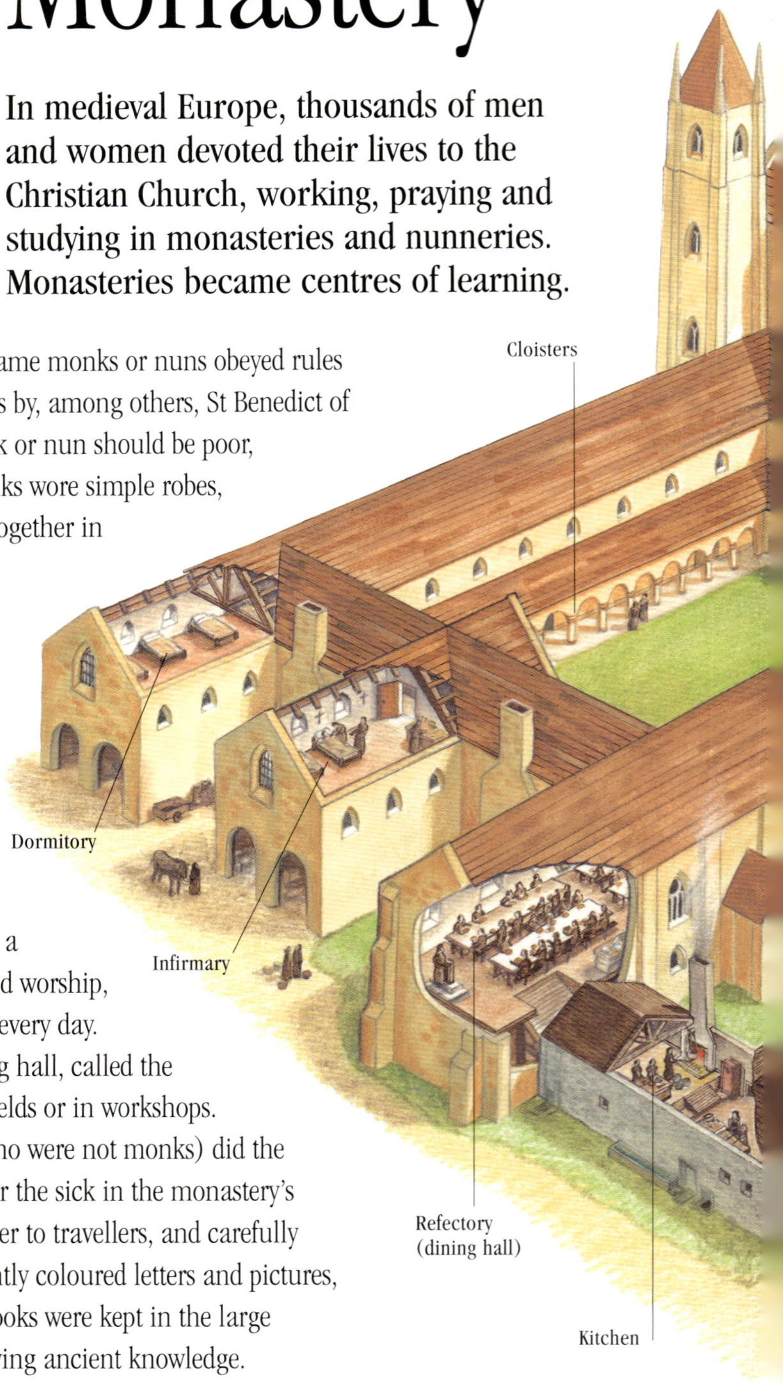

There were several organizations, or orders, of monks. These included the Benedictines, Carthusians and Cistercians. In the 1200s, new orders of travelling preachers, known as friars, were formed. Friars of the Franciscan order (founded by St Francis of Assisi) did not live inside monastery walls, but wandered the countryside preaching Christianity to the people.

A monastic community *followed a daily routine of work and worship. At its heart was the chapel. There were herb gardens and cloisters (covered walks), an infirmary for the sick, workshops and farm buildings.*

Founded in 909, Cluny Abbey *in France is one of many abbeys in Europe built during the Middle Ages. An abbey was a large community of monks or nuns, who lived quietly within its walls.*

CHRISTIAN PILGRIMS

Pilgrims in the Middle Ages made long journeys to visit holy places or shrines, which could hold the bones or tomb of a saint or some other holy relic. In England, the most famous shrine was that of St Thomas à Becket at Canterbury.

Knights and Castles

500s Byzantines build strong stone castles and walled cities.
800s Arabs build castles in the Middle East and North Africa.
950 Earliest known French castle built at Doue-la-Fontaine, Anjou.
1000s Normans develop the motte (mound) and bailey (enclosure).
1078 In England, building of the Tower of London begins.
1100s Stone keeps become the main castle stronghold.
1142 Crusaders take over Krak des Chevaliers in Syria.
1150–1250 Thousands of castles are built across what is now Germany.
1180s Castles with square-walled towers are built.
1200s Concentric or ring-wall castle design is used in Europe.
1205 Krak des Chevaliers is rebuilt by the Knights Hospitallers.
1220s Castles with round-walled towers are first built.
1280s Edward I of England orders many castles to be built in England and Wales.
1320s Cannons are first used in Europe.
1400s Castle building declines in Europe.

Knights were the most heavily armoured soldiers of the Middle Ages. Clad in metal, they rode to battle on horseback. Their base was the castle, a strong fortress. There were castles all over Europe, the Middle East and India, and as far east as Japan. A castle was also home to a lord and his family.

A jester *would entertain the lord of the castle and his guests during a medieval banquet.*

The earliest medieval castles were earth mounds with wooden stockades on top. Castles like these were built by the Norman invaders of England in 1066, often on the site of earlier Saxon and Roman forts. These early castles were soon enlarged and strengthened, using water-filled ditches, called moats, stone walls protected by towers, and a massive central stronghold called a keep. Castles were often built on hilltops for good visibility, or to guard harbours, rivers and vital roads.

The building of the central keep Tower of London*, called the White Tower, was started in 1078 by William the Conqueror. Since then, the castle has been used as a royal palace, a weapons store, a place of execution, a prison and as the royal mint where coins were made.*

Jousting was combat on horseback between two knights with blunt-tipped lances. A joust was a social occasion with a large audience. In a tournament, groups of knights fought mock battles, sometimes with fatal accidents. Safety measures, including blunt swords, were only introduced in the 1300s.

Castles were private fortresses for the lords who owned them. A castle was also a family home. Early castles were cold and draughty, with no glass in the windows and dry reeds on the stone floor. The lord and his followers feasted in the great hall. Food was brought by servants from the kitchen. At night, everyone slept on the floor around the central fire, except the lord and his lady, who retired to a private room called the solar. Before about 1300, people rarely took baths, and lavatories emptied straight into the moat. The castle was defended by foot soldiers and mounted knights. When a castle was attacked, the defenders needed enough food and water to withstand a siege lasting weeks or even months. Castle walls had to be thick enough to withstand catapults, tunnels and battering rams. In due course, cannons and barrels of gunpowder placed in tunnels proved so effective at blasting down walls that castle building came to an end.

Knights carried shields to ward off blows *and to identify themselves. A shield carried its owner's family badge, which was called a coat of arms.*

The Crusades

For European Christians, the Crusades were holy wars, with the promise of plunder in the service of the Church. For more than 200 years, Christian and Muslim armies fought for control of the Holy Land, the territory around Jerusalem in the Middle East.

1096 First Crusade, called by Pope Urban II. Peter the Hermit leads a peasant army across Europe.
1099 Crusaders defeat the Turks and capture Jerusalem.
1147 Second Crusade. German and French armies are defeated.
1187 Saladin captures Jerusalem.
1189 Third Crusade, led by Frederick I 'Barbarossa' of the Holy Roman empire, Philip II of France and Richard I of England.
1191 Crusaders capture the port of Acre in Palestine.
1202 Fourth Crusade attacks Egypt.
1204 Crusaders capture Constantinople.
1221 Fifth Crusade. Crusaders fight the sultan of Egypt.
1228 The Sixth Crusade ends when Muslims hand over Jerusalem.
1244 Muslims retake Jerusalem.
1249 Seventh Crusade is led by Louis IX of France.
1270 Eighth Crusade also led by Louis. He and many of his men die of plague in Tunis.
1291 Acre, last crusader stronghold, is captured.

***Crusaders found** the weather in the Holy Land very hot, and soon learned from Muslim soldiers that it was best to wear airy, loose robes over their armour.*

Many Christian pilgrims visited Jerusalem, which was a holy city to Jews and Muslims, as well as to Christians. But Jerusalem was held by Muslim Turks, and in 1095 they banned Christian pilgrims from the city. This angered both the western Christian Church, based in Rome, and the eastern Christian Church in Constantinople. From Rome, Pope Urban II called on Christians to free Jerusalem, and so launched the First Crusade, or war of the cross. In 1096, a European force joined with an army from Constantinople. Their leaders were inspired by religious faith, but also by a desire to increase territory and wealth. In three years, they captured Jerusalem and went on to set up Christian kingdoms in Palestine. None of the seven later crusades matched this success.

***Saladin (1138–93)** was the greatest of the Muslim leaders. He took Jerusalem, and in 1192 made peace with Richard I, allowing Christian pilgrims to enter the city.*

***The Church of the Holy Sepulchre** in Jerusalem is built on the site where Christ is said to have been crucified and buried. Jerusalem remains a holy city to Christians, Jews and Muslims today.*

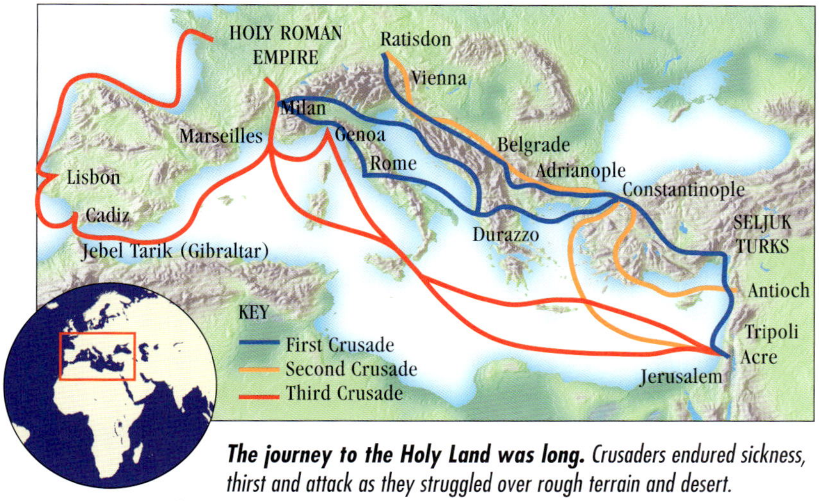

The journey to the Holy Land was long. *Crusaders endured sickness, thirst and attack as they struggled over rough terrain and desert.*

CHILDREN'S CRUSADE OF 1212

Inspired by two boy preachers, 50,000 children in two groups, one from France and one from Germany, set off for the Holy Land. Some died on the journey, and many others were sold as slaves in North Africa.

The Crusades inspired many stories of bravery and honour on both sides. But disasters also happened. Before the First Crusade even set out, a peasant army known as the People's Crusade wandered across Europe and was eventually massacred by the Turks. Then the Fourth Crusade of 1202 turned aside to loot the Christian city of Constantinople.

The Crusaders never did win back the Holy Land. But Europeans learned more about eastern science, food and medicine as trade between Europe and Asia grew.

Both sides built strong castles. *To capture a castle, soldiers besieged it, sometimes for months. They battered at the gates and tried to blow up the walls, while being bombarded with missiles from inside.*

1162 Work begins on the cathedral of Notre Dame in Paris, which by 1210 is a city with paved streets, walls and 24 gates.

1136 Fire destroys many old, straw-thatched buildings in London.

1200s Many new towns are founded in Europe. City states develop in Italy and Germany.

1209 A new London Bridge is built.

1260 The German towns of Lubeck and Hamburg form a trade association, which is later known as the Hanseatic League.

1285 English merchants are banned from selling their goods in churchyards.

1300 The wool trade is at its peak in England. Large churches are built in prosperous wool towns.

1348–49 People flee towns during the Black Death in England.

1377 London by now has at least 50 guilds and a population of more than 35,000 people.

1400s Morality plays, in which actors stage tales of good against evil, are performed in churches or in the streets.

A Medieval Town

In the Middle Ages, towns in Europe were noisy and crowded by day, but quiet and dark at night. The silence was broken only by watchmen calling out the hours. Churches, guilds, fairs and markets all drew people into the towns.

If you walked through a medieval town, you took care where you stepped, because people threw out their rubbish into the muddy streets. Open drains ran alongside and smelled foul. People either fetched water from the town well or bought it from the water-seller, hoping it was clean. Pigs and chickens wandered in and out of small yards. Houses were built close together, with the top floors often jutting out over the streets. Since most houses were made chiefly of wood, they caught fire easily. At night, the curfew bell warned people to cover or put out their kitchen fires.

Stained-glass windows *told stories in pictures. In church, people who could not read looked at the colourful windows to learn more about Bible stories and the Christian faith.*

Market day in a medieval town. *People brought in farm produce to sell, visited stalls and shops, gossiped and drank at the ale house. Acrobats, actors and dancing bears amused the crowds.*

MONEY MAKES MONEY

European merchants usually carried silver coins, but Arabs preferred gold. As international trade increased, Italian merchants set up the first banks, using written bills of exchange to pay for goods instead of heavy bags of coins.

This image *shows tradesmen at work in their shops. Tailors stitch cloth and a grocer sets out his goods. Up the street a barber is shaving a customer.*

Many houses doubled as workshops and shops. Craftworkers and traders formed groups called guilds to organize their businesses and to set standards of work. Guilds also staged pageants and plays in the streets. Some towns were famous for their fairs, which attracted merchants from all over Europe, as well as entertainers, fake doctors and pickpockets.

In towns, work was to be found building magnificent cathedrals, churches and defensive walls. Large trading cities in Europe, such as Hamburg, Antwerp and London, grew rich from buying and selling wool and other goods. About 90 cities in northern Europe formed the Hanseatic League to fight pirates, win more trade and keep out rivals.

The Mongols

'Inhuman and beastly, rather monsters than men...' is how the English historian Matthew Paris described the Mongols in the 1200s. Mongol armies conquered a vast area of land that formed the largest empire in history. When Kublai Khan became leader of the Mongols, he moved from the steppes of Central Asia to rule the most splendid court in the world, in China.

***Genghis Khan** was ruthless in battle, but kept peace in his empire and ruled fairly, if sternly. Trade flourished during his rule.*

1206 Temujin is chosen to be khan of all the Mongols He takes the name Genghis Khan.

1211 The Mongol army attacks China.

1215 Beijing, capital of China, is captured.

1216 Kublai Khan is born.

1219 The Mongols sweep west to attack the empire of Khwarezm.

1224 Mongol armies invade Russia, then Poland and Hungary.

1227 Genghis Khan dies. In 1229, his son Ogadai is chosen as the new khan.

1237 Mongol generals Batu and Subotai invade northern Russia.

1241 Ogadai dies. His armies pull back from Europe.

1260 Kublai is elected Great Khan of the Mongols.

1271 Marco Polo sets out from Venice for China.

1274 Kublai Khan tries to invade Japan, but is driven back by a storm.

1281 A second Mongol attack on Japan is foiled by a typhoon, which the Japanese call kamikaze, the 'divine wind'.

1294 Kublai Khan dies.

1368 The Mongols are driven from China.

1395 Tamerlane invades parts of southern Russia.

1398 Tamerlane takes Delhi in India.

1405 Death of Tamerlane.

The Mongols lived on the plains of Central Asia, from the Ural mountains to the Gobi Desert. They were nomads, wandering with their herds and living in portable tents (yurts). Their leaders were called khans. In 1206, Temujin Khan brought all the tribes under his rule and was proclaimed Genghis Khan, 'lord of all'. In a lifetime of conquest, he seized an empire that extended from the Pacific Ocean in the east to the river Danube in the west, incorporating the once mighty Persian empire. The Mongols continued their attacks after Genghis Khan died. In 1237, a Mongol army led by Batu Khan, one of Genghis' sons, invaded Russia.

In Europe, people panicked as word spread of the Mongols' speed and ferocity in battle. Mongol soldiers travelled with five horses each and they were experts with bows and lances. In victory, they were merciless, slaughtering the people of a city and carting away treasure. Western Europe was saved only when the Mongols turned homeward on the death of their leader Ogadai Khan in 1241.

***The Mongols roamed** in search of fresh grassland for their sheep, horses and goats. They carried their felt houses (yurts) with them on ox carts.*

***Mongols preferred** to fight on horseback. Warriors controlled their horses with their feet, leaving their hands free to shoot bows and hurl spears. Mongol cavalry charges usually overwhelmed the enemy.*

In China, Kublai Khan (1216–94) founded the Yuan dynasty, which lasted until 1368. Yuan means 'origin of the universe'.

***Genghis Khan's empire** extended from the river Danube in the west to the Pacific in the east. The capital was Karakorum.*

Genghis's grandson, Kublai Khan, overthrew the ruling Song dynasty in China. By 1279, he controlled most of the country and moved his capital to Beijing. China had the world's biggest cities, including Kaifeng and Hangzhou (each with more than one million people).

Kublai Khan strengthened his empire by building long roads to connect territories. He also tried to invade Japan twice, without success. After his death in 1294, the Mongol empire began to decline and by the mid 1300s had largely broken up. Then in 1369, Timur 'Leng' ('the lame'), known as Tamerlane, made himself ruler of Samarkand in Central Asia. He set out to re-create the Mongol empire, and conquered Persia, Iraq, Syria, Afghanistan and part of Russia. In 1397, he invaded India, and died on the way to China in 1405.

***Merchants travelled in caravans** (groups of laden camels and horses) for protection against bandits. From China, they followed the Silk Road across mountains and deserts to the markets of the Middle East. The Silk Road provided the only regular contact between Europe and China.*

MARCO POLO

In 1271, an Italian merchant named Marco Polo (1256–1323) travelled to China from Venice. He stayed for 24 years, touring China in the service of Kublai Khan. Later, he wrote about China's cities and inventions. Today, however, there is some debate about whether he even visited China or whether he simply made up his stories.

***The Chinese began** making paper in about AD 105. In the imperial workshops, paper makers used hemp or mulberry tree bark for fibre. Pulp was spread on mesh trays to dry into sheets.*

1344 Bubonic plague breaks out in China and India.
1347 The plague reaches Genoa in Italy and spreads farther west.
1348 In the summer, the disease hits southern England. In the winter, it reaches London.
1349 The Black Death spreads to Ireland, Wales and Scotland. Also affected are France, Spain, Germany and Russia.
1350 The epidemic reaches Scandinavia.
1353 The Black Death epidemic eases. As many as 20 million people in Europe are dead.
1358 A peasants' uprising in northern France is savagely put down.
1361–63 Subsequent outbreak of the plague.
1381 The Peasants' Revolt in England, with rioting in the southeast (in Essex and Kent).
1400 Further outbreaks of the Black Death continue until this date.

The Black Death

The Black Death was the most horrific natural disaster of the Middle Ages. It was a devastating plague that killed many millions of people in Europe and Asia. One Italian historian wrote: 'This is the end of the world.'

A picture of the time *shows a procession of penitents whipping themselves in the streets. Many people believed that the Black Death was a punishment from God.*

The plague came to Europe from Asia in 1347. Disease ravaged a Mongol army fighting in the Crimea (southern Russia). The Mongols catapulted diseased corpses over the walls of a fortress defended by Italians. When the Italians sailed home to Genoa, they carried the disease with them.

The disease was bubonic plague, which was passed to humans from infected rats through flea bites. The name 'Black Death' came from the black spots that appeared on victims, who also developed swellings in their armpits and groins and coughed up blood. Many died the day they fell ill.

No medieval doctor knew why the Black Death struck or how to cure it. To many Christians it seemed to be a punishment from God, and some took to the streets, whipping themselves as a penance for the sins of humanity.

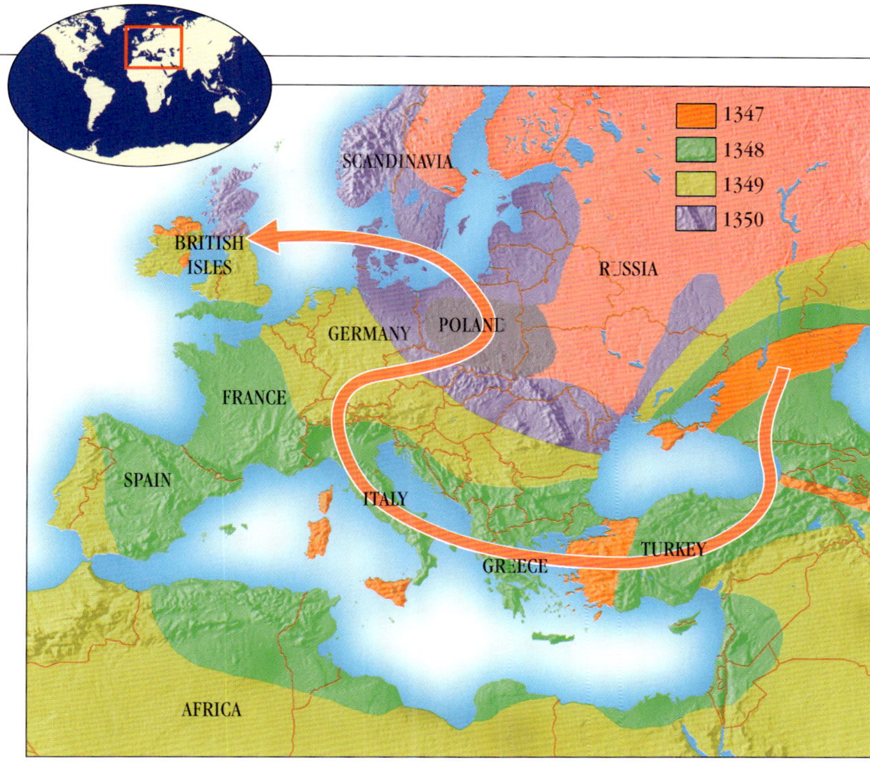

The Black Death raged from China to Scandinavia. As it spread, panic-stricken people fled from the towns. Wherever they went, the plague went with them. So many people died (more than 20 million, or a third of the people in Europe) that villages were left deserted and fields overgrown. The Church lost many priests, the only educated men of the time. Half of England's monks and nuns died, and three archbishops of Canterbury died in one year.

From East Asia, *the plague swept into the north and west of Europe.*

Repeated plague attacks throughout the 14th century left Europe short of people to work and farm the land, and pushed up wages. Unrest over wages and taxes led to an uprising in France in 1358 and to the Peasants' Revolt in England, led by Wat Tyler, in 1381.

Neither town governments *nor local doctors could fight the plague. Many people fled, leaving the sick to die. Carts carried the dead away.*

BLACK DEATH

The black rat carried the fleas that transmitted the disease. The rats travelled on ships from port to port, and, as they moved, the Black Death spread at terrifying speed. There were rats and fleas in every medieval town and in most houses. Rubbish in the streets and poor sanitation made towns an ideal breeding ground for disease. Many towns lost half their populations to the plague, and some villages were abandoned.

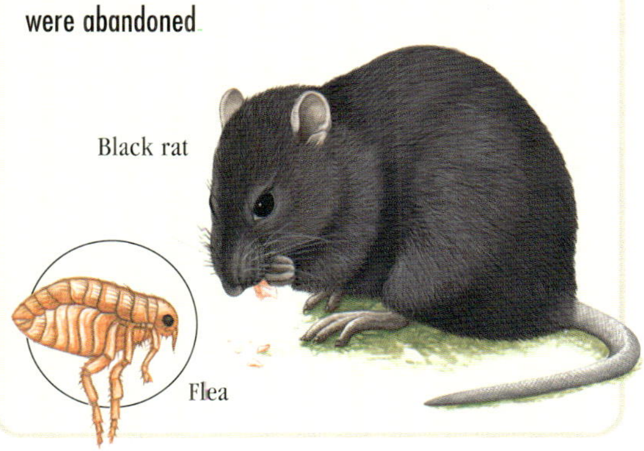

750 Arab armies have overrun most of North Africa. Islam spreads westwards.
770 Soninke people begin to build the kingdom of Ghana, led by King Maghan Sisse.
800 Ife kingdom in Nigeria becomes prominent.
800s Arabs and Persians set up trading posts in East Africa.
900s Ghana controls gold and salt trade and buys cloth from Europe.
969 Fatimid dynasty conquers Egypt.
1043 Mandingo empire of Jenne is founded in West Africa.
1062 Muslim Berbers (Almoravids) build their capital of Marrakech.
1070 Ghana is conquered by the Almoravids.
1100 All of Muslim Spain is now part of the Almoravid empire.
1163 Almohads overthrow Almoravids and rule northeast Africa and Spain.
1173 Saladin declares himself sultan of Egypt.
1200s Founding of Benin kingdom under the first oba, Eweka.
1250 Mamelukes rule in Egypt.
1307 Mali empire at its height under Mansa Musa, with its capital at Timbuktu.
1440–80 Reign of the most famous oba of Benin, Ewuare the Great.

African Kingdoms

In this period, the abundant riches of the mightiest kingdoms in Africa impressed Muslims and Europeans who visited their courts. Much of this wealth came from trade in gold, salt and slaves.

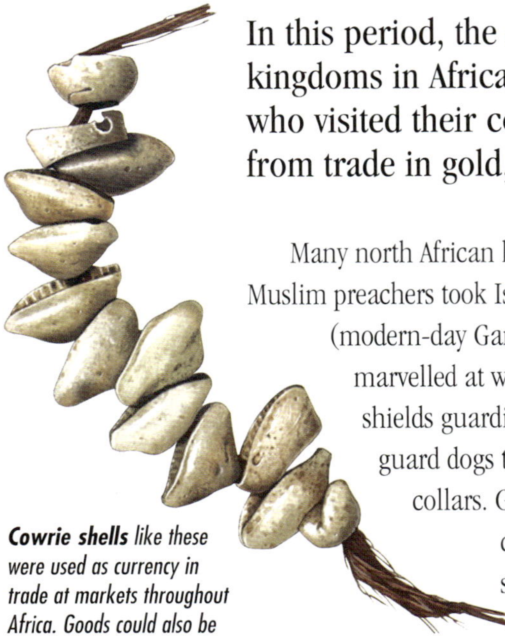

***Cowrie shells** like these were used as currency in trade at markets throughout Africa. Goods could also be exchanged, or 'bartered', for other goods that were worth a similar value.*

Many north African kingdoms were Muslim. From these kingdoms, Muslim preachers took Islam to West Africa. In the kingdom of Ghana (modern-day Gambia, Guinea, Mali and Senegal), Muslim traders marvelled at warriors who carried gold-mounted swords and shields guarding the king in his capital, Koumbi Saleh. Even the guard dogs that were kept in the royal pavilion wore gold collars. Ghana reached the peak of its power in the 10th century, when it controlled both the gold and salt trade in the region.

In the 1300s, Muslim camel caravans crossed the Sahara Desert to the city of Timbuktu. They carried cloth and luxury items, which were exchanged for slaves, leather goods and kola nuts (used as a drug). Timbuktu was the capital of Mali, an Islamic kingdom that soon replaced Ghana as the most powerful empire in West Africa. Mali's most famous ruler, Mansa Musa, made a pilgrimage to Mecca in 1324, with an entourage of 60,000 followers. His fame spread as far as Europe, where his kingdom was shown on maps as a land that was filled with gold.

***Many people in Africa** were skilled in metalworking. This bronze hand altar shows a Benin king with his wives, servants and soldiers. The lost-wax process was used to make bronzes of superb quality.*

Farther south were kingdoms just as splendid, such as Ife, Oyo and Benin, where trade made powerful rulers rich.

The craftworkers of Benin made cast bronze figures, the finest metal sculptures in Africa. Benin's ruler, who was called the oba, lived in a walled city with his 100 or so wives. The people of Benin traded with the Portuguese, who began sailing along the West African coast in the 1400s.

In East Africa, people living in what are now Somalia, Kenya and Tanzania traded in ivory, animal skins and slaves with cities on the coast. These were visited by ships from Arabia and India. The east coast prosperity lasted until almost 1500, when the Portuguese took control of trade in the region and the trading cities were destroyed.

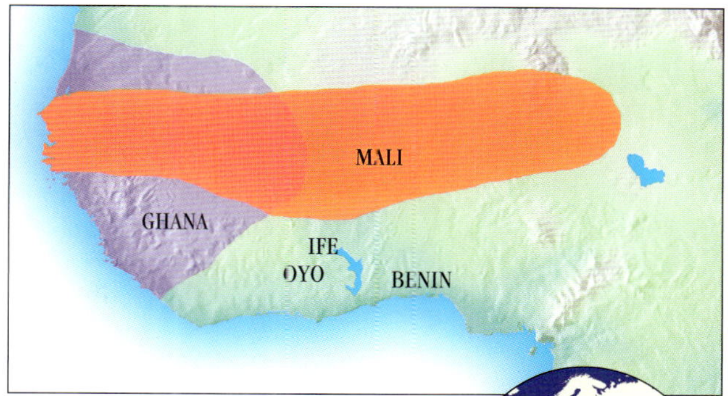

The kingdom of Ghana *rose to power by the 900s, but was later swallowed up by the Islamic empire of Mali. Other African kingdoms also flourished in West Africa, including Ife, Oyo and Benin.*

Mansa Musa *on his pilgrimage to Mecca in 1324. He lead a large army that contained camels, horses and foot soldiers. His fame spread as far as Europe.*

582 Buddhism reaches Japan.
794 Imperial court moves to Heiankyo (modern-day Kyoto).
995 Literary and artistic achievements under Fujiwara Michinaga.
c. 1002 Murasaki Shikibu writes *Tale of Genji*, the world's first novel.
1192 Minamoto Yoritomo sets up military government or shogunate.
1219 Hojo clan rules Japan until 1333.
1274 Mongols try to invade Japan, but are driven back by a terrible storm.
1333 Daigo II overthrows Hojo shoguns and rules until 1336.
1338 Ashikaga family rule as shoguns until 1573.
1543 Shipwrecked Portuguese introduce firearms to Japan.
1549 Francis Xavier introduces Christianity to Japan.

Japan's Warlords

Emperors in medieval Japan had little power, relying on warlords, or shoguns, who led armies of warriors and ruled the land.

Japan's emperors were dominated by powerful military families. From these soldier clans came the shoguns, such as the powerful Minamoto Yoritomo (1147–99). The shoguns drove off attacks from Mongol China with their fiercely loyal samurai warriors. Like a knight in Europe, a samurai held land that was farmed by peasants, while he hunted or trained with sword and bow. The samurai eventually came to form an elite warrior class. They practised Zen Buddhism, a philosophy brought to Japan from China in 582.

From the 1300s, Japan was torn apart by civil wars between daimyos – lords who built castles to guard their lands. The daimyos led armies of samurai warriors. The most powerful daimyo was Hideyoshi Toyotomi (1537–98), a peasant who rose to become a samurai warlord. He controlled all Japan from 1585 until his death. One of his lieutenants, Ieyasu, became shogun in 1603 and founded the Tokugawa dynasty.

A Samurai warrior *wore a steel horned helmet and fought with bow, sword and lance. His body armour was made in pieces from leather or lacquered iron strips, making it very flexible.*

DIVINE WIND

The Japanese believed the gods protected them. In 1274 and 1281, Kublai Khan sent fleets to conquer Japan. The first fled before a storm. The second was sunk by a typhoon (shown here as a god), which the Japanese called kamikaze, or 'divine wind'.

The Hundred Years' War

1337 Edward III goes to war with France, claiming the throne.
1340 Sea battle of Sluys (off Belgium) won by English.
1346 English victory at the Battle of Crécy.
1356 English victory at Poitiers, led by Edward III's son, the Black Prince.
1380 France's Charles V dies. Charles VI succeeds him.
1399 Henry of Lancaster seizes English throne, becoming Henry IV.
1415 Henry V of England gains control of France after victory at Agincourt.
1429 Joan of Arc relieves the siege at Orleans.
1431 Joan of Arc is burned to death.
1436 Charles VII captures Paris.
1453 Bordeaux is captured by the French. End of the Hundred Years' War.

Edward III became king of England in 1327. He believed he also had a claim to the French throne, so, in 1337, he declared war on France. War between England and France lasted on and off until 1453.

Edward's forces won a sea battle at Sluys and two great land victories at Crécy and Poitiers, but were driven back by the French king, Charles V, and his commander Bertrand du Guesclin. In 1360, Edward gave up his claim to the French throne in return for land.

Years of truce followed until England's King Henry V renewed his claim to the throne in 1414. He led his troops to France where, in 1415, they defeated a much larger French army at Agincourt. To make peace, Henry married the French king's daughter, but he died in 1422 before his baby son could become king of France. Fighting continued as the French were inspired by a peasant girl named Joan of Arc (1412–31), who claimed to hear voices from God. She fought until she was captured and burned her as a witch. Under the weak rule of Henry VI, the English lost Paris, Rouen and, by 1453, all French lands except Calais.

***Soldiers fought** with (top row, left to right) halberd, longbow, (second row) sword, cannon and crossbow. Only knights wore full armour. If knocked from his horse, a knight was often imprisoned and ransomed.*

***The death of Joan of Arc.** The English hoped this would end French resistance, but the French were inspired to fight on and win back their lands.*

40,000 years ago People move from Southeast Asia to the islands of Indonesia, New Guinea and Australia.
c. 25,000 years ago Aborigines settle in southeast Australia. This part of Australia later becomes the island of Tasmania (when the sea level has risen, about 12,000 years ago).
c. 4000 BC People from New Guinea settle in the Solomon Islands (Melanesia).
c. 1000 BC People from Melanesia sail east to settle on Fiji. Other people from Polynesia also make voyages to colonize the Fijian islands.
AD 100 Polynesian settlers arrive in the Hawaiian Islands.
c. 400 The first settlers land on Easter Island. They probably came from Polynesia, though some historians claim that the island was colonized by South Americans.
c. 750 Maoris start to settle New Zealand. They probably came from eastern Polynesia. They did not use the name Maori until much later.
900 Earliest recorded rulers of Tonga, an island group in the South Pacific settled earlier by Polynesians, who probably came from Samoa.

Pacific Voyagers

The first people to settle Oceania – Australia, New Zealand and the Pacific islands – almost certainly came originally from Asia. They made some astonishing voyages, crossing vast stretches of the world's largest ocean in wooden canoes.

The first humans to settle in New Guinea and Australia had arrived there by 40,000 years ago. Until about 10,000 years ago, these two land masses formed one large continent, of which Tasmania (now an island) was also a part. So it was relatively easy for humans from Asia to migrate there, either over land or by crossing narrow stretches of water.

The first people to reach Australia probably arrived from the islands of Southeast Asia. Although they never made metal tools, they survived in Australia's often harsh environments, spearing fish and using boomerangs to kill animals for food. They became expert at finding seeds, insect grubs, roots, tubers and fruits to eat. The modern Aboriginal peoples of Australia preserve some of these ancient skills.

Humans settled the islands of the western Pacific, known as Melanesia, by 'island-hopping'. However, reaching the more remote islands of Micronesia (such as Guam, the Marianas and Nauru) and Polynesia (including Fiji, Tonga and Samoa) was more difficult.

***The Maoris of New Zealand** built wooden stockades, called pas. Warriors fought from platforms on the walls. To capture an enemy's fort was a great triumph. The victors took the food stored inside.*

Aboriginal paintings on rocks *and tree bark often depicted animals and people. They were painted in pigments made from coloured earth and were drawn to keep ancestor spirits alive.*

Mysterious stone statues *scattered around Easter Island. The tallest figure is 11 m high. No one knows why the stone heads were carved and set up.*

A Maori war canoe sets out on a raid. *Like other Pacific islanders, the Maoris built wooden canoes for sea travel, often twin-hulled like modern catamarans. Some settlements were the result of accidental voyages, others of planned migrations.*

About 4,000 years ago the intrepid colonists set sail in outrigger canoes loaded with essentials – coconuts, taro, yams, bananas, breadfruit, pigs and chickens. They relied on skill and luck to land on islands dotted across the Pacific Ocean. Canoe voyagers travelled as far west as Easter Island and, about 2,000 years ago, they reached the Hawaiian islands.

One of the last places the voyagers colonized was New Zealand. Polynesian Maoris had landed in New Zealand by about AD 750. Australia was isolated, apart from occasional visits from Indonesian and possibly Chinese traders, until the 1500s. The great southern continent and the Pacific islands remained unknown to Europeans.

The Age of Discovery

The 1400s mark the end of the Middle Ages. In Europe, the new ideas of the Renaissance and the Reformation transformed the way people thought about themselves and the world, and the way they lived.

p106 Tokugawa Ieyasu (1543–1616), the shogun of Japan.

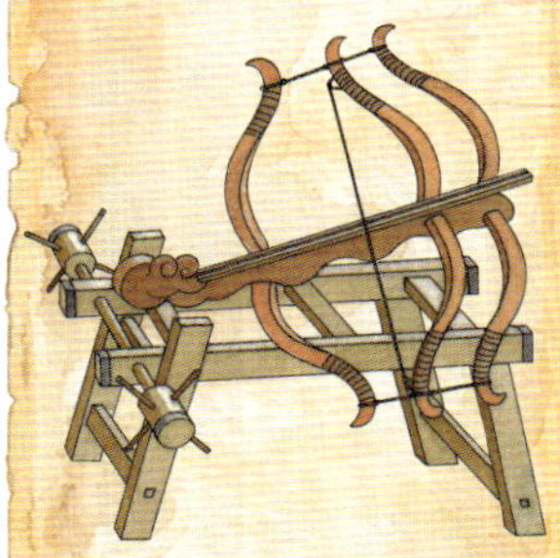

p101 A Chinese artillery crossbow could fire an arrow that could pierce armour up to 200 m away.

p108 Coffee, tea, cinnamon and cloves were valuable goods traded by the Dutch East India Company.

p90 European explorers sailed in ships called carracks with three masts and square sails. Columbus's ship Santa Maria may have looked like this.

Three events are often picked out as marking the end of the medieval period and the start of the modern age. They are the fall of the city of Constantinople (now called Istanbul) in 1453, which ended the last traces of the old Roman empire; the development of printing in the 1450s, which made books cheaper and more widely available; and the first voyage of Christopher Columbus to the Americas in 1492.

The 'Age of Discovery' was a time when the peoples of the world came into increasing contact with each other. Cultures in America, Africa and Asia had greater contact with Europe. Europeans increased their power in the world through trade, through the use of new technology, such as cannon and muskets, and through a restless search for new lands and wealth.

p89 A gold raft depicting El Dorado, a legendary ruler whose body was said to be dusted with gold every year.

p89 The Spanish were fewer in number than the Incas. But they had horses, armour and guns. Many Incas fought bravely, but with their king murdered, they were quickly defeated.

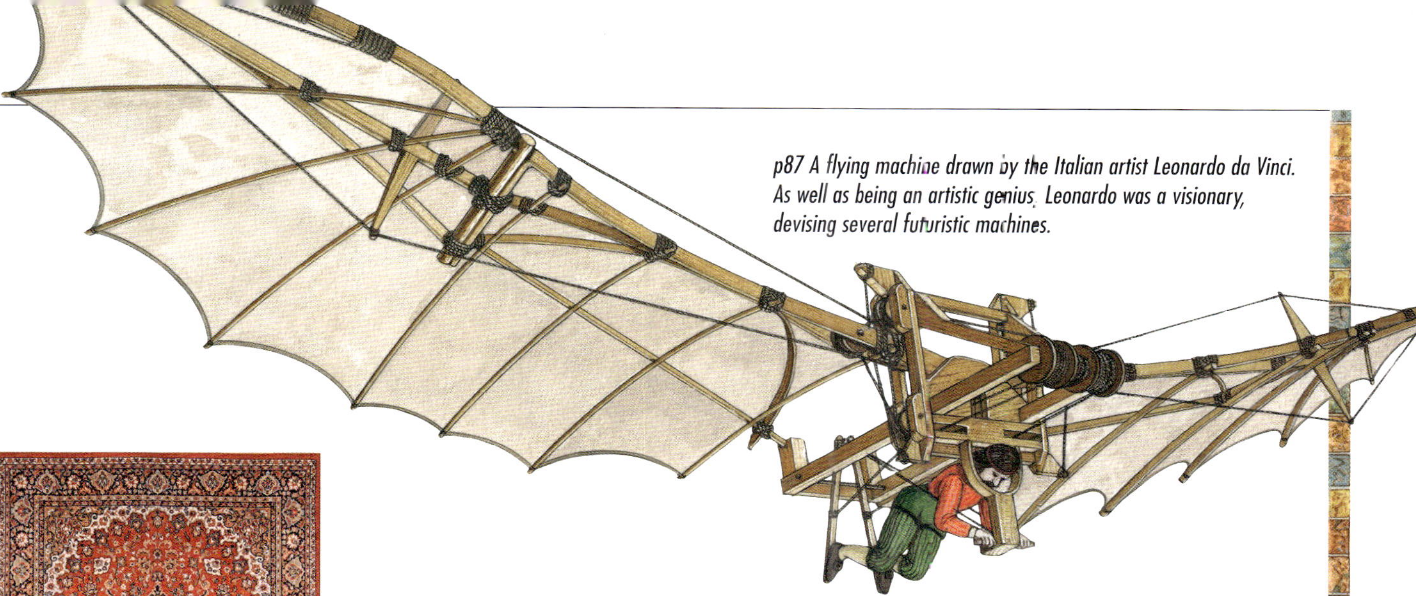

p87 A flying machine drawn by the Italian artist Leonardo da Vinci. As well as being an artistic genius, Leonardo was a visionary, devising several futuristic machines.

p99 A Persian carpet of the 1500s. Designs traditionally included flowers and geometric shapes.

This sent explorers and adventurers across the oceans to far-flung parts of the Earth and even right around the globe. By the 1600s, several European countries had established permanent colonies overseas.

This period also saw the development of many new ideas and challenges to old, traditional beliefs. Quarrels between different religious groups frequently led to bitter wars. There were power struggles between monarchs and parliaments, as democratic principles and government slowly developed. From the start of the 1500s, there were startling advances in science, with inventions such as the telescope and microscope revealing new wonders out in space and much closer to home. These discoveries prompted great thinkers of the day to formulate new theories about the world, its relation to space and about humans' place within it. Great scientists such as Copernicus, Galileo and Newton challenged the old ideas, and new theories began to shake the foundations of society.

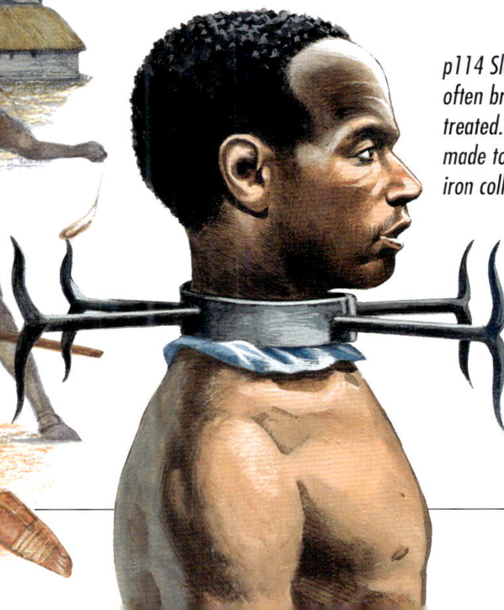

p114 Slaves were often brutally ill-treated. Some were made to wear heavy iron collars.

The Renaissance

The Renaissance was a 'rebirth' of interest in the art and learning of ancient Greece and Rome. Many historians say that it marked the end of the Middle Ages and the beginning of our modern world. It began in Italy, and in the 1400s spread throughout Europe, changing the way people thought about the world.

The Renaissance began among the scholars, artists and scientists of Italy. They had new ideas, but also turned to the past, rediscovering the learning of ancient Greece and Rome. Many old handwritten books were brought to Italy by scholars fleeing from the city of Constantinople (the ancient capital of the Eastern Roman empire), which was captured by the Ottoman Turks in 1453. With a greater knowledge of ancient science and beliefs, European scholars were inspired to think again about established religious teaching.

Dante Alighieri, *whose poem* The Divine Comedy *explores love, death and faith. Dante wrote in his own language, Italian, and not Latin, which was the language of scholars.*

Moveable metal type *can be used again and again. Each letter is set to form the words and then inked to print on the page. Once the printing has been completed, the letters can be taken out again and used to print another book.*

1306 Italian artist Giotto di Bondone paints frescoes that are more life-like than earlier medieval paintings.

1308 Dante Alighieri begins writing *The Divine Comedy* in his native Italian, not Latin.

1387 Geoffrey Chaucer begins *The Canterbury Tales*, written in English.

1416 Italian sculptor Donatello breaks new ground with free-standing figures, including his nude *David*.

1453 Constantinople is captured by the Turks; many of its scholars flee to Italy.

1454 Johannes Gutenberg perfects printing with movable type. By 1476, William Caxton is printing in London.

1466–1536 Life of Erasmus. He publishes studies of the Old and New Testaments.

1478 Lorenzo de Medici makes Florence a centre of art and learning. Sandro Botticelli paints *Primavera*.

1508 Michelangelo paints the ceiling of the Sistine Chapel in the Vatican, Rome.

1513 Italian Niccolo Machiavelli writes *The Prince*, on the theory of government.

1516 Sir Thomas More publishes *Utopia*.

1543 Nicholaus Copernicus develops his theory about the solar system.

1590 William Shakespeare is writing plays in England.

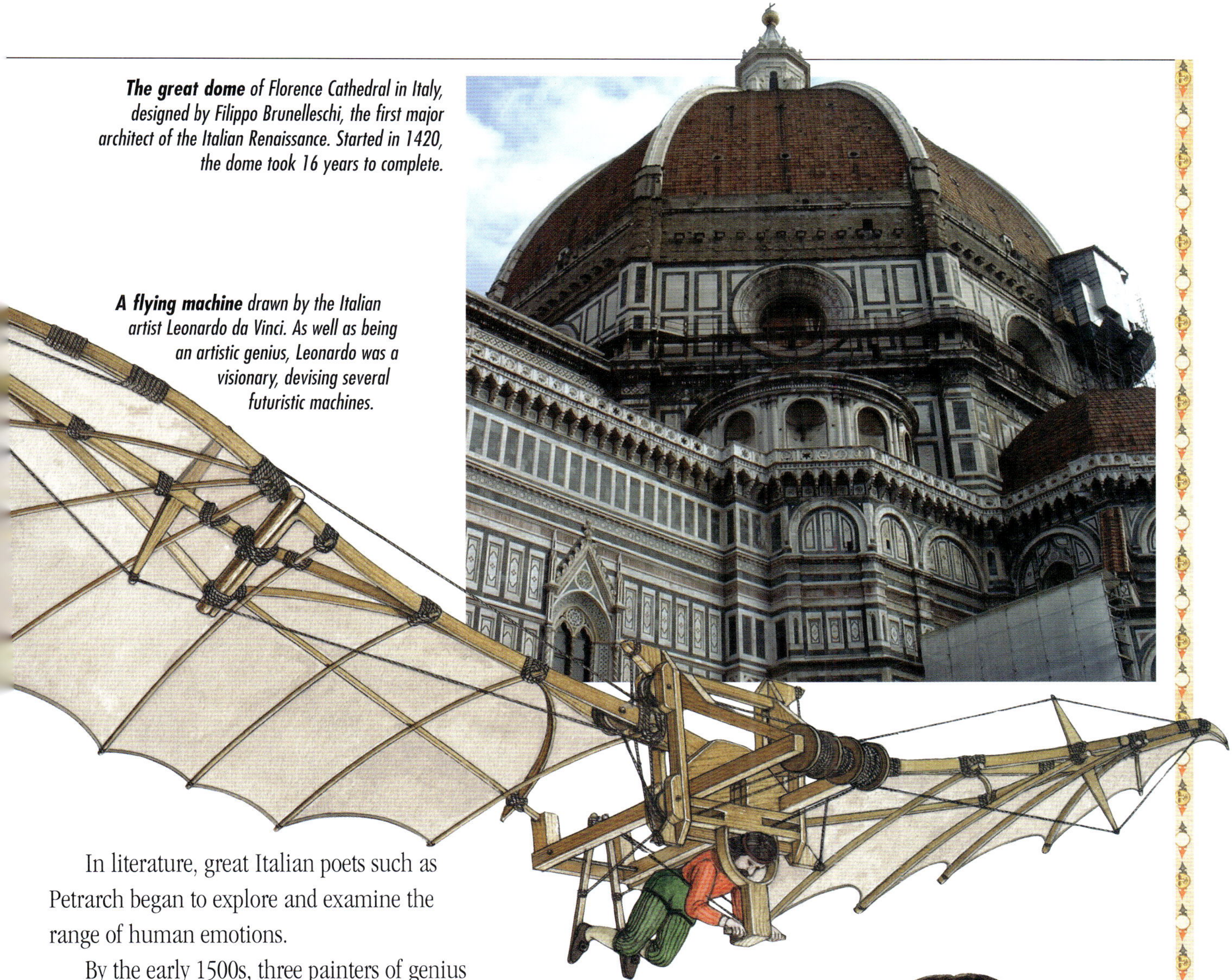

The great dome *of Florence Cathedral in Italy, designed by Filippo Brunelleschi, the first major architect of the Italian Renaissance. Started in 1420, the dome took 16 years to complete.*

A flying machine *drawn by the Italian artist Leonardo da Vinci. As well as being an artistic genius, Leonardo was a visionary, devising several futuristic machines.*

In literature, great Italian poets such as Petrarch began to explore and examine the range of human emotions.

By the early 1500s, three painters of genius – Leonardo da Vinci, Michelangelo and Raphael – were bringing a new energy and realism to art. Architects designed new and elegant buildings that echoed the classical styles of ancient Greece and Rome.

The Renaissance was fuelled by new technology. Printing with movable type, developed by Johannes Gutenberg in Germany, made books cheaper and more plentiful, so new ideas could be read by more people. Some new ideas were astounding, such as Copernicus's theory that the Sun and not the Earth was at the centre of the solar system.

THE NEW UNIVERSE

In 1543, the Polish astronomer Nicolaus Copernicus published an idea that changed the shape of the entire universe. He put the Sun, not the Earth, at the centre of the universe. This challenged the established theory of the second-century Greek astronomer Ptolemy and also the teachings of the Christian Church.

The Aztecs and Incas

c.1200 Aztecs settle in the Valley of Mexico.
1200 Incas begin to conquer neighbouring peoples throughout the Andes region.
1325 Traditional date for the founding of Tenochtitlan.
1438 Inca empire begins, under Pachacuti, the ninth Inca (king).
1440–69 Reign of Montezuma I. The Aztec empire is extended.
1450–1500 Under Topa Inca and his son, Huayna Capac, the Inca empire is extended from Peru into modern-day Bolivia, Chile, Ecuador and Colombia.
1500 The Aztecs rule more than 10 million people.
1502 Montezuma II becomes Aztec emperor.
1519 Spaniards led by Hernando Cortés march on Tenochtitlan.
1520 The Aztecs rise up against the Spanish invaders. Montezuma is wounded and dies.
1521 Cortés and his men attack and capture Tenochtitlan. End of the Aztec empire.
1527 Death of the emperor Huayna Capac; civil war starts.
1532 Francisco Pizarro attacks the Incas and captures Cuzco.

***The heart of the Aztec empire** was the fertile Valley of Mexico where the capital, Tenochtitlan, and most of the major cities were located. These thrived as busy market centres. The empire extended south and east into present-day Guatemala.*

The Aztecs were fierce warriors. They conquered an empire that extended right across Mexico, and was at its height in the early 1500s. From the mountains of Peru, the god-emperor of the Incas ruled a highly organized kingdom. Spanish invasion ended both empires.

Tenochtitlan, the Aztec capital, was founded in 1325 on an island in the middle of Lake Texcoco (now the site of Mexico City). Tenochtitlan was a walled city of 100,000 people. Causeways linked the island to the mainland, and smaller islands were specially built as places to grow food.

The Aztecs worshipped the Sun. Each year priests sacrificed thousands of victims to the Sun-god in the belief that this would bring good harvests and prosperity. Aztec farmers grew corn, beans and tomatoes, and their merchants traded throughout the empire. The ruling class were warriors. All warriors had to capture at least one enemy warrior for sacrifice, and conquered peoples were forced to pay taxes to the emperor.

***Aztec warrior chiefs** wore feather headdresses (feathers and jaguar skins were traded throughout the empire). But most people wore simple clothes woven from plant fibres.*

In 1519, a Spanish expedition led by Hernando Cortés attacked the Aztecs. Emperor Montezuma II welcomed them, believing Cortés was the god Quetzalcoatl, but the emperor was taken prisoner. Aztec spears and clubs were no match for Spanish guns, and by 1521 the Aztec empire was at an end.

GODS AND SACRIFICE

One of the reasons that the Aztecs went to war was to capture prisoners to sacrifice to the gods. They believed that the hearts and blood of their victims nourished the gods. Priests cut open the bodies using sacrificial knives like the one shown here. Sacrifices had to be performed on the right day, according to the sacred 260-day calendar.

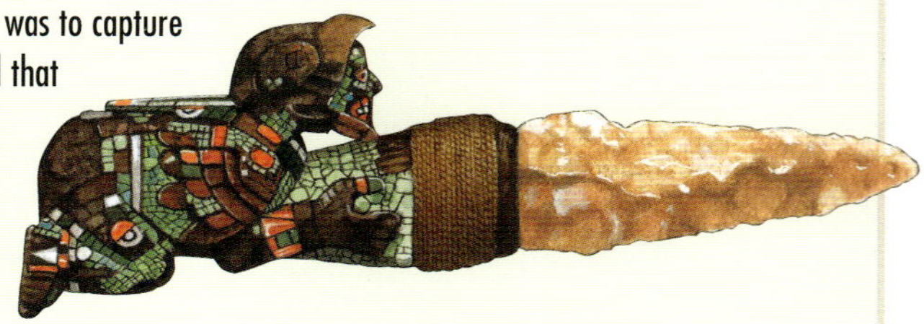

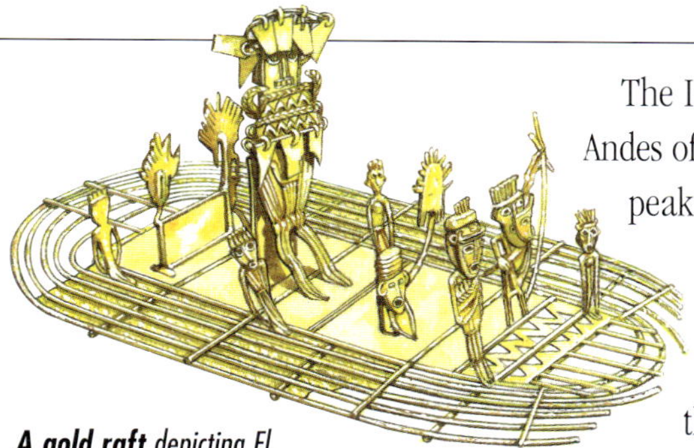

***A gold raft** depicting El Dorado, a legendary ruler whose body was said to be dusted with gold every year. Such tales made European invaders greedy for gold.*

The Incas took over from the Chimu as rulers of the Andes of South America. Their civilization reached its peak in the 1400s under the ruler Pachacuti.

Pachacuti reformed the way the kingdom was run. He appointed a central administration to control the building of towns and to ensure that farms and workshops were run efficiently. From the capital, Cuzco, he and his successors expanded the Inca empire to include parts of Chile, Bolivia and Ecuador.

The Incas built stone cities and fine roads, which were used by traders. Goods were bartered as the Incas did not use money. Farmers used terraced fields on the mountain slopes to grow corn, cotton and potatoes. The Incas' many skills included bridge-building and medicine, although they never developed writing or the wheel.

In 1525, the Inca empire was at its greatest extent. But in 1527, after Emperor Huayna Capac died, the empire was split between his two sons and civil war broke out. In the 1530s, a Spanish expedition led by Francisco Pizarro arrived, seeking gold. The Europeans were impressed by Cuzco's palaces and temples, and by the fortress of Sacsahuaman, which was built from huge stones that fitted together perfectly without mortar.

Though few in number, the Spaniards had horses and guns. In 1532, Pizarro captured the Inca ruler Atahualpa and demanded a room full of gold and two rooms full of silver. The ransom was paid, but Atahualpa was killed anyway. The Inca armies were swiftly defeated, although resistance to Spanish rule continued until 1572.

***The Incas communicated** over long distances by sending fast runners with messages in the form of quipus (knotted cords). A message could be sent more than 200 km in a day along a system of paved roads.*

***The Spanish were fewer in number** than the Incas. But they had horses, armour and guns. Many Incas fought bravely, but with their king murdered, they were quickly defeated.*

Voyages of Discovery

In the late 1400s, Europeans began to explore the oceans. In stronger ships capable of longer voyages, they went in search of trade, treasure and new lands. Their voyages took them west to the Americas and east to Asia.

After the Byzantine empire fell to the Ottoman Turks in 1453, the old land trade routes between Europe and Asia were cut off. Europeans, anxious to get spices that were essential for flavouring and preserving their food, had to find a new way to reach India and the islands of Indonesia. This need, coupled with a growing curiosity and a spirit of adventure, sent Europeans to sea.

The first nation to go exploring was Portugal. Its prince, Henry the Navigator, took a keen interest in ship building and navigation. He directed his sailors west into the Atlantic Ocean and south to explore along the west coast of Africa. They set up forts along the African coast to protect the trade routes and traded for gold and ivory. Spanish, French, Dutch

***European explorers sailed** in ships called carracks with three masts and square sails. Columbus's ship* Santa Maria *may have looked like this.*

Cross-staff

Astrolabe

Compass

***Seafarers used simple navigation instruments** such as the astrolabe and cross-staff to fix their ships' positions by the Sun and the stars. The magnetic compass showed North, but was not always reliable.*

1419 Portuguese sail to the Madeira Islands.
1431 Portuguese reach the Azores.
1488 Bartolomeu Dias of Portugal explores the west coast of Africa and rounds the Cape of Good Hope.
1492 Christopher Columbus, an Italian, leads a Spanish expedition to America.
1494 Spain and Portugal divide the Americas between themselves by the Treaty of Tordesillas.
1497 John Cabot, an Italian in the service of England, sails to Canada. The Portuguese explorer Vasco Da Gama sails round Africa to India.
1499 Italian Amerigo Vespucci sails to South America.
1500 Pedro Alvares Cabral from Portugal sails to Brazil.
1509 Spain begins settlement of the Americas.
1513 Spanish explorer Vasco Nuñez de Balboa is the first European to see the Pacific.
1517 Portuguese traders reach China.
1522 First round-the-world voyage is completed by Ferdinand Magellan's Spanish crew.
1524 Italian Giovanni da Verrazano searches for a northwest passage from Europe to Asia.

and English sailors followed. Some explorers, like Christopher Columbus, headed farther west, and ended up in the Americas – much to their surprise, as they did not realise that the American continent existed!

Portugal and Spain began to settle and plunder the Americas, dividing it between themselves by treaty. By 1517, the Portuguese had landed in China (by sailing east around Africa to India and onward). Nearly 30 years later, they reached Japan.

The ships used by the explorers were small, but more seaworthy than the clumsy vessels of the Middle Ages. These ships used a mixture of square and lateen (triangular) sails for easier steering and greater manoeuvrability. Sailors had only crude maps and simple instruments to guide them on voyages that lasted many months. In 1519, a Portuguese captain, Ferdinand Magellan, set out from Spain with five ships. The ships sailed around South America, across the Pacific Ocean to the Philippines (where Magellan was killed) and across the Indian Ocean to Africa. Only one ship, commanded by Sebastian Del Cano, found its way home to Spain, becoming the first ship to sail around the world.

Pepper

Tomato

NEW WORLD FOODS

As well as gold and silver, European explorers brought back new foods from the Americas. Potatoes, tomatoes and peppers, plants native to America, were all unknown in Europe before 1500. Potatoes were a luxury at first, served only to the rich at banquets. Chocolate, from the cacao tree, was first brought to Spain from Mexico in 1520. Also from the New World came tobacco, turkeys and maize.

Potato

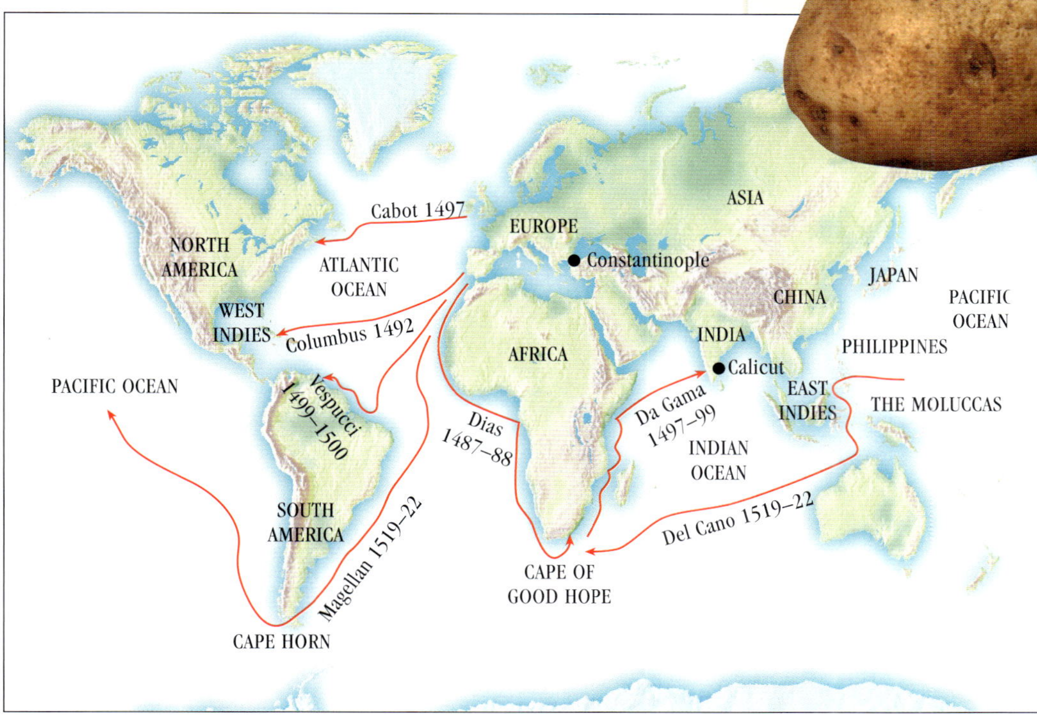

***The voyages of discovery** revealed to Europeans that the world was larger than many ancient geographers had believed. Sailors crossed oceans and met peoples unknown to earlier Europeans.*

711 Muslims invade southern Spain (which includes what later becomes Portugal).
Early 1000s Muslim central rule of Spain collapses into civil war.
1143 Portugal gains independence from Castile.
Late 1200s Granada is the only Moorish kingdom left in Spain.
1469 Aragon and Castile become one kingdom.
1492 Moors are forced out of Granada. Jews are expelled from Spain. Columbus sails to the Americas.
1512 Ferdinand seizes Navarre to complete unification of Spain.
1521 Spain conquers the Aztec empire in Mexico.
1535 Spain conquers the Inca empire in Peru.
1556 Philip II becomes king of Spain.
1565 Spain colonizes the Philippines.
1568 War in the Spanish Netherlands begins.
1571 Battle of Lepanto: Spain and Austria defeat a Turkish fleet.
1580 Spain conquers Portugal and holds it until 1640.
1588 Spanish Armada sails to invade England, but fails.

Spain and Portugal

Medieval Spain was divided between Christian and Muslim kingdoms. After several wars, two monarchs ended Muslim rule in Spain. They were Ferdinand of Aragon and Isabella of Castile.

***Philip II ruled Spain** from 1556 to 1598. A devout Catholic, he dreamed of a Spanish-led Catholic empire embracing Europe and America.*

In 1469, Ferdinand and Isabella were married, uniting Spain's two strongest Christian kingdoms. By 1492, their forces had captured Granada, the last Muslim outpost in Spain. The new rulers were intolerant of other religions and set up the Spanish Inquisition to seek out heretics – both Christians who held different beliefs from the Roman Catholic Church and people of other faiths, such as Jews.

In the 16th century, Spain became Europe's strongest nation. Its army fought wars in Europe (against the Dutch, for example) and its navy controlled the profitable trade in gold and silver from Spain's new empire in the Americas.

Spanish power reached its peak during the reign of Charles I (1516–56). He became Holy Roman Emperor in 1519, which gave him control of lands in what is now Germany, Austria and the Netherlands, as well as parts of France and Italy.

***Catherine of Aragon** (1485–1536) was the daughter of King Ferdinand and Queen Isabella of Spain. In 1509, she became the first of the six wives of King Henry VIII of England.*

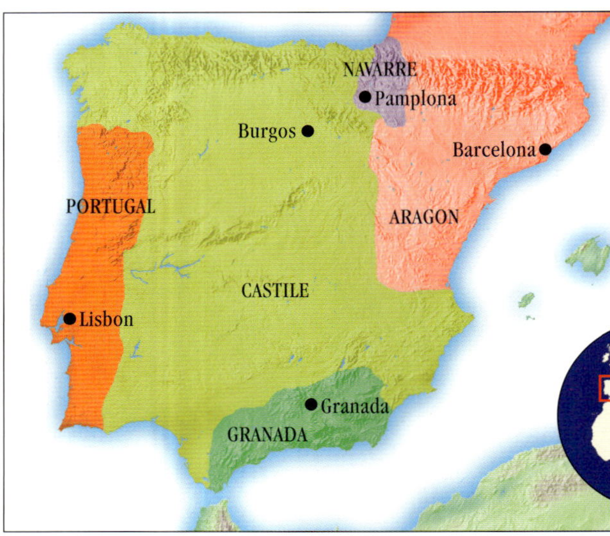

***In the early 1400s,** Spain was not yet one kingdom. Aragon and Castile were the strongest Christian kingdoms, while Granada was ruled by Muslim emirs.*

Arabic script *on Spanish stonework. The Muslims left a rich legacy of architecture in cities such as Granada and Cordoba in southern Spain.*

Christopher Columbus *had to win the support of King Ferdinand and Queen Isabella for his westward voyage. He set sail in 1492, convinced that the Atlantic was a narrow ocean.*

On his death, his lands were divided between his son Philip II (who ruled Spain, the Netherlands and Spanish colonies in the Americas) and his brother Ferdinand (who became Holy Roman Emperor).

By 1580, the Spanish empire included Portugal. Portugal had led the way in European exploration of the oceans. Its sailors had opened up new trade routes to Asia. The Portuguese already controlled an overseas empire that included large stretches of coastline in East and West Africa, Brazil and India, as well as trading posts such as Goa in India, Macao in China and many islands in Southeast Asia.

The Monument to the Discoveries *in Lisbon was built in 1960 to commemorate the 500th anniversary of the Death of Henry the Navigator. Henry is shown at the front of the monument holding a model of a caravel.*

HENRY THE NAVIGATOR

Prince Henry of Portugal (1394–1460) had a passion to explore. He brought together seamen, shipbuilders and mapmakers to plan voyages to the Madeira islands and south along the coast of Africa. These voyages used carracks (large, three-masted ships that used square and lateen sails) and caravels (above). Caravels were light sailing ships that were developed in the 15th century. They were fast for the period and are thought to have been used on many voyages of discovery, including Columbus's trip to the Americas.

1300s European rulers try to contact the legendary Prester John. Great Zimbabwe is the heart of a powerful Bantu kingdom.
1335 The Songhai ruling dynasty is founded.
1341 Suleiman is king of Mali to 1360.
1430s Portuguese begin exploring along the west coast of Africa.
1460s Portuguese explorers buy ivory, pepper, palm oil and slaves from the kingdom of Benin.
1464 Songhai breaks away from Mali's control.
1468 Sonni Ali captures Timbuktu.
From 1480s Portuguese traders set up forts as bases to trade with African rulers.
1488 Portuguese explorer Bartolomeu Dias rounds the Cape of Good Hope.
1493 Songhai is at its peak. Askia Muhammad I takes over the Mandingo empire.
1506 The kingdom of Kongo has its first Christian king, Alfonso I.
1511 A Portuguese explorer reaches Great Zimbabwe, now in decline.
1520 Portuguese mission to Ethiopia (lasts until 1526).
c. 1530 The slave trade from Africa to the Americas begins.
1591 Songhai is defeated by Moroccans, aided by Spanish and Portuguese soldiers.

African Empires

Africa was a continent of many kingdoms and empires. The richest African rulers commanded trade in gold, ivory and slaves – goods that by 1500 were attracting European traders.

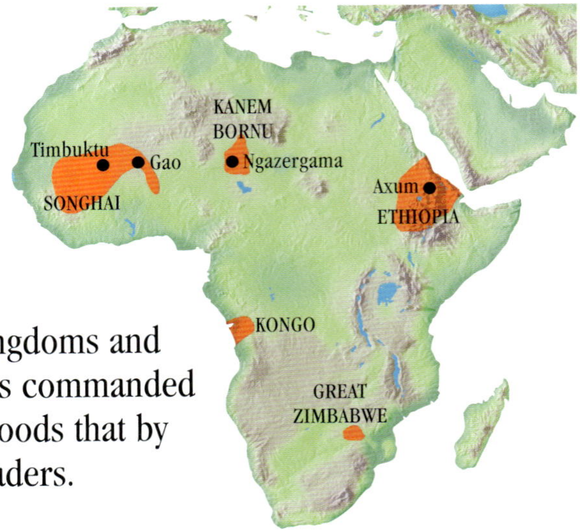

African kingdoms, *c. 1400–1600. Because transport across much of Africa was so difficult, Africans often had more contact with Europeans and Asians (who traded with them by sea) than with other African states.*

Portuguese traders sailing the coast of West Africa heard tales of wondrous kingdoms located in the heart of the continent. The strongest was called Songhai, a Muslim kingdom that controlled trade across the Sahara Desert. In 1464, King Sonni Ali freed Songhai from control by the Mali empire, and expanded its borders. A new Songhai dynasty was founded in 1493 by Askia Muhammad I, who gained great wealth from the trading cities of Jenne and Timbuktu. Songhai rule lasted until 1591, when the army was defeated by a Moroccan force, which was much better armed with guns.

Another Muslim empire, Kanem-Bornu, extended through parts of present-day Chad, Cameroon, Nigeria, Niger and Libya. Kanem-Bornu thrived on trade between northern and southern Africa. It reached its peak in about 1570, under Idris Alawma.

Ethiopian Christians *cut down into solid rock to build their cross-shaped churches, which were hollowed out inside. Fifteen rock churches survive at Lalibela (then named Roha), capital of the Ethiopian empire in the 1200s.*

In northeast Africa was the Christian empire of Ethiopia. Europeans heard tales of its legendary ruler, Prester John. Here, people lived by farming and cattle herding.

By 1450, a settlement at Great Zimbabwe in southern Africa had reached its greatest extent. Built over about 400 years, Great Zimbabwe was probably a royal stronghold overlooking a valley that was home to up to 20,000 people. It was surrounded by massive walls and a high tower. The people who lived in this prosperous kingdom used copper and iron, and traded in gold with the region of Sofala on the east coast (present-day Mozambique). By 1500, however, the civilization that built Great Zimbabwe was in decline, and people had abandoned the stronghold.

PRESTER JOHN

Travellers told tales of Prester ('priest') John, the fabulously rich Christian king of Ethiopia. One story claimed he had a magic mirror in which he could see everything that went on in his empire. Another story tells of giant ants that dug up gold for his treasury.

Timbuktu, on the southern edge of the Sahara Desert, was the centre of the gold and salt trade, and merchants came from as far as Morocco to sell cloth and horses there. Muslim scholars from the city advised the ruler of the Songhai empire, Askia Muhammad I.

The Reformation

1498 Savonarola, an Italian friar who preached Church reform, is burned at the stake in Florence.

1517 Martin Luther pins 95 written arguments critical of the Catholic Church on a church door in Wittenberg, Germany. This sets off the Reformation.

1519 Ulrich Zwingli starts the Reformation in Switzerland.

1521 Luther is expelled from the Church.

1532 John Calvin starts the Protestant movement in France.

1534 Ignatius Loyola founds the Jesuits. Henry VIII becomes head of the Church of England.

1536 Dissolution of the monasteries in England.

1541 John Knox takes the Reformation to Scotland.

1549 A new prayer book, the *Book of Common Prayer*, is introduced in England.

1562 Religious wars in France between Catholics and Huguenots (Protestants).

1568 Protestant Dutch revolt against Spanish rule.

1581 The Netherlands declares independence from Spain. This is not recognized by Spain until 1648.

1588 Defeat of the Spanish Armada off Britain's coast.

1598 Edict of Nantes gives Protestants and Catholics in France equal rights.

***Martin Luther** believed that people were saved by faith alone, that the Bible was central to that faith, and that church services should be in everyday languages, not in Latin.*

***The Spanish sent the Armada** to England in 1588 to restore Catholic rule. An English fireship attack off Calais helped fight off the planned invasion. The great Spanish fleet was eventually wrecked by storms around the coasts of northern Britain.*

The Reformation was a protest movement aiming to reform the Catholic Church. It came about at a time when there was a new interest in humanism – the belief that humans are in control of their own destinies. Aware of the growing discontent with the way the western Christian Church was run, reformers suggested new forms of worship, to create a new relationship between the people, the Church and God.

In 1517, Martin Luther, a German monk, protested publicly at what he saw as the Church's corruption and called for reform. His campaign led to the creation of a religious movement known as the Reformation. His ideas were taken up and spread by other reformers throughout Europe, such as Ulrich Zwingli in Switzerland and John Calvin in France. This led to the formation of the Protestant ('protesting') Church.

John Calvin, *religious reformer, was born in France. He believed that only people chosen by God would be saved from damnation. His reforms became known as 'Calvinism'.*

The technology of printing spread these new ideas far and wide. The Bible, which previously had been available only in Latin (the language of scholars) was translated into local languages for all to read. Some rulers used this discontent with the Church for their own ends. Henry VIII of England, for example, wanted to divorce Catherine of Aragon. When the pope refused to grant the divorce, Henry broke with the Catholic Church in Rome to get his own way.

Starting in 1545, the Catholic Church fought back with a movement known as the Counter Reformation. It sent out Jesuit priests to campaign against the spread of Protestantism and to convert the peoples of the Spanish empire to Catholicism. The split between Catholics and Protestants in Western Europe led to many wars as countries struggled with new religious alliances. Catholics and Protestants persecuted one another in countries throughout Europe, often in the cruellest ways.

King Henry VIII *made himself head of the Church in England. He always considered himself a Catholic, despite his quarrel with the pope in Rome over his divorce from Catherine of Aragon.*

1288 Osman becomes ruler of the Ottoman Turks.
1402 Tamerlane rules most of the Ottoman empire until his death in 1405.
1453 Constantinople is captured by the Ottomans. They rename it Istanbul.
1501 Safavid dynasty in Persia is founded by Shah Ismail I.
1516 Ottoman Turks conquer Egypt, defeating Mamelukes.
1520 Suleiman I becomes sultan of the Ottoman empire.
1526 Battle of Mohacs in Hungary is won by the Turks.
1529 At the siege of Vienna, the Turks fail to capture the city.
1534 Turks capture Tunis, Baghdad and Mesopotamia.
1565 Turks attack Malta, but are fought off by the Knights of St John.
1571 Battle of Lepanto. Don John of Austria destroys the Ottoman fleet, led by Ali Pasha.
c.1600 The Ottoman empire declines. It eventually ends in 1918.
1685 Turks lay siege to Vienna but again fail to capture the city.

The Ottoman sultan *Suleiman I made the Ottoman empire a power to be respected and feared. Europeans called him Suleiman the Magnificent.*

Ottomans and Safavids

The Ottoman capture of Constantinople in 1453 marked the beginning of a Turkish golden age. The Ottoman Turks controlled the eastern Mediterranean and the Near East, and their armies moved west to threaten Europe. They also fought many wars against the Safavids, their Muslim rivals in Persia.

After taking Constantinople, the Ottoman Turks renamed the city Istanbul. It became the centre of a Muslim empire that, at its peak, encircled the eastern Mediterranean. Most of the Ottoman conquests were made during the rule of Suleiman I (1520–1566). The Turks invaded Persia (modern-day Iran), captured Baghdad, took control of the island of Rhodes and crossed the river Danube into Hungary, where they won the Battle of Mohacs in 1526.

By 1529, the Turkish army was outside the city walls of Vienna and looked likely to invade western Europe. The siege of Vienna was lifted, however, and Europe relaxed. But Ottoman warships continued to control the Mediterranean. Turkish pirates, such as the ferocious Barbarossa (Khayr ad-Din Pasha), raided ports, captured merchant ships and carried off Christians to be slaves. Ottoman sea power was checked in 1571, when a European fleet defeated the Turks at the Battle of Lepanto in the Gulf of Corinth, Greece.

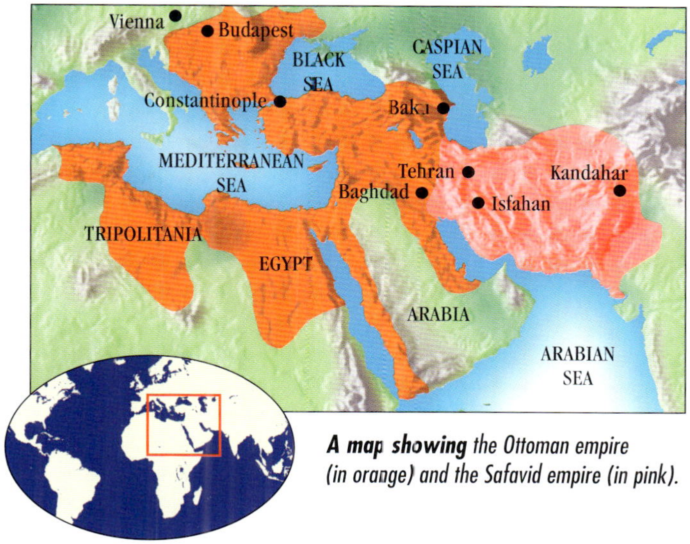

A map showing *the Ottoman empire (in orange) and the Safavid empire (in pink).*

A traditional Persian carpet. *Designs usually included flowers and geometric shapes.*

The Battle of Lepanto *in 1571 was fought between a large Turkish fleet and a smaller European fleet. The Turks were defeated, losing at least 20,000 men. The Europeans lost about 8,000.*

Istanbul's Blue Mosque *was built on the orders of Sultan Ahmet I (reigned 1609–1616). After capturing the city in 1453, the Muslim Ottomans took over Christian churches and built magnificent new mosques such as this one.*

Suleiman tried three times to conquer Persia, which from 1501 was under the rule of the Safavid dynasty, founded by Shah Ismail I. Here the people were Shiites, not Sunni Muslims as in the Ottoman empire. Safavid rivalry with the Ottomans continued under Shah Abbas I (1557–1628). From his capital of Isfahan, Shah Abbas I ruled not only Persia but also most of Mesopotamia (modern-day Iraq). Wars between the two empires continued throughout the 16th century and helped to keep the Ottoman Turks from advancing into Europe.

The Mughal Empire

The Mughal dynasty ruled a mighty empire in India for nearly 200 years. The dynasty was founded by Babur in 1526. Under his grandson Akbar, India saw a rich flowering of Mughal art and learning.

1526 Mughal dynasty founded by Babur. His victory at Panipat against the sultan of Delhi, Ibrahim Lodi, gives him control of northern India.
1530 Humayun becomes emperor.
1540 Humayun is defeated by Sher Shah, a ruler of eastern India, and exiled to Persia.
1556 Start of Akbar's reign; he wins a second battle of Panipat against the Hindus.
1565 Akbar extends his rule to southern India.
1567 Akbar subdues the Rajput princes, storming the fortress of Chitor with mines and artillery.
1575 Akbar conquers Bengal.
1627–57 Rule of Shah Jahan.
1658–1707 Rule of Aurangzeb.
1664 Hindu Marathas overrun western India.
1720s Mughal empire breaks up.

The golden age of Mughal India began in 1556 under the rule of Babur's grandson Akbar (then aged only 13). Akbar widened the empire using war and diplomacy. His conquests included Bengal, with its riches of rice and silk. Akbar ruled until 1605.

Akbar was succeeded by his son Jahangir and he was succeeded in 1627 by Shah Jahan. Shah Jahan was a great patron of the arts and paid for many splendid buildings, including the Taj Mahal in Agra. In 1657, he fell ill, and an argument broke out between his sons over who should now rule. His third son Aurangzeb killed his brothers, locked up Shah Jahan and seized the throne. Aurangzeb, the last great Mughal ruler, expanded the empire to its greatest extent. After his death in 1707 the Mughal empire began to break up.

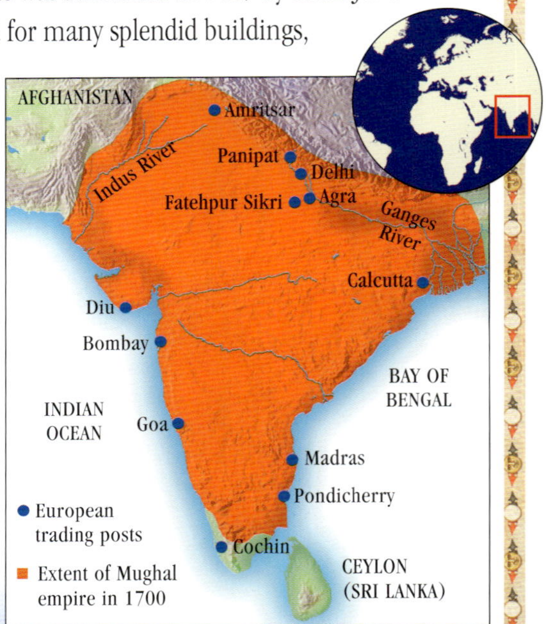

A map of the Mughal empire at its peak. *Akbar ruled from Agra and Fatehpur Sikri.*

The Taj Mahal *was built between 1631 and 1648 as a tomb for the favourite wife of Mughal emperor Shah Jahan. 20,000 workers and artists helped create this beautiful white marble building.*

1368 Foundation of the Ming dynasty in China.
1398 Death of the first Ming emperor, Hong Wu.
1405–33 Zheng He leads seven voyages to India and East Africa. He may have reached Australia.
1421 Beijing is made the Chinese capital.
1449 The Ming emperor is captured by the Mongols. He resumes the throne in 1457.
1505–60 A period of poor government by two emperors.
1514 Portuguese traders arrive in China, followed by the Dutch in 1522.
1551 Voyages beyond Chinese waters are banned.
1557 The Portuguese set up a trading base at Macao.
1560 Ming forces drive off Mongols and pirate raids. China's population nears 150 million.
1575 Spain begins to trade with China.
1592–98 Ming armies help Koreans fight off Japanese invaders.
1618–1630s Manchus rebel against Ming rule. High taxes anger many Chinese people.

Ming China

This is a 'Ming vase'. *The Ming period was one of elegant artistry, especially in porcelain.*

Christian missionary *Matteo Ricci, an Italian, went to China in 1583 and spent 30 years there. In 1601, he visited the emperor in Beijing, giving two clocks as gifts.*

In the 1300s, the Mongol grip on China weakened. A revolt drove out the last Yuan (Mongol) emperor, and in 1368 a Buddhist monk calling himself Ming Hong Wu became China's new ruler. The Ming dynasty ruled China for almost 300 years.

Under Ming Hong Wu, the first Ming emperor, Chinese self-confidence and national pride returned. An able and efficient ruler, Hong Wu established peace and prosperity. He reformed Chinese society by abolishing slavery and by confiscating large estates and redistributing them among the poor. China began to reassert its power over its neighbours, and its strong army was able to fight off foreign attacks.

At sea, Chinese ships made a series of voyages during the early 1400s as far as Africa and Arabia. The fleets were commanded by Admiral Zheng He.

Ming emperors supported the arts and built many fine palaces. From 1421, they lived within the Forbidden City in Beijing, a huge complex of palaces, temples and parks. Only the emperor's family and the officials and servants of the royal household were permitted inside the Forbidden City.

China's first contacts with European traders began in the 1500s, when Portuguese ships arrived. By 1557, the Portuguese had set up a settlement in Macao.

The Chinese rarely looked beyond their borders and after the mid-1500s the government banned voyages overseas. Ming rule lasted until 1644.

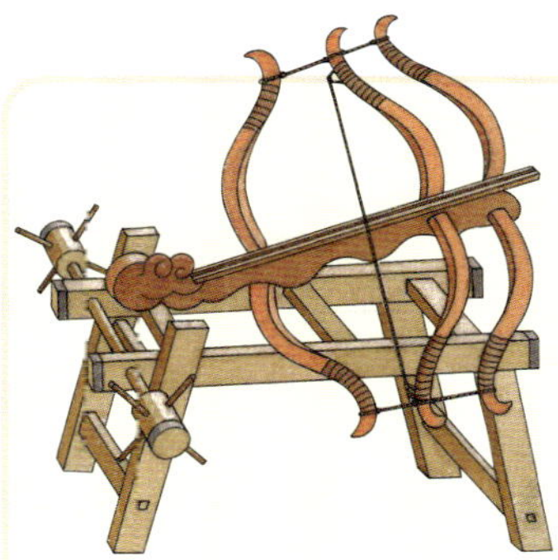

CROSSBOW
An arrow fired from a powerful Chinese artillery crossbow could travel up to 200 metres and pierce a wooden shield. The Chinese developed a number of other ingenious weapons, including gunpowder rockets and bombs, which they first used about AD 1000.

Chinese soldiers *defended their empire against foreigners such as Japanese warlords (samurai), who tried to invade Korea in the 1590s, but later withdrew.*

1500s Portuguese navigators begin to explore the Pacific.
1519–21 Ferdinand Magellan's ships cross the Pacific Ocean during the first-ever circumnavigation of the globe.
1526 Portuguese land on Papua New Guinea.
1567 Spanish explorer Mendana de Neyra visits the Solomon Islands.
1577–80 English explorer Sir Francis Drake explores the Pacific during his round-the-world voyage.
1606 Dutch sailor Willem Jansz sights the north coast of Australia.
1615 Luis Vaez de Torres of Spain explores coasts of New Guinea and northern Australia.
1616 Dutch sailor Dirk Hartog and his crew land at Shark Bay, on the west coast of Australia.
1627 The Dutch East India Company Captain Francois Thysssen sails along the southern coast of Australia.
1642 Dutch sailor Abel Tasman explores the coast of Tasmania and New Zealand's South Island.

Oceania Explored

European sailors first crossed the Pacific Ocean in the 1500s and trade ships were regularly sailing to the Indian subcontinent and the Far East during the latter half of this century. However, Australia, New Zealand and many of the Pacific Islands remained undiscovered by Europeans until the 1600s.

***The Aborigines of Australia** had a way of life perfectly in tune with their environment. Before the 1700s, their only contacts with the outside world were occasional trade exchanges with Asian fishermen and merchants.*

It seems certain that Chinese and Indonesian sailors knew about the northern coastline of Australia long before the first European ships arrived in the southern Pacific. Asian fishermen and seafarers traded with the Aborigines, handing over iron knives, for example. Rumours and stories of an unknown 'Southern Land' reached Europe during the 1500s, and a landmass starts to appear on maps drawn after 1540.

The first European to see Australia and return was Dutch explorer Willem Jansz. He sailed into the northern Gulf of Carpentaria in 1606, where he saw what he described as 'wild black men'. The first known landing on Australia did not occur for another ten years until 1616, when a Dutchman named Dirk Hartog landed there.

Hartog was the skipper of a ship bound from the Cape of Good Hope to Java, but he was blown off course. He sailed too far east, and landed on the west coast of Australia. Other Dutch ships took the same route and saw this new land. They explored its western and southern coasts, but did not settle.

In 1642, Abel Tasman, another Dutch captain, sighted the island of Tasmania, which he named Van Diemen's Land. Sailing on eastwards, his ship came in sight of a bigger island. He had discovered New Zealand's South Island.

***To mark his landing in Australia** in 1616, Dirk Hartog put up a metal plate on the shore of what is now Dirk Hartog Island. The plate was later returned to the Netherlands, and can be seen in an Amsterdam museum. The Dutch never attempted to settle in Australia.*

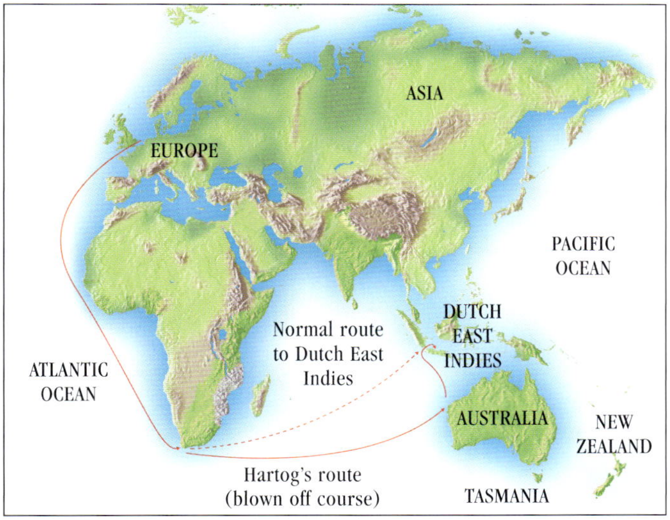

Dirk Hartog's route to the spice islands *in 1616 should have taken him north of Australia (dotted line) to the Dutch East Indies (Indonesia). But driven off course by winds known as the Roaring Forties, he and his crew reached the west coast of Australia.*

Unfortunately, Tasman's first contact with the Maori people who lived there ended violently, with four of the European sailors killed. Tasman reported that the new land was best left alone. And so it was, until the arrival of James Cook over 100 years later in 1769.

Crossing the vast Pacific Ocean was a risky adventure. The first expedition to do so was led by the Portuguese explorer Ferdinand Magellan in 1519–21. This expedition was the first circumnavigation of the world. However, Magellan did not live to see the voyage completed as he was killed in the Philippines in April 1521. Five months later, the remains of his fleet returned to Spain. Only one ship completed the voyage of the five that set out and just 17 European sailors returned out of an original crew of more than 270. More than 50 years later, the English sailor Francis Drake made the second round-the-world voyage from 1577–80, landing in Australia on the way. Much later, in the 1680s, the English pirate William Dampier explored the coasts of Australia and New Zealand. There seemed little trade or treasure to be gained from visiting this region, so Europeans largely ignored the new southern lands until the 1700s.

Francis Drake *sailed around the world in the* Golden Hind. *He was the second explorer to make the voyage.*

The first European visitors *to New Zealand were very respectful of the warlike Maoris, whose weapons included clubs, spears and long staves.*

1618 War starts with the Defenestration of Prague.
1619 Ferdinand II is crowned Holy Roman emperor.
1620 Ferdinand's army enters Bohemia and defeats Protestant King Frederick.
1625–29 Denmark and England join the war in support of the Dutch.
1630 King Gustavus II Adolphus of Sweden joins the war on the side of the Protestants.
1631 Swedish victory at the Battle of Breitenfeld.
1632 Gustavus is killed after the Battle of Lützen.
1634 Sweden withdraws following defeat at Nordlingen.
1635 Richelieu takes France into the war against the Habsburgs.
1637 The French and their allies start to defeat Spain.
1643 French victory at Rocroi over Spain.
1648 The Treaty of Westphalia ends the Thirty Years' War.
1659 Spain and France cease fighting. France becomes the most powerful country in Europe.

The Thirty Years' War

The French statesman Richelieu *(1585–1642) ruthlessly suppressed Protestantism in France, but to defeat Spain he supported the Protestant states in the Thirty Years' War.*

The religious conflicts in Europe that started after the Reformation continued into the 1600s. The Thirty Years' War began in 1618 as a protest by the Protestant noblemen of Bohemia (now part of the Czech Republic) against their Catholic rulers, the Holy Roman emperors.

Bohemia's noblemen chose Protestant Frederick of Bohemia to become their king. Then, in 1619, Ferdinand II, a member of the powerful Habsburg royal family, became the new Holy Roman emperor. Ferdinand was determined to return the entire Holy Roman empire back to Catholicism, so he sent his army to attack the state of Bohemia in order to overthrow their new Protestant ruler and replace him with a Catholic one.

By 1620, Ferdinand's army had defeated Frederick's troops, forcing him and his family to flee to the Netherlands, which was largely Protestant. Catholicism was now the only form of Christianity allowed in Bohemia. At this time, Spain was also ruled by members of the Habsburg family and, in 1621, they joined the war on the side of the Holy Roman empire and sent an army to fight against the Protestant Dutch. In 1625, the Dutch turned to Denmark and England for help and both countries sent forces. Many English soldiers were killed not by fighting, but from plague. Just four years later, in 1629, Habsburg armies had also defeated the Danes.

The Protestant Swedish king Gustavus II Adolphus led his army to war against Spain and the Holy Roman empire in 1630. He won in Saxony at Breitenfeld in 1631 and again at Lützen in 1632.

In 1618, *a group of Bohemian nobles threw two Catholic governors out of a window in Prague Castle. This act, known now as the 'Defenestration of Prague', sparked off the Thirty Years' War.*

However, Gustavus was killed during a cavalry charge at the Battle of Lützen when he was separated from his own forces. Two years later Sweden withdrew from the war.

Finally, France entered the war in 1635. Even though it was largely a Catholic nation, France joined the Protestant side in order to weaken the power of the Habsburg family in Europe. At first, Spain was victorious, but from 1637 the French and their Protestant allies were able to defeat them. The Treaty of Westphalia ended a war that, together with disease, had halved the populations of many German states.

Europe after the war ended in 1648. *Many small German states were devastated, while France emerged as Europe's strongest nation.*

King Gustavus II Adolphus *of Sweden leading his troops into battle, as was his custom. He went to war against the Habsburgs to defend Protestant beliefs, and also to protect Swedish trade in the Baltic, which was being threatened by Spain.*

1543 Birth of Tokugawa Ieyasu.
1550 Ieyasu is sent as a hostage to the Imagawa family.
1560 Ieyasu returns to his own lands and allies himself with the warlord Nobunaga.
1582 Nobunaga commits suicide. He is succeeded by Hideyoshi.
1584 After several small battles, Ieyasu allies himself with Hideyoshi.
1600 Ieyasu defeats rival warlords at the battle of Sekigahara.
1603 Ieyasu becomes shogun. The Tokugawa period begins.
1605 Ieyasu abdicates, but retains great power.
1613 Edo has about 150,000 people. 80,000 of them are samurai.
1616 Death of Ieyasu.
1637 All foreigners apart from the Dutch are forced to leave Japan.
1830s Peasants and samurai rebel against the Tokugawas.
1867 The last Tokugawa shogun is overthrown.

Tokugawa Japan

The Tokugawa, or Edo, period in Japan marked the end of a series of civil wars that had ravaged the country and introduced a long period of stability and unity. It began in 1603, when Tokugawa Ieyasu became the first of the Tokugawa shoguns – the powerful military leaders and effective rulers of Japan.

__Shogun Tokugawa Ieyasu__ (1543–1616) encouraged agriculture and Confucianism in Japan. He firmly controlled the nobles and their families.

In 1543, when Tokugawa Ieyasu was born, Japanese warlords were fighting each other for control of the country. As a boy, Ieyasu learned the skills of fighting from a rival family he had been sent to as a hostage. When he finally returned home to his own family, he began a long and well-planned struggle for power. By 1598, Ieyasu had the biggest army in Japan and the most productive estates, which were centred on the fishing village of Edo. In 1603, the emperor appointed him to the position of shogun, giving him power to run the country on the emperor's behalf.

Ieyasu turned Edo into a fortified town (later known as Tokyo). He reorganized the country into regions, each led by a daimyo, who controlled the local warriors (samurai).

Ieyasu abdicated in 1605, but he continued to hold on to real power. By 1612, he was fearful that Christianity might undermine his postition. To combat this, he discouraged visits to Japan by foreign Christian missionaries.

__Samurai warriors__ fought on foot or on horseback. They wore armour and masks to make them look more frightening, as well as for protection.

Ieyasu died in 1616, but his policy of discouraging Christian missionaries was continued and in 1637 missionaries were banned altogether. All Japanese Christians had to give up their religion or be put to death. The shogun next banned all foreign traders from Japan, apart from the Dutch who were allowed to send one trading ship a year to the port of Nagasaki. Japan flourished, despite its isolation from the rest of the world. The Tokugawa dynasty ruled until 1867.

Kabuki drama, *with its elaborate costumes and make-up, developed as a popular art form in the 1600s.*

ORNAMENTAL WOMEN

Under the Tokugawas, wealthy Japanese women were regarded as ornaments. They wore high-soled platform shoes and complicated ornamental hairstyles that greatly restricted their movement. The rules of the society they lived in were rigid, too. People were expected to commit suicide if they or their families were disgraced in any way.

Osaka castle *was built by the warlord Toyotomi Hideyoshi, who ruled Japan from 1585 to 1598. Under the Tokugawas, the power of such warlords was greatly reduced.*

The Dutch Empire

1568 William of Orange leads a Dutch revolt against Spanish rule.
1576 Spanish troops destroy Antwerp. Many inhabitants move to Amsterdam.
1577 The Netherlands makes a pact with England to fight against the Spanish.
1579 Seven northern provinces of the Netherlands form the Union of Utrecht.
1581 The Republic of the United Netherlands declares independence. William of Orange is elected ruler.
1599 The Dutch take control of the Moluccas from Portugal.
1602 The Dutch East India Company is founded.
1621 The Dutch West India Company is founded.
1648 Spain recognizes Dutch independence at the end of the Thirty Years' War.
1651–74 Three Anglo-Dutch wars between the Netherlands and England are fought over trade.
1689 William III of Orange and his wife Mary (daughter of James II of England) are offered the English throne.

William of Orange *(1533–84) led the Dutch in several revolts against Spanish rule. He was elected the first ruler of the Republic of the United Netherlands, but was killed by a Spanish agent.*

Until 1581, the countries we know today as Belgium, Luxembourg and the Netherlands (Holland) were part of the Low Countries, a group of 17 provinces. The people of the Netherlands (the Dutch) won their independence from Spanish rule in 1581. They sent ships west and east to trade, and, by the 1600s, a Dutch empire had come into being.

From 1516, the Dutch were ruled by Spain as part of the Holy Roman empire. This came about because the Holy Roman Emperor Charles V was also king of Spain. Charles's son Philip II was an ardent Catholic, whereas most of the people in the northern Low Countries were Protestant. The Spanish tried to crush the Protestants, but the Dutch, led by William of Orange, rose in revolt. Seven northern provinces broke away from Spanish rule, declaring themselves the Republic of the United Netherlands in 1581.

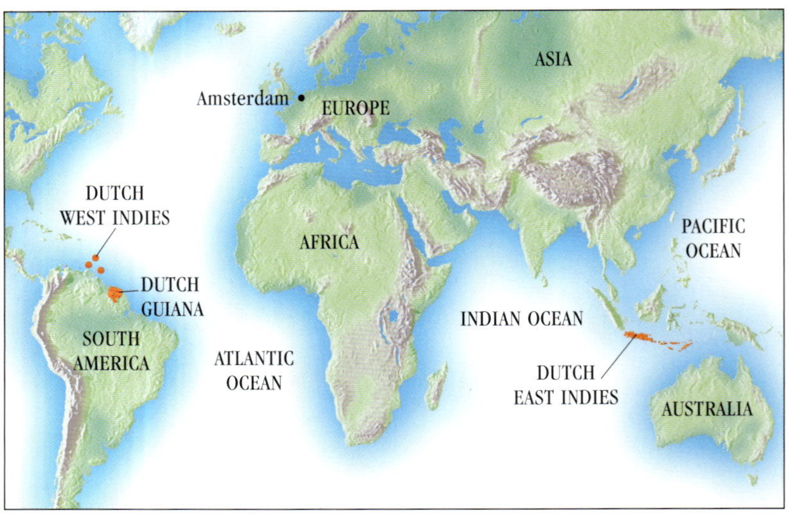

This map shows the Dutch trading empire. *As well as slaves, goods traded included spices, sugar and rice. The chief Dutch city, Amsterdam, was home to merchants and bankers.*

Coffee, tea, cinnamon and cloves *were among the valuable goods traded by the Dutch East India Company.*

***Dutch East India Company** traders sailing from the Netherlands to the East Indies would break their journey at the southern tip of Africa (the Cape of Good Hope) to buy supplies for their onward journey. The Dutch set up a colony there in 1652.*

While still at war with Spain, the Dutch began to build a trading empire overseas, in the Caribbean and Asia. In 1599, they began to take control of the Moluccas, or Spice Islands, from Portugal. In 1602, the Dutch East India Company was set up to encourage trade with the East Indies (Indonesia). Its headquarters, founded in 1619, were at Batavia (now Jakarta) on the island of Java. The company later took control of Ceylon (now Sri Lanka) and several ports in India.

Other Dutch merchants headed west, and, in 1621, set up the Dutch West India Company. This controlled islands in the Caribbean, and Dutch Guiana in South America. It traded in slaves, sugar and tobacco. Their jealously guarded trading empire increased Dutch wealth, but led to rivalry and wars with England in the late 1600s.

***One of the most famous** Dutch artists from this period is Rembrandt van Rijn (1606–69). After the Netherlands gained independence from Spain, there was a flowering in Dutch art.*

1542 By this time, Spain has claimed Florida, New Mexico, California, Arizona and Texas.
1536 Jacques Cartier claims the St Lawrence River in Canada for France.
1608 French explorer Samuel de Champlain founds Quebec.
1610 Henry Hudson discovers Hudson Bay in Canada.
1614 Colonist John Rolfe marries Pocohontas, a Native American princess.
1619 The first slaves from Africa arrive in Virginia to work on tobacco plantations.
1621 Following their first successful harvest, the Pilgrim Fathers hold the first Thanksgiving Day celebration.
1630 By this date there are about 16,000 English settlers in Massachusetts.
1636 Harvard College is founded in Cambridge, Massachusetts.
1664 The English capture New Amsterdam from the Dutch and rename it New York.
1670 The Hudson Bay Company is set up to encourage trade, especially in furs, between Canada and England.
1679 Fur traders from France are the first Europeans to see Niagara Falls.
1682 The explorer La Salle claims the whole Mississippi river valley for France.
1683 The first German settlers arrive in Pennsylvania.

Colonizing North America

The Spanish and French were the first Europeans to explore North America. French traders and missionaries explored the north, which they named Canada. To the south, the Spanish founded what is now New Mexico, and explored California and Texas.

***Native Americans** taught the settlers how to grow their new crops. They exchanged animal furs for guns and alcohol.*

The first serious attempts at European colonization were made in the 1580s by English explorer Sir Walter Raleigh, in an area he named Virginia. These early colonies failed, but in 1607 Raleigh set up a more successful colony named Jamestown. The colonists struggled against hunger, disease and battles with the Native Americans, whose land they were occupying, but they survived. In 1620, a group of religious dissenters, the Pilgrim Fathers, left Plymouth in England and sailed to North America seeking a place where they could practise their religion in peace. They landed near Cape Cod in Massachusetts, and founded a small settlement – the Plymouth Plantation. Only with help from the Native Americans were they able to survive. In 1624, the Dutch West India Company founded the colony of New Netherlands on the Hudson River, and, in 1625, the Dutch built a trading post on Manhattan Island, naming it New Amsterdam.

French colonization started in Canada. Samuel de Champlain founded Quebec in 1608, and from there explored beyond the St Lawrence River, claiming all of the land for France.

***Sir Walter Raleigh** (1552–1618) was a favourite of Queen Elizabeth I, England's 'Virgin Queen'. He named Virginia in her honour. In 1615, he led an expedition to South America in search of gold, but failed. On his return he was imprisoned by King James I, and later executed.*

Later, other French explorers travelled along the Mississippi River and claimed the whole river valley for France, naming it Louisiana, after King Louis XIV of France.

A replica of the Mayflower, *the ship that took the Pilgrim Fathers to America in 1620. They planned to land in Virginia, but were blown north, near to Cape Cod. It was midwinter, and only 54 of the 102 passengers survived until spring.*

European settlers *cut down trees to build simple log cabins to live in, and barns for their animals. The cleared land was fenced in and used for growing crops such as maize and squash. Turkeys were kept for food, and tobacco, indigo and rice were grown for export to Europe.*

EUROPEANS FIGHT FOR NORTH AMERICA

The English, French and Spanish claimed large areas of North America for themselves, even though many Native Americans already lived there. Some Europeans tried to convert the Native Americans to Christianity. The colonists fought battles with Native Americans and with rival colonists over land ownership.

The English Civil War

1625 Charles I becomes king. He marries Henrietta Maria of France.
1629 Parliament tries to curb Charles's power and is dismissed.
1637 Charles forces the English Prayer Book on Scotland.
1639 Rebellion breaks out in Scotland.
1640 Charles calls, dismisses, then recalls parliament.
1642 Charles tries to arrest five Parliamentarians. Civil war begins.
1645 New Model Army defeats Royalists at Naseby.
1646 Charles surrenders to the Scots.
1647 Charles is handed over to parliament. He escapes to the Isle of Wight.
1648 Charles, aided by Scots, starts second civil war, but is defeated.
1649 Charles goes on trial for treason. He is executed on 31 January.
1651 Charles's son goes into exile in France.
1653–58 Cromwell rules as Lord Protector.
1660 Restoration of the monarchy; Charles II comes to the throne.

The English Civil War broke out during the reign of the Stuart ruler Charles I, who became king in 1625. Charles led a royal army who fought against the army of parliament. Charles lost the Civil War and was executed. For a time, England became a republic under the control of Oliver Cromwell.

***Oliver Cromwell** (1599–1658). He helped recruit, train and command the New Model Army. As Lord Protector, he tried to impose parliamentary rule on Scotland and Ireland by force.*

***The king's soldiers** were called Royalists. Some wore their hair long and dressed flamboyantly in wide-brimmed hats and shirts of fine linen. Most soldiers on both sides wore leather jerkins and iron breastplates to protect their chests.*

There were religious, economic and political reasons for the war. Puritans (extreme Protestants) thought Charles favoured Catholics – he had a French Catholic wife, Queen Henrietta. Charles believed that only God gave him the right to rule and to choose his advisers. He came into conflict with parliament over raising taxes, and from 1629 tried to rule without parliament.

In 1640, Charles had to recall parliament, to raise money through taxes to fight against rebelling Scottish Protestants. He later tried to arrest his five leading opponents in the House of Commons, but they escaped. Mobs rioted in support of the members of parliament and Charles had to leave London. Both sides then raised armies of volunteers.

Neither side won the first major battle, which was fought in August 1642 at Edgehill. Thanks largely to Cromwell's New Model Army, Parliamentarians beat the Royalists decisively at the Battle of Naseby in 1645. There followed a series of Royalist defeats and Charles's headquarters at Oxford were captured in 1646.

***Parliament's cavalrymen** wore long boots with spurs. Iron helmets with neck- and face-guards protected them from sword blows. In 1645, the Parliamentarian force was reorganized into the New Model Army. This highly trained and well-disciplined force defeated the Royalist army in a series of battles which led to the end of the Civil War.*

This map shows the main battles of the war. *The pink area is land held by Charles I after 1644, when he lost control of the north. Parliament controlled the rest of the country.*

Charles fled to the Scots, who handed him over to parliament. He escaped and plotted with the Scots to fight again (1648), but his forces were soon crushed. Charles was tried for treason, found guilty, and executed on 31 January, 1649. In 1651, his son Charles, invading with Scots help, was beaten at Worcester on 3 September 1651. This battle ended the Civil War. After that point, England was governed as a Commonwealth (republic) by parliament, until its members quarrelled and parliament was dissolved by Oliver Cromwell. From 1653, Cromwell took over the governing of the country and ruled as Lord Protector, with the backing of his army. He divided the country into 11 districts and appointed military leaders to run them. Some of these leaders were strict Puritans who were unpopular because they closed down alehouses and stopped popular pastimes and sports. When Cromwell died in 1658, his son Richard took over as Lord Protector, but he was soon removed from office. In 1660 a new parliament invited Charles II back from exile.

King Charles I *was a small, shy man, with a slight stammer. But he was a good horseman, and he loved art – he brought the finest painters of the time to England, including Anthony van Dyck and Peter Paul Rubens.*

The execution *of King Charles I took place in Whitehall, London, on 31 January, 1649. During the execution, Charles wore two shirts so that he did not shiver in the cold and make people think that he was afraid. As he placed his head on the block, he spread out his arms, the signal for his readiness for the executioner to bring down the axe on his neck.*

1441 The Portuguese bring gold and slaves to Europe from West Africa for the first time.

1448 The Portuguese set up the first trading post in Africa.

1493 Christopher Columbus introduces sugar cane from Europe to the Caribbean.

1502 The Spanish take the first slaves from Africa to America to work on plantations.

1570s The Portuguese take slaves from Africa to Brazil to work on sugar plantations.

1619 African slaves arrive in Virginia to work on tobacco plantations.

1681 By now, there are about 2,000 slaves in Virginia.

1683 By now, almost all the native peoples of the Caribbean have been wiped out.

1700s The slave trade is at its peak. Cities such as Bristol, Liverpool and Nantes grow rich on the profits.

1730 About 90 per cent of Jamaica's population is of African origin.

1780s People start to campaign against slavery.

The Slave Trade

Africa has a long history of slavery. Until the early 1500s, most slaves were prisoners of war. Some were sold to Arab traders. Then Europeans visited the coasts of Africa and began shipping slaves to the New World.

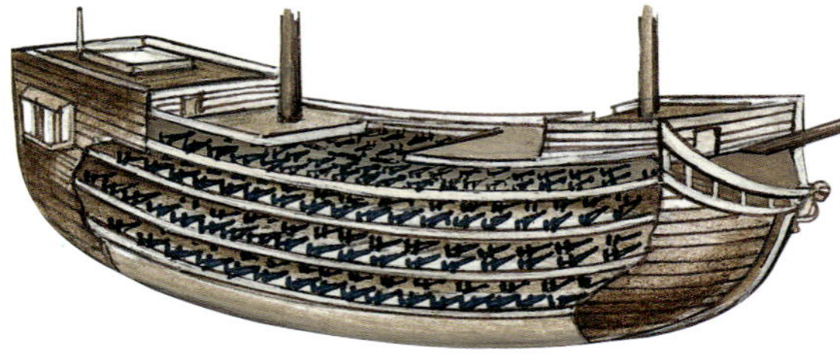

Slave ships *carried more than 400 people, packed in as tightly as possible. The voyage from West Africa to the Americas could last as long as 12 months.*

European explorers to the New World set up colonies on mainland America and the islands of the Caribbean. They grew crops such as sugar cane on large plantations, and in many places enslaved the native population to do the work for them. But terrible conditions and European diseases killed many native people, so the colonists started to look elsewhere for workers to replace them. Some convicts were brought from Europe, but they soon fell ill and died. The colonists then looked to Africa for slaves.

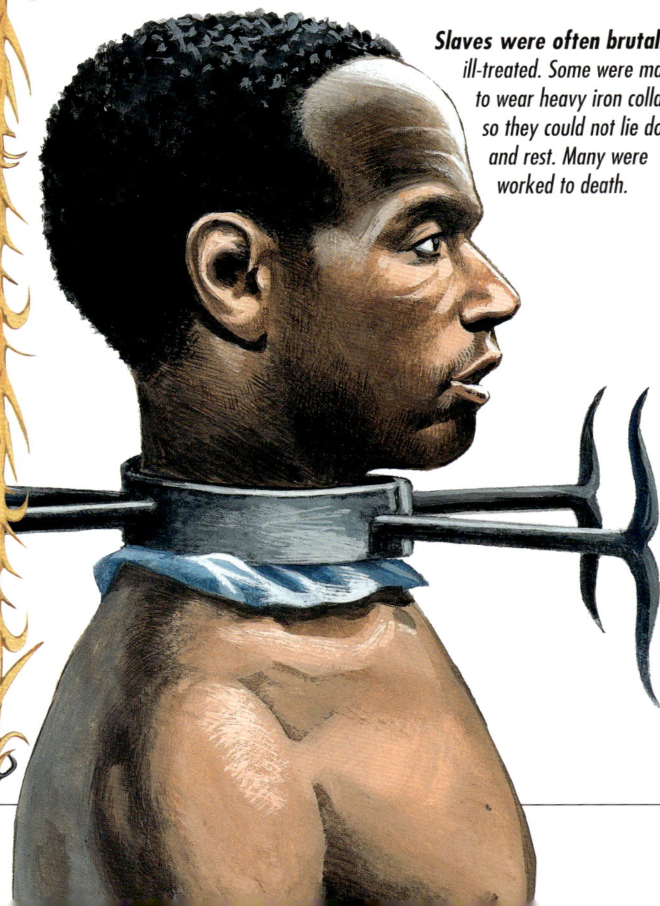

Slaves were often brutally *ill-treated. Some were made to wear heavy iron collars so they could not lie down and rest. Many were worked to death.*

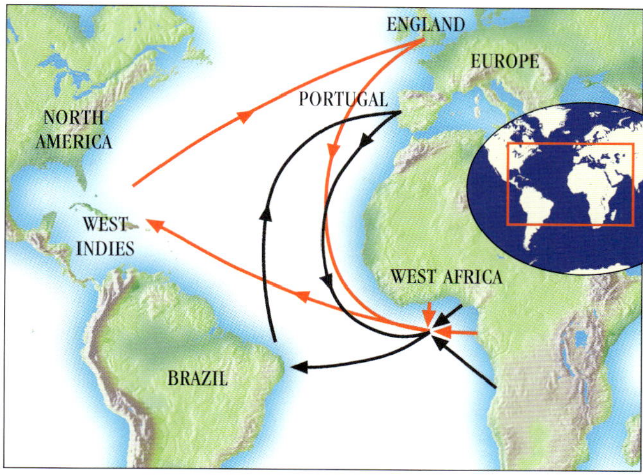

From Europe, ships sailed to Africa with guns and cloth to buy slaves. *The slaves were carried to the Americas, where they were sold. On the return journey to Europe the ships carried sugar, rum and cotton.*

On a sugar plantation, *slaves worked in the fields and processing factories. The work was heavy, conditions were bad and hours were long. Some plantation owners even beat and starved the slaves who worked in their grand houses.*

A SLAVE AUCTION

When African slaves arrived in the Caribbean, South America or the colonies of North America, they were sold at auction to the highest bidder. Africans from different cultures and with different languages were grouped together to work.

Soon huge numbers of people were being captured in central Africa. Chained together, they were forced to march to the coast, where they were sold to European slave traders. Then, still chained, they were crammed into slave ships and taken across the Atlantic. Conditions on board ship were terrible, with not enough light, air, food or water, and as many as a third of the slaves died on each eight-week journey to America.

Slaves faced a hard life on the plantations. They were often badly fed and whipped for the smallest mistake. Many died soon after arriving at the plantations. The strongest rarely survived for more than ten years, and few ever saw Africa again.

The slave trade reached its peak in the 18th century, when between six and seven million people were shipped from Africa to America. The impact on some traditional African societies was devastating. From the 1780s, European reformers at last began to realize how cruel slavery was and started to campaign against it.

1638 Birth of Louis, son of Louis XIII of France and Anne of Austria.
1643 Louis succeeds to the throne as Louis XIV.
1648 At the end of the Thirty Years' War, France is the most powerful nation in Europe.
1653 Cardinal Jules Mazarin finally puts down the five-year uprising known as the Fronde and Louis returns to Paris.
1660 Louis marries Marie-Thérèse of Austria, daughter of the king of Spain.
1661 Mazarin dies and Louis takes control of France.
1667 Start of war with Spain over the Netherlands. Louis gains control of Flanders, but has to retreat in 1668.
1672 Start of six-year Dutch war, which ends in victory for France.
1678 Louis moves his court to Versailles.
1685 Persecution of the Huguenots (French Protestants) forces many of them to leave France.
1689–97 War of the Grand Alliance, led by Britain against France, ends in French defeat.
1701–13 War of the Spanish Succession, in which Louis fights for control of the Spanish empire.
1715 Death of Louis XIV at the age of 77.

***Louis XIV** (1638–1715) was glorified by artists and writers as the 'Sun King'. He ruled France for 72 years.*

Louis XIV

Louis XIV of France was the most powerful of all European monarchs in the 17th century. He was an absolute ruler, which means that he governed the entire nation of France alone. This brought him into conflict with both the nobility and the ordinary people.

Louis XIV came to the throne in 1643, when he was just five years old. His mother ruled on his behalf until 1651. The council of nobles, a group of France's social elite who helped to run the country, argued with her constantly, because it wanted a share of the power. There was also a rebellion by the people in 1648, over the heavy taxes that they had to pay. When the nobles revolted, too, Louis fled from Paris and did not return until 1653. He was determined such a rebellion would never happen again.

In 1661, Louis dismissed the council of nobles and took into his own hands the government of France. At this time, France had become the most powerful nation in Europe.

***The palace of Versailles** (built 1662–1710). The nobility were encouraged to live here, under King Louis XIV's watchful eye.*

***The gardens at Versailles** were designed by Andre Le Nôtre between 1661 and 1700. Later additions include a mock village which was built in 1774 on the grounds for Marie Antoinette, the wife of Louis XVI.*

Louis XIV's chief adviser, Jean Colbert, reorganized taxes and reformed the legal system. He set up new industries and a network of roads and canals, and increased the size of the merchant fleet to encourage foreign trade overseas. Louis spent much of France's wealth on building a magnificent new palace at Versailles near Paris, and also on wars throughout Europe. He wanted to expand French territory to reach the Alps, the Pyrenees and the Rhine river. Between 1667 and 1697, he fought three major wars with other European powers, including Spain and Great Britain.

The French peasants were heavily taxed to pay for the king's extravagant building projects and wars, while the nobles and clergy paid nothing. Two bad harvests left thousands of people starving, but protests were quickly crushed. When Louis died in 1715, his five-year-old great-grandson succeeded him, inheriting a country left financially weak after years of warfare.

MOLIERE

Louis XIV was a great patron of the arts and literature. One of his favourite dramatists was Jean Baptiste Poquelin, known as Molière (1622–73), the father of modern French comedy. From 1659 to 1673, Molière wrote and directed many plays at Versailles. He also acted in his plays.

Revolution and Industry

The two centuries between 1700 and 1900 were a time of conflict, revolution and change in many parts of the world. Empires were won and lost, governments toppled while agriculture and industry developed rapidly.

The countries of northwest Europe grew more powerful, while Spain and Portugal declined. The 13 American colonies declared their independence from Britain in 1776 to become the United States of America. They were helped by the French, who in 1789 had their own revolution. The French overthrew their king and became first a republic and then an empire. By 1793, this had led to wars between France and Austria, Britain, the Netherlands, Portugal, Prussia, Russia and Spain.

p123 Chinese vases made from fine porcelain were exported to the West during the Qing dynasty.

p122 Catherine the Great became ruler of Russia in 1762.

p139 The Spinning Jenny was invented by James Hargreaves.

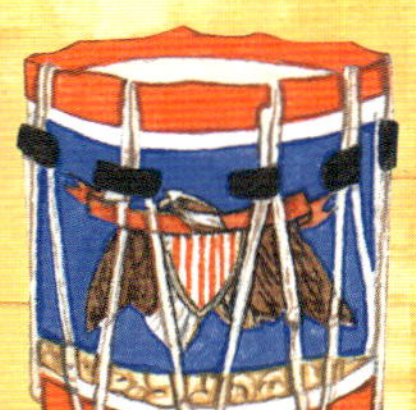

p148 The American Civil War involved many new weapons, including ironclad warships.

p121 Improved telescopes gave astronomers clearer images of the universe.

p129 George Washington led his troops across the Delaware River and went on to defeat the British at the Battle of Trenton in 1776.

p134 The Duke of Wellington led the British army in Spain and Portugal, and defeated Napoleon at Waterloo, in what is now Belgium.

p132 *Captain James Cook met Maoris for the first time, while charting the coast of New Zealand. Cook was killed by islanders in Hawaii in 1779.*

The Spanish and Portuguese colonies in South America took advantage of the wars in Europe to gain their independence. Later conflicts united the states of Germany and Italy into two countries. In the United States of America, conflict over slavery led to a civil war. Revolutions in agriculture, industry and transport affected the lives of even more people, especially in Europe and America. New methods of farming made it possible to feed more people, and large numbers left the countryside to make a living in the expanding towns. Factories in towns used machines to produce vast quantities of goods once made by hand.

To provide raw materials and a ready market for these factory goods, many European countries built up empires overseas. Britain tightened its control on India and laid claim to Australia and New Zealand. The rising power was the United States, where millions of European settled, forcing Native Americans from their homelands.

p152 *Zulu warriors killed 1,700 soldiers of the British army at the start of the Zulu War in 1879.*

1632–1704 Life of English philosopher John Locke. He believed that all men were equal and free and that the authority of government comes only from the consent of the governed.

1687 Sir Isaac Newton sets out his theories about light and the visible spectrum, the three laws of motion and the existence of gravity.

1743 Benjamin Franklin sets up the American Philosophical Society in Philadelphia. Its members are interested in science as well as philosophy.

1751 The first volume of the *Encyclopédie* is published.

1751 Linnaeus publishes his *Philosophia Botanica*.

1755 Samuel Johnson's *Complete Dictionary of the English Language* is published. It contains over 43,000 words.

1768 The *Encyclopaedia Britannica* is first published.

1788 *The Times* newspaper is first published in London.

1791 Thomas Paine's *The Rights of Man* influences Americans in their fight for independence.

1792 Mary Wollstonecraft's *A Vindication of the Rights of Women* argues for equal opportunities in education.

The Enlightenment

***The* Encyclopédie,** *compiled by the French writer and critic Denis Diderot, was written by experts in many subjects and aimed to cover all branches of knowledge. First published between 1751 and 1772, the work comprised 17 volumes of text and 11 volumes of pictures.*

The Enlightenment was the name given to a time of new ideas, beginning in the 1600s and lasting until the end of the 1700s. It was also called the 'Age of Reason', because people began to look for reasons why certain things happened as they did. Modern science developed from this line of questioning. New ideas about government and how people should live were also central to the Enlightenment.

Some European rulers took up Enlightenment ideas with enthusiasm, as did ordinary people who were no longer willing to be told what to do, and who wanted a say in government. Other people feared that this new way of thinking would overturn the old world for ever. The French philosopher René Descartes (1596–1650) argued that only an idea that could be shown to be true, by evidence or by reasoning, was true. Such arguments troubled the heads of the Christian Church.

François Marie Arouet *used the pen-name Voltaire. He was a scientist, thinker and writer, noted for his wit. He declared: 'I may disagree with what you say, but I will defend to the death your right to say it.'*

These arguments also troubled kings and queens throughout Europe who believed they had a 'divine' (God-given) right to rule. Another French thinker, Voltaire, criticized both the Church and government of his day. So did Jean-Jacques Rousseau, whose ideas helped to shape the events that led up to the American and French revolutions.

The Enlightenment was a period of many practical discoveries as well as philosophical theories. The English scientist Isaac Newton published theories on light and the spectrum, as well as his laws of motion and the existence and effects of gravity. Other scientists took to studying the living world in great detail, including the Dutch scientist Carl von Linné (Linnaeus), who started to define the various parts of the plants and animal kingdoms. These scientists were aided by the development of improved scientific equipment, such as more powerful telescopes and microscopes.

Other leading lights of the Enlightenment were Benjamin Franklin, scientist, inventor and statesman; Adam Smith the economist; David Hume the historian; the philosopher Immanuel Kant; and the writer Mary Wollstonecraft. The belief that every person had the right to knowledge, freedom and happiness inspired a new revolutionary and democratic fervour, which was to shape the world of the 19th century.

INFLUENTIAL WOMEN

New ideas were exchanged at meetings of artistic and educated people. They gathered, often in the homes of wealthy women, to discuss the latest scientific discoveries, plays, books and issues of the day. Two such women were Madame Geoffrin and Marie-Anne Lavoisier, wife of the chemist Antoine Lavoisier.

Linnaeus *was the first person to classify the plant and animal kingdoms, defining and grouping living things into species. In 1751, he published* Philosophia Botanica *which contained many detailed studies of hundreds of plant species.*

The telescope *opened new worlds of discovery. Improved telescopes made by Newton in 1668 and Cassegrain in 1672 used mirrors to reflect light, and gave astronomers clearer images of the universe.*

The Russian Empire

1672 Peter the Great is born.
1696 Peter becomes sole ruler of Russia.
1700–21 Great Northern War against Sweden.
1703 St Petersburg is founded. Peter calls it his 'window on Europe'.
1712 St Petersburg becomes Russia's capital and main port.
1722–23 War with Persia gives Russia access to the Caspian Sea.
1725 Peter the Great dies.
1729 The future Catherine the Great is born in Prussia.
1745 Catherine marries her cousin, Peter III, heir to the Russian throne.
1762 Catherine becomes empress of Russia after her husband's death.
1773 A revolt by the serfs is brutally crushed.
1787 On a tour of Russia, Catherine meets healthy, well-fed, well-dressed actors while the real serfs are hidden from sight.
1796 Catherine dies and is succeeded by her son.

Peter the Great changed Russia from an isolated, backward nation into a major European power. Nearly 40 years after his death, another great ruler, Catherine the Great, carried on his ambition.

***Peter the Great** ruled Russia from 1682 to 1725. He was an immensely tall, strong, energetic man. But he could also be brutal – he imprisoned and tortured his own son.*

***Catherine the Great** was ruthless and ambitious. She was interested in new ideas, but her plans to improve Russia's education system and to reform the law came to nothing.*

In 1682, aged just ten, Peter the Great (Peter I) became Tsar of Russia. At first, he ruled with his half-brother Ivan V. When Ivan died in 1696, Peter ruled on his own until 1725. Russia had been growing rapidly since 1639, but it was still backward compared with the rest of Europe. Peter was determined to change this. For 18 months he toured Europe, meeting kings and scientists, and people in industry, farming and ship-building. In the Netherlands, he even worked in a shipyard for a while. When he returned to Russia, Peter built up the navy and army, encouraged industries and farming, and built new roads and canals to help trade. Peter also acquired a Baltic coastline for Russia through war with Sweden. This gave Russia a seaport that was not ice-bound in winter. He moved Russia's capital from Moscow to St Petersburg on the Baltic. When Peter died in 1725, Russia was more secure and advanced than it had been when he came to power.

In 1762, Catherine II (the Great) came to the throne. Like Peter, she encouraged western ideas and gained territory for Russia, fighting the Ottoman empire in 1774 and 1792, and Sweden in 1790. She also claimed much of Poland. Conditions did not improve for the Russian serfs, however, and a revolt in 1773 was harshly put down.

***Carriages used** runners instead of wheels so they could glide through the snow like a sleigh during the long Russian winters.*

1618 United Manchu tribes take control of the Chinese province of Liaotung.
1630s The Chinese start to rebel against the high taxes imposed by the Ming dynasty.
1644 The Manchus take control of Beijing and overthrow the Ming dynasty.
1661 Kangxi becomes the second Qing emperor. He conquers Taiwan, Outer Mongolia, parts of Siberia and Tibet.
1692 Kangxi gives Jesuit missionaries permission to spread Christianity to the Chinese.
1704 All missionaries, except the Jesuits, are expelled for not tolerating Chinese traditions.
1722 Death of Kangxi.
1736 Qianlong, grandson of Kangxi, becomes emperor of China and rules for 60 years.
1770 Manchu power begins to decline. Qianlong closes all but one port to foreign traders and tries to keep China isolated from the world.
1792 The British are refused permission to increase trade by the emperor.
1796 Qianlong abdicates, but dominates government even in retirement.
1840 The Qing dynasty declines following rebellions in China and successful attacks by foreigners.

Manchu China

In the early 1600s in China, rebellions broke out against the Ming emperor's unpopular government and its high taxes. At the same time, tribes in Manchuria (the region to the northeast of China) were uniting.

Beautifully shaped vases *made from fine porcelain and decorated with patterns of flowers and animals were exported to the West during the Qing dynasty.*

By 1618, the Manchu were strong enough to take control of and hold on to the Ming province of Liaotung. Then, in 1644, a rebellion in China led to the capture of Beijing, the capital. Ming officials asked the Manchus to help them defeat the rebels. Instead, the Manchus seized power and set up a new dynasty, the Qing, which ruled China for more than 250 years.

Under the Qing dynasty, China flourished once more. Production of silk, porcelain, lacquerware and cotton expanded, and trade increased.

In 1792, Britain sent its first ambassador to China with a request for greater trade rights. The emperor refused, wanting China to stay isolated. This meant China was slow to take up new technology, and by the 1840s the weakened empire was unable to resist Western pressure.

The Qing empire *(in orange) was larger than China today (boundary shown in blue).*

Beijing expanded greatly under the Ming, *who built many new palaces and temples, and a new wall and moat around the city. The Qing left the inner city unaltered, but built new palaces and temples outside the city wall.*

The Agricultural Revolution

1701 British inventor Jethro Tull invents the horse-drawn seed drill.
1715 The Dutch reclaim large areas of land from the sea.
1730 Four-crop rotation is introduced in England.
1759–1801 In Britain the Enclosure Acts enclose huge areas of common land.
1796 A school for farmers is set up in Hungary.
1800 In Britain, selective breeding has more than doubled the weight of the average cow from 100 years earlier.
1840 Publication of the first book on using chemicals in farming.

Until the end of the 17th century, farming methods in Europe remained unchanged from the Middle Ages. Most people still lived in the country and were able to grow just enough food to feed themselves, with a little spare to sell at the local market.

The fantail windmill *was invented in 1745. The fantail moved the main sails when the wind's direction changed. Before this, a windmill's main sails needed moving whenever the wind's direction changed, so that they faced into the wind.*

People farmed small strips of land, scattered over three or four large, open fields that surrounded their village. To keep the land fertile, each year one field was left unplanted, or fallow, and so produced nothing. This system worked well while the population was small. However, in time the population increased, and more people moved to the newly expanding towns where there was no land on which to grow crops. If everyone was to be fed, better ways of growing crops had to be found.

Some of the earliest experiments in agriculture were carried out in the Netherlands, where more land was needed that was suitable for farming. The Dutch drained lakes and reclaimed large areas of land from the sea, building dykes. They used pumps powered by windmills to keep the water out. Dutch farmers could not afford to leave any fields unplanted. Instead, they experimented with crop rotation, in which four different crops were planted in the same field over a four-year period. This idea was later copied in Britain. Other agricultural breakthroughs were made: the plough was improved and the horse-drawn seed drill and hoe were invented. These allowed several rows of seeds to be sown at the same time, and later weeded.

In many places, the land was reorganized. Large, open fields were divided into smaller ones, separated by hedges or walls. Laws were passed in Britain giving landowners the right to enclose common land, which everyone had previously used for grazing.

As more people moved to the new industrial towns, fewer farmers had to provide more food. Agricultural changes between 1700 and 1850 helped farmers to feed the growing population.

New, larger breeds of farm animals *were bred during the 18th century, so that they could supply more meat, milk and wool.*

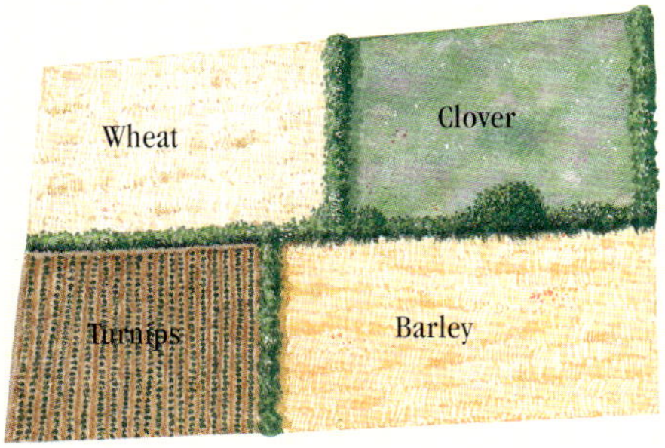

CROP ROTATION

Crop rotation increased the fertility of the soil. A farmer planted wheat in the first field, turnips in the second, barley in the third and clover in the fourth. Each year the crops were rotated, so in the second year wheat was grown in the second field, and so on.

A horse-drawn seed drill *made a series of even holes into which seeds fell. A worker then raked over the holes. Before this, seeds were scattered on the ground by hand. They fell unevenly and often failed to germinate, or were eaten by birds.*

1700 Austria takes Hungary from the Ottomans. The last Spanish Habsburg monarch dies and Spain is ruled by the Bourbons of France.

1711 Charles VI, Archduke of Austria, becomes Holy Roman emperor.

1713 Frederick William succeeds as king of Prussia.

1740 Maria Theresa succeeds Charles VI. Rivals challenge her right to rule. Frederick II (the Great) becomes king of Prussia.

1756–63 Seven Years' War. France, Austria and Russia clash with Britain and Prussia.

1765 Maria Theresa rules the Holy Roman empire with her son Joseph.

1772 First partition (division) of Poland by Austria, Prussia and Russia.

1780 Maria Theresa is succeeded by Joseph II.

1781 Joseph II introduces reforms and frees the serfs.

1786 Frederick the Great dies.

1795 Second partition of Poland between Austria, Prussia and Russia. Poland ceases to exist until 1919.

Austria and Prussia

Europe in the 18th century was dominated by absolute monarchs, whose power was not limited by any elected assembly. They built palaces and attracted artists and intellectuals to their 'enlightened' courts. Two of the most powerful states were Austria and Prussia.

***Maria Theresa** (1717–80) inherited the throne of Austria in 1740. War broke out among her rivals, but her position was secured in 1748.*

Austria was ruled by the Habsburgs, a family that had dominated Europe since the 13th century. In the early 1500s, the Habsburg Charles V, then Holy Roman emperor, divided his huge realm. One half was ruled from Spain, the other from Vienna in Austria. In 1700, the Spanish Habsburgs died out, but the Austrian Habsburgs were still powerful. From 1740 Maria Theresa ruled Austria (which included Hungary, recaptured from the Turks). She restored its power and made Vienna the artistic centre of Europe. Artists and architects from all over Europe came to work on its grand building projects. Maria Theresa was succeeded in 1780 by her son Joseph II.

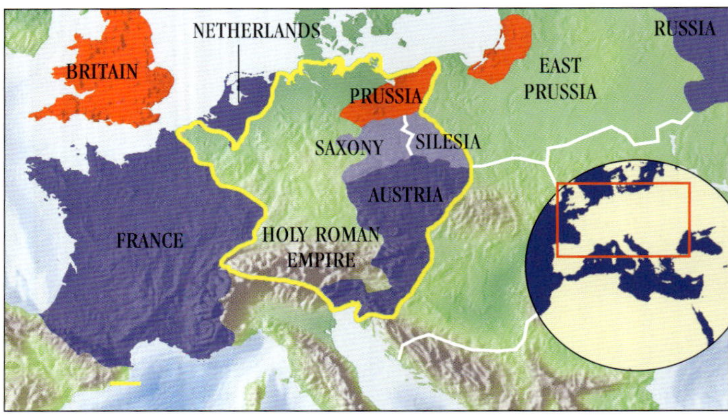

***In the Seven Years' War** (1756–63), France, Austria and Russia opposed Prussia and Britain. At the end of the war, Prussia gained Silesia, which was seized from Austria. Britain took control of France's colonies in India and America.*

***Frederick the Great** (1712–86) of Prussia was a cultured man, but also a stern administrator. He encouraged the study of science and agriculture, and improved education.*

Joseph was influenced by the Enlightenment. He freed the serfs and abolished privileges enjoyed by nobles.

Frederick II (the Great) became king of Prussia in 1740. An outstanding general, he inherited a well-organized state with a powerful army, which he used to make Prussia a major power in Europe.

The Schönbrunn Palace in Vienna *(built 1696–1711) was the Habsburgs' summer palace. Planned to rival Versailles, the French king's palace just outside Paris, it had 1,440 rooms.*

Wolfgang Amadeus Mozart *(1756–91) playing at the court of Maria Theresa. Mozart first played at court when he was only six years old.*

Birth of the United States

1765 Protests start against British taxes in the American colonies.
1770 At the Boston Massacre, British troops fire on a crowd of colonists and kill five of them.
1773 The Boston Tea Party; in Boston harbour, colonists throw ships' cargoes overboard as a protest against the tax on tea.
1775 The American War of Independence starts.
1776 On 4 July, the Continental Congress adopts the Declaration of Independence.
1777 The British are defeated at Saratoga, New York. France sides with America. The British capture Philadelphia, Pennsylvania.
1778 The British capture Savannah, Georgia.
1779 Spain joins the war on America's side.
1780 The Dutch join the war on America's side. British victory at Charleston, South Carolina.
1781 After a siege at Yorktown, Virginia, the British surrender.

British troops, *trained for fighting in European wars, found fighting in America very different. Standing in close-packed ranks, firing volleys of shot, they presented easy targets for American guerilla tactics. British infantrymen wore red long-tailed coats, and so were known as 'redcoats'.*

By the mid 1700s, there were 13 British colonies in North America. Britain had also won control of Canada, by defeating France in the Seven Years' War (1756–63). Britain had no thought of changing the way it governed its American colonies, but the colonists, denied a say in governing themselves, rebelled. The American Revolution led to the colonies' independence as the United States.

Britain taxed its American citizens to help pay for the defence of North America. There were about two million British Americans. They produced most of their own food and other goods, but were unhappy at having to pay taxes on imported tea and legal documents. Also the British Americans had no representatives in the British Parliament, and declared that 'taxation without representation is tyranny'. Britain reacted by sending soldiers to quell any protests.

PAUL REVERE

Paul Revere is one of the heroes of the War of Independence. He rode from Boston to Lexington to warn of the approach of British soldiers. Although he was captured, his mission was successful. Revere was immortalized in a famous poem by Longfellow.

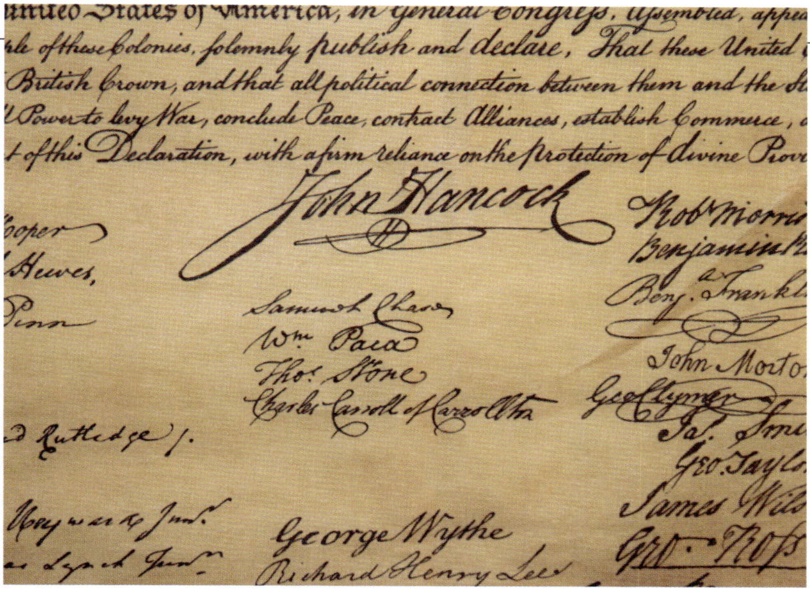

***The Declaration of Independence** was signed on 4 July, 1776 by delegates from the 13 colonies. It separated them from Great Britain and created the United States.*

In April 1775, an armed confrontation between colonists and British troops took place at Lexington in Massachusetts. The colonists formed an army of their own, commanded by George Washington, and on 17 June the two armies clashed at Bunker Hill, near Boston. The British were successful, but the War of Independence, or American Revolution, had begun.

While fighting continued, colonial leaders signed the Declaration of Independence on 4 July, 1776. The British government refused to accept it. Under Washington's command, the colonists' army began to defeat the British. France, Spain and the Netherlands all joined the colonists' side. The six-year war ended in 1781, when the British surrendered at Yorktown. Two years later, Britain recognized the independent United States of America.

***On Christmas night** 1776, George Washington led his troops across the icy Delaware River and went on to defeat the British at the Battle of Trenton. This was one of the first major American victories in the War of Independence.*

1789, 15 May The Estates General meets for the first time since 1614. The third estate breaks away and forms the National Assembly.
1789, 14 July The French Revolution starts when a mob seizes the Bastille.
1789, 26 August The Declaration of the Rights of Man is made.
1789, 5 October The king and his family are seized by a mob and taken to Paris as prisoners.
1791 The royal family try to escape but are returned to Paris.
1792 France is declared a republic.
1793 Louis XVI is executed in January, Marie Antoinette in October. The Reign of Terror starts. The Netherlands, Austria, Britain, Prussia and Spain are at war with France.
1794 Robespierre's execution ends the Reign of Terror. France is governed by the Directoire, a committee of five.
1795 Napoleon Bonaparte's rise to power starts when he defends Paris against rebels.

The French Revolution

The French Revolution of 1789 shook all of Europe. It began as a protest for fairness, food and democracy. The French people, most of whom were denied a say in government, rose up against the 'old order'. The years of bloodshed led to the emergence of a dictator, who made himself emperor – Napoleon Bonaparte.

In 1793, Maximilien Robespierre *(1758–94) started the Reign of Terror. Over the next nine months, thousands of opponents of the Revolution were put to death, until he himself was denounced and guillotined.*

In the 18th century, society in France was divided into three classes, or estates. The first estate was the nobility, the second was the clergy and the third was everyone else. Only people in the third estate paid taxes. Educated people, by now familiar with the ideas of the Enlightenment, knew how unfair the system was. Their discontent increased in 1788, when a bad harvest pushed up prices, leaving many people facing starvation. After years of extravagant kings and costly wars, the government had little money to deal with the crisis. When, in 1789, King Louis XVI called a meeting of the Estates General (the nearest France had to a parliament) to raise more money, the third estate said that if they had to pay taxes, they should have a say in how the country was run. Louis XVI refused this request.

The rebels, calling themselves the National Assembly, refused to leave Versailles until the king listened to their demands. In Paris, a mob attacked the Bastille, a royal prison, and riots broke out all over France. The National Assembly made a 'Declaration of the Rights of Man'. These included liberty, equality and the right to resist oppression. Louis XVI and his family were arrested and held until 1793. Finally, the king was put on trial and executed in January of that year. This was the start of the Reign of Terror.

During the Reign of Terror *about 500,000 people were arrested and 17,000 of them put to death by public execution on the guillotine. Many of the first victims were aristocrats, condemned as 'enemies of the people'.*

During the Terror, led by Maximilien Robespierre, thousands of people were put to death. Austria, Britain, the Netherlands, Prussia and Spain all went to war with France. Alarmed by this turn of events, Robespierre's colleagues ordered his execution. The threat of civil war in 1795 led to the rise of an ambitious French soldier, Napoleon Bonaparte.

***The Colonne de Juillet** in Paris stands on the site of the Bastille prison which was destroyed by the revolutionary mob on 14 July, 1789.*

MARIE ANTOINETTE
Marie Antoinette (1755–93), daughter of Maria Theresa of Austria, was married to King Louis XVI of France. At first, she was popular, but her extravagance soon turned people against her. On hearing that Parisians were rioting over bread shortages, she is reputed to have said: 'Let them eat cake!'

1768–71 Captain James Cook's first voyage to the South Pacific.
1772–75 Captain Cook's second voyage to the South Pacific.
1776 Captain Cook's third and last voyage to the South Pacific. In 1779, he is killed in a quarrel with Hawaiians.
1788 Convicts are transported from Britain to Australia.
1793 The first free settlers from Britain arrive in Australia. They settle in Botany Bay.
1803 Settlers from Britain start going to Tasmania for the first time.
1813 By this date merino sheep (from Spain) have been introduced into Australia. Settlers have spread north and west, beyond the Blue Mountains.
1840 Maori leaders sign the Treaty of Waitangi. It offers land rights and full British citizenship. The treaty is not honoured and war breaks out (1843–48).
1851 Discovery of gold in Victoria results in the Australian Gold Rush.

Australia and New Zealand

In the late 1700s, European interest in Australia and New Zealand and the peoples living there, the Aboriginals and Maoris, was reignited. Settlement of Australia by Britain began in 1788, and in 1840 New Zealand became a British colony. Emigrants from Europe settled in both countries.

British navigator James Cook made three voyages to the Pacific during the 1700s. His first expedition left in 1768. Cook sailed around New Zealand, then to the eastern and northern coasts of Australia. He landed at Botany Bay on the southeast coast and claimed the territory for Britain. On his second journey he explored many of the islands dotted around the Pacific Ocean.

Captain James Cook *and his men met Maoris for the first time while charting the coast of New Zealand (1769–70). Cook was killed by islanders in Hawaii in 1779.*

Remains of the penal settlement at Port Arthur, Tasmania. *Port Arthur was colonized in 1830 and acted as a timber station. Convicts were kept here until 1877 when the settlement started to decline.*

ABORIGINES AND MAORIS
Many Aboriginal Australians were ill-treated by Europeans. Some were shot, others died from European diseases. Many simply lost the will to live. The Maori of New Zealand numbered about 100,000 when James Cook arrived. After the Treaty of Waitangi, Maori rights were not protected, war broke out, and in 1848 the Maori were defeated.

The third voyage, in 1776, took Cook back to New Zealand. He then explored the Pacific coast of South America, before sailing to Hawaii.

In 1788, the First Fleet sailed from Britain, transporting convicts to the penal colony of Port Jackson in Australia. Some prisoners stayed on as free men, and from 1793 were joined by settlers. Towns were built and explorers crossed the continent. The settlers showed little respect for the Aboriginal Australians whose lands they were taking. Transportation of convicts to Australia ended in 1850.

In New Zealand, the French arrived after Cook, but found the Maoris hostile. Contact continued with visits by whalers, seal hunters and Christian missionaries in the early 1800s. In 1840, by the Treaty of Waitangi, Maori leaders gave up their lands and New Zealand became a British colony.

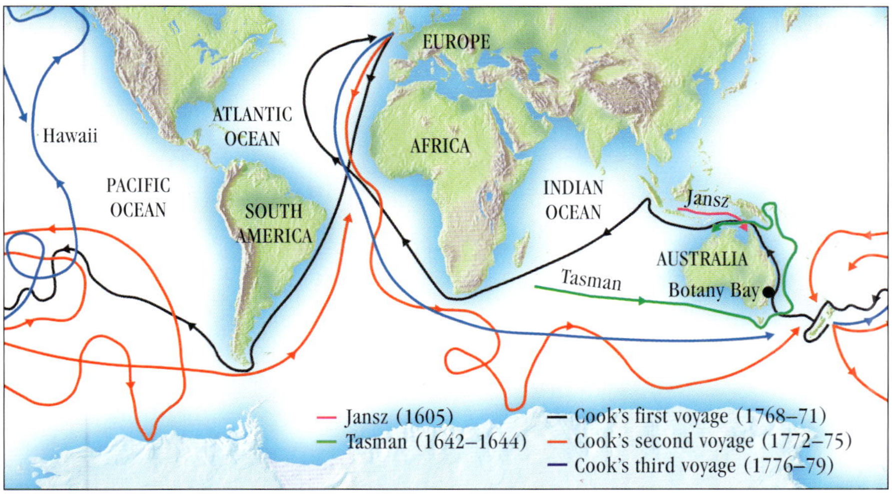

***This map shows** the voyages to Australia and New Zealand of the 17th-century Dutch explorers Willem Jansz and Abel Tasman, and the three epic explorations (1768–79) of Britain's James Cook.*

1785 Napoleon becomes an officer in the French army.
1795 Napoleon defends Paris against rebels and prevents civil war breaking out.
1797 A French army led by Napoleon drives Austrians from much of northern Italy.
1798 The French fleet is defeated by Nelson at the Battle of the Nile in Egypt.
1799 Napoleon returns to France and seizes power.
1804 Napoleon declares himself emperor of France.
1805 The French fleet is defeated by Nelson at the Battle of Trafalgar. Napoleon's army defeats the Austrians and Russians at the Battle of Austerlitz.
1806 Napoleon's army defeats the Prussians at Jena.
1807 Napoleon's army defeats the Russians at Friedland. France takes control of Portugal.
1808 The Peninsular War starts when Napoleon puts his brother Joseph on the throne of Spain.
1809 Napoleon marries the Austrian emperor's daughter, Marie Louise.
1812 Napoleon's army invades Russia, but is defeated by the winter weather. The French army is defeated at Salamanca, Spain.
1814 Napoleon is forced to abdicate and is exiled to the island of Elba, off Italy.
1815 Napoleon escapes from Elba. He is defeated finally at the Battle of Waterloo.

Napoleon's War

Napoleon Bonaparte (1769–1821) rose from the rank of artillery officer to become emperor of France. Determined to unify Europe under his rule, his wars of conquest dominated the start of the 19th century.

***In land battles, Napoleon was a master** at using artillery (wheeled guns). At sea, he tried to starve Britain into making peace by cutting its trade links, but he was unable to defeat the British navy.*

Napoleon was born on the island of Corsica, off the south coast of France. He joined the French army in 1785. He supported the French Revolution and in 1793 defeated anti-revolutionary forces at Toulon. In 1795, he was called to Paris to defend the city against rebels, and in 1796 was appointed to command the French army in Italy. He won control of Italy from Austrian forces, and then headed for Egypt, hoping to disrupt the British trade route to India. He defeated the Egyptians in 1798 at the Battle of the Pyramids, but was then stranded when the British navy destroyed the French fleet at the Battle of the Nile. Napoleon returned to France and set about making himself sole leader in place of the committee, the Directoire, that ruled the country – it fell in 1799. Most people welcomed a strong ruler, and in 1802 Napoleon was made First Consul. He brought in a new code of laws, the Code Napoleon, embodying some of the principles of the French Revolution. In 1804, he had himself crowned emperor.

Napoleon enjoyed a string of successes on the battlefield against France's enemies: Prussia, Austria and Russia. However, he could not subdue Britain. Naval defeat by the British admiral Horatio Nelson at the Battle of Trafalgar in 1805 ended his hopes of invading Britain. In 1807, he led his army through Spain to invade Portugal, and made his brother king of Spain. Britain responded by sending troops, beginning the long Peninsular War.

In 1812, Napoleon led his Grand Army into Russia. At the head of a force of more than 600,000 men, Napoleon advanced from Poland into Russia and reached as far as Moscow. However, Napoleon was driven back by the bitter Russian winter.

***A caricature of the Duke of Wellington** (who had a boot named after him). He led the British army in Spain and Portugal, and defeated Napoleon at Waterloo, in what is now Belgium.*

Attacked by Russian cavalry, the Grand Army returned to Poland with just 10,000 fully fit troops.

By 1813, the French empire was collapsing. Napoleon abdicated as emperor in 1814 and he was exiled to the island of Elba, off the coast of Italy. Escaping from exile, he raised a new army and made a final effort for victory and peace. Defeat at Waterloo in 1815 ended his hopes, and he was exiled to Saint Helena, in the middle of the Atlantic Ocean, where he died in 1821.

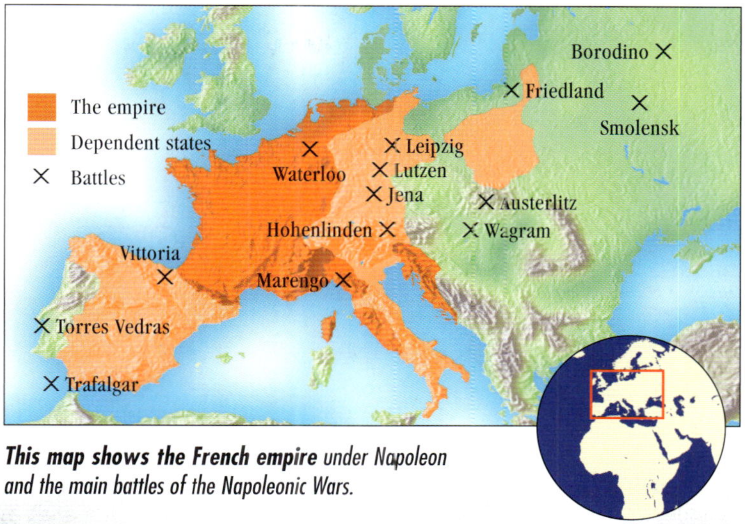

This map shows the French empire *under Napoleon and the main battles of the Napoleonic Wars.*

At the Battle of Austerlitz *in December 1805, a French army of 73,000, under the command of Napoleon and his marshals Soult and Bernadotte, defeated an army of 87,000 Austrians and Russians.*

1759 General James Wolfe captures Quebec for Britain.
1763 The Treaty of Paris gives all of French North America to the British.
1774 The Quebec Act recognizes the rights of French Canadians in British-ruled Canada.
1775 Americans try to invade Canada.
1791 Britain creates Upper and Lower Canada.
1806 Population of Upper Canada reaches 71,000. Population of Lower Canada is approximately 250,000.
1821 Hudson's Bay Company takes control of territory west of the Great Lakes.
1841 Upper and Lower Canada reunited.
1855 The British North American colonies achieve self-government.
1867 Canada becomes a dominion of the British empire.
1886 Canadian Pacific Railway spans Canada.

Canada

In 1759, the British captured Quebec from the French, and by 1763 New France (French Canada) had become British Canada. The Canadian people developed a unique culture of French, British and Native American traditions.

***The Royal Canadian** Mounted Police or 'Mounties' were founded in 1875, with 300 riders to patrol the wilderness.*

Canada was a vast land with few people. During the American Revolution (1775–83), thousands of United Empire Loyalists moved from America to Canada. Canadians later resisted American attempts to invade them during the War of 1812. Britain split Canada into two: Lower Canada (mostly French-speaking) and Upper Canada.

At first, only the eastern part of the country was settled by Europeans. The west and Arctic north were left to Native Americans and Inuit peoples. But soon, fur traders and explorers pushed west, followed by farmers and railway builders. Britain reunited Upper and Lower Canada in 1841, and in 1867 Canada became a self-governing dominion.

In 1869 the Red River Rebellion, an attempt by French-speaking settlers to set up a provisional government, failed to break up Canada, and by the 1890s the country extended from the Atlantic Ocean to the Pacific Ocean and included the Yukon territory.

***The building of the first railway** across Canada, the Canadian Pacific Railway, in the 1880s, united the eastern and western halves of the huge country.*

1815 Spain sends a strong force to South America to put down any unrest.
1816 José de San Martín leads Argentina to independence from Spain.
1818 Chile becomes independent from Spain.
1819 Colombia wins independence from Spain.
1819–30 Simón Bolívar rules as president of Gran Colombia.
1821 Simón Bolívar wins independence for Venezuela.
1822 Brazil wins independence from Portugal.
1822 At Pichincha, Simón Bolívar defeats Spanish forces to free Ecuador.
1823–26 Simón Bolívar is made dictator of Peru.
1824 Bolívar wins independence for Peru after Spanish forces are defeated at Battle of Ayacucho.
1825 New republic of Bolivia is named after Simón Bolívar.
1828 Uruguay wins independence from Spain.
1829 Venezuela becomes independent of Gran Colombia.
1830 Simón Bolívar dies of the illness tuberculosis.

South American Independence

José de San Martín *freed Argentina from Spanish rule, then led his army over the Andes mountains to help the people of Chile gain their independence.*

In 1800, Spain and Portugal still ruled vast areas of North and South America. Most local people hated being colonists, paying taxes to distant governments. After the Napoleonic Wars in Europe brought chaos to Spain and Portugal, the colonies decided to try to win their independence.

The main fight against Spanish rule was led by Simón Bolívar from Venezuela and José de San Martín from Argentina. San Martín gained freedom for his country in 1816, but Simón Bolívar's fight was longer and more difficult. He had joined a rebel army that captured Caracas, capital of Venezuela, in 1810, but was then defeated by the Spanish. Bolívar became the army's leader in 1811 and spent three years fighting the Spanish. When he was defeated a second time, he went into exile in Jamaica. In 1819, he led an army over the Andes from Venezuela to Colombia, where he defeated the Spanish in a surprise attack at the Battle of Boyaca. In 1821, he freed Venezuela, and then in 1822 he freed Ecuador and Panama. He made them all part of a new state, called the Republic of Gran Colombia, with himself as president. Finally, Peru was liberated and part of it was renamed Bolivia after Bolívar.

At the Battle of Ayachucho *in 1824, Simón Bolívar's army defeated the Spanish to win independence for Peru.*

1698 Thomas Savery develops a steam engine to pump water out of mines.
1709 Abraham Darby invents coke smelting.
1712 Thomas Newcomen improves the steam engine.
1733 John Kay invents the flying shuttle, speeding up weaving.
1742 First cotton factories in England.
1764 James Hargreaves invents the Spinning Jenny.
1769 James Watt designs a more efficient steam engine. Richard Arkwright invents a spinning frame powered by water. Josiah Wedgwood makes pottery.
1779 The first iron bridge is built.
1799 Steam engines power mills making paper, flour and textiles.
1811 Start of 'Luddite' protests against new machinery.
1815 Humphry Davy invents a safety lamp that warns miners of explosive gas.
1825 First passenger railway in England (Stockton to Darlington).
1842 The British parliament bans all women, and children aged less than ten, from working underground in coal mines.

The Industrial Revolution

***The Rocket,** designed and built in England (1830), was the first intercity steam locomotive.*

The Industrial Revolution began in Britain in the mid-18th century. Society was transformed as people moved from the countryside to the towns to work in factories.

Two events in the early 18th century helped to make the Industrial Revolution possible. The first was Abraham Darby's discovery that coke was a better fuel than charcoal for smelting iron. The second was Thomas Newcomen's invention of an improved steam engine, used for pumping water out of coal mines. It was now possible to produce more coal and better-quality iron for industry.

Until the 1760s, most goods were hand-made by people working at home or in small workshops. Metalworkers made nails, pins and knives, and spinners and weavers produced woollen and linen cloth. But the 1700s saw a rising demand for cotton cloth, which at first was imported from India. Later, raw cotton was imported, for manufacture into cloth in Britain.

***Children** aged only five could work in coal mines until 1842. Some pulled heavy loads; others sat all day in darkness, opening and closing doors to let the air circulate.*

Pit machinery at an English coal mine in 1792. *In the centre is a steam pump used to drain water from the mine. Steam engines were used to power machinery in factories too.*

In 1733, the invention of a flying shuttle speeded up the weaving process so much that spinning wheels could not produce enough yarn to keep the weavers supplied. Then, in 1764, James Hargreaves invented the Spinning Jenny, which allowed one person to spin eight threads at once. This was followed five years later by Richard Arkwright's heavy spinning frame, which was powered by water. Factories were built near fast-flowing streams to house these new machines, and the cotton industry boomed. By 1790, James Watt's improvements to the steam engine meant that steam power could be used to drive machinery. This also increased the demand for coal to heat the water to make steam, and for iron to make the engines and other machinery. Canals (and later railways) were built to bring raw materials to the factories and take finished goods away. Towns grew rapidly, but housing and working conditions were often very poor and many people suffered from hunger, disease, or accidents at work.

The first public railway, *from Stockton to Darlington in England, opened in 1825. From 1830, steam locomotives were used to draw covered passenger carriages.*

SPINNING JENNY

James Hargreaves, inventor of the Spinning Jenny, was a poor spinner. He named his new machine after his daughter Jenny. Other hand-spinners feared his machines would put them out of work, and destroyed them.

Europe in Turmoil

1830 Revolt in France sees Louis-Philippe replace Charles X as ruler.
1831 Belgium declares independence from the Netherlands.
1832 Greece becomes independent from the Ottoman empire.
1838 In Britain, the People's Charter demanding political reforms is published. Its supporters become known as Chartists.
1844 Friedrich Engels makes a study of the lives of workers in Manchester, England.
1848 The Year of Revolutions affects most of Europe.
1852 In France, the Second Republic is replaced by the Second Empire.

Irishman Feargus O'Connor *(1794–1855) was elected to the British parliament in 1832. He campaigned for votes for all men, and led the Chartists from 1841 until 1848.*

In 1815, at the end of the Napoleonic Wars, Europe was in disorder. Old governments, with old ideas, were restored, but a new age of industrialism and democracy was dawning. At first, people's demands for change were either ignored or crushed. Revolution seemed the only weapon to people all across Europe who still had no say in how they were governed.

Revolt broke out in France in 1830, when Louis-Philippe was chosen as a 'citizen-king' to replace the unpopular Charles X. Reports of the uprising spread, sparking off protests in other countries.

The revolutions *of 1848 started with a small revolt in Sicily on 20 January. This inspired a revolt in France on 24 February. Soon the spirit of protest had spread across Europe.*

Within two years, Greece declared its independence from Turkish rule, and Belgium from the Netherlands.

In 1848, so many revolutions and protests broke out throughout Europe that it became known as the 'Year of Revolutions'. In Britain, the Chartists demonstrated for political reforms and votes for all men. In France, a group of rioters in Paris, who were demanding votes for all men and a new republic, were shot by soldiers. In Belgium, Denmark and the Netherlands political reforms were made peacefully.

In Germany, many people wanted all the German states to be united into one country, and Italians wanted a united Italy. In contrast, the many groups of people who made up the vast Austrian empire wanted the empire to be divided into separate states to reflect the many different cultures.

Riots broke out in Berlin in 1848. *Men, women and children were attacked by Prussian soldiers as demands for reform and a united Germany were crushed.*

The revolutions in 1848 were crushed by the end of 1849. The ideas that drove them did not go away, however. Many governments realized that they would have to make some reforms. Reformers looked for new ways of governing and distributing wealth more fairly. The German socialists Karl Marx and Friedrich Engels published their ideas in *The Communist Manifesto* in 1848. This was to have a huge impact on future events.

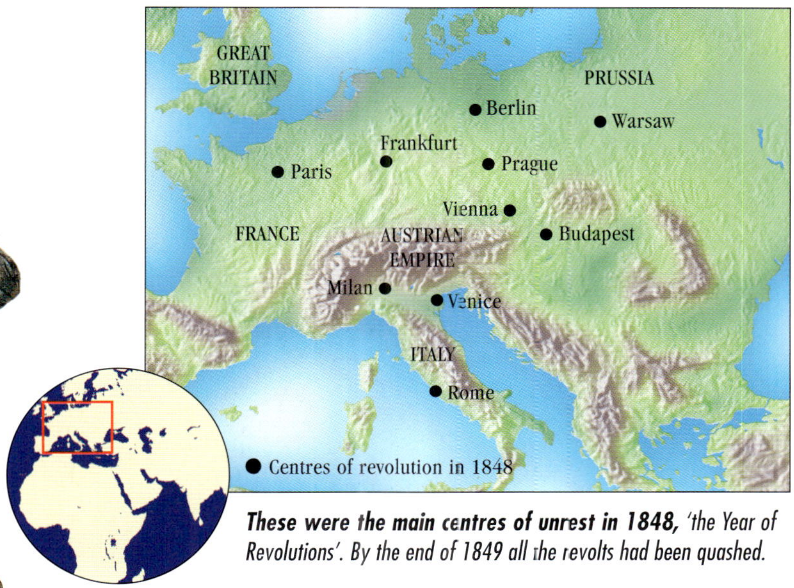

These were the main centres of unrest in 1848, *'the Year of Revolutions'. By the end of 1849 all the revolts had been quashed.*

Colonizing Africa

1795 The African Association sends Mungo Park to explore the Niger river.
1805 Mungo Park drowns while leading an expedition along the Niger.
1806 Britain takes control of Cape Colony from the Dutch.
1807 The British slave trade is abolished.
1822 Liberia in West Africa is founded as a country for freed slaves.
1828 Frenchman René August Caillie is the first European to visit Timbuktu, Mali, and return alive.
1830 The French invade Algeria.
1835 Start of the Great Trek; the Boers leave Cape Colony and head north.
1841 David Livingstone goes to Africa to work as a missionary and doctor.
1845 The British Bible Society sends James Richardson across the Sahara Desert.
1852 Livingstone starts a four-year journey across Africa, following the Zambezi river.
1858 Richard Burton and John Speke are the first Europeans to see Lake Tanganyika.
1866 Livingstone sets out on an expedition to find the source of the Nile. Three years later, the journalist Henry Stanley is sent to look for him.
1879 Stanley is hired by the king of Belgium to help him set up an empire in Africa.

***Table Mountain** above Cape Town, South Africa. Cape Town was established by the Dutch in 1652 as a resupply station for its trade ships.*

Although Europeans had been trading with Africa since the 16th century, they knew very little about the interior of the continent. They hardly ever ventured beyond the trading posts on the coast.

In Britain, curiosity about the interior of Africa grew, and, in 1788, an association was formed to encourage exploration and trade there. At the same time, many Europeans started to campaign against slavery. The British slave trade was abolished in 1807, with slavery finally ending throughout the British Empire in 1833. In 1822, Liberia was founded in West Africa as a home for freed American slaves.

Christian missionaries travelled from Europe to Africa to set up churches and schools. Settlers also went to Africa, with most of them making for Cape Colony (South Africa), which the British captured from the Dutch in 1806. This was the largest European settlement in Africa.

***The Zulus** were the most formidable soldiers in southern Africa. They fought the Boers and the British, but were finally defeated by the British in 1879.*

The Victoria Falls, *or Mosi-oa-tunya (the 'Smoke that Thunders'), on the Zambezi river. The first European to see the falls was David Livingstone in 1855.*

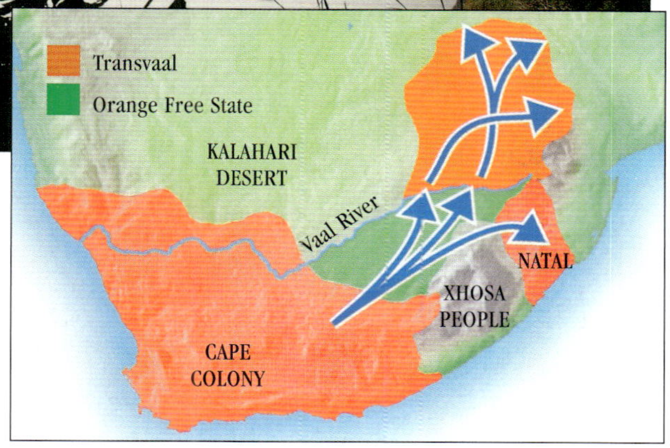

The route of the Boers' Great Trek *is shown in blue. They went in search of new lands north of the Vaal river (Transvaal). Some tried to settle the Zulu lands of Natal, but were defeated. Later, the British took over Natal.*

Most of the colonists were Dutch farmers, known as Boers. By 1835, many of them were unhappy living under British rule, and they set off on the Great Trek into the interior. After much hardship they formed two new republics, the Transvaal and the Orange Free State. But when they reached the Zulu lands they came into conflict with the Zulus. Eventually the Zulus were defeated by the British in 1879.

Many British expeditions explored Africa's interior along its great rivers. From 1768 to 1773, James Bruce explored Ethiopia, and, in two expeditions from 1795 to 1806, Mungo Park explored the Niger river. From 1852 to 1856, David Livingstone crossed the continent following the Zambezi river. In 1866, he set out to look for the source of the Nile, but lost contact with Britain for almost three years. An expedition led by Henry Stanley found him on the shores of Lake Tanganyika. Stanley went on to explore the Congo river, paid by the king of Belgium, who wanted his own African empire. This was the start of Europe's scramble to control the entire continent.

Journalist and explorer Henry Stanley *found David Livingstone encamped at Ujiji on the shores of Lake Tanganyika in 1871.*

1763 Britain takes control of India.
1788 First British settlement in Australia.
1815 Treaty of Vienna gives Cape Colony (South Africa), Ceylon (Sri Lanka), Mauritius, Malta and French islands in the Caribbean to Britain.
1819 Foundation of the British colony of Singapore.
1829 Britain claims the whole of Australia.
1830 Britain starts to control the Gold Coast (Ghana).
1839–42 Britain fights Opium Wars to open China to trade.
1840 With the Treaty of Waitangi Britain gains New Zealand.
1842 China cedes Hong Kong to Britain at the end of the First Opium War.
1843 The Gambia becomes a British colony.
1853–56 The Crimean War.
1857–58 Indian Mutiny leads to British government taking control of India from the East India Company.
1867 Malacca and Penang become British dominions.
1875 Britain buys shares in the Suez Canal Company.
1876 Victoria is crowned Empress of India.
1882 Britain controls Egypt.
1887 French form Indochina, from Cambodia and Cochinchina, Tonkin and Annam (Vietnam).
1893 Laos is added to French Indochina.

European Empires

By the 17th century, European trade with Asia was so important that the British, Dutch and French set up companies to control their interests. These companies laid the foundations for colonies. During the long reign of Queen Victoria, Britain became the world's most powerful nation, ruling a huge empire.

__Officials of the East India Company__ had many servants and were often carried around in enclosed litters, called palanquins.

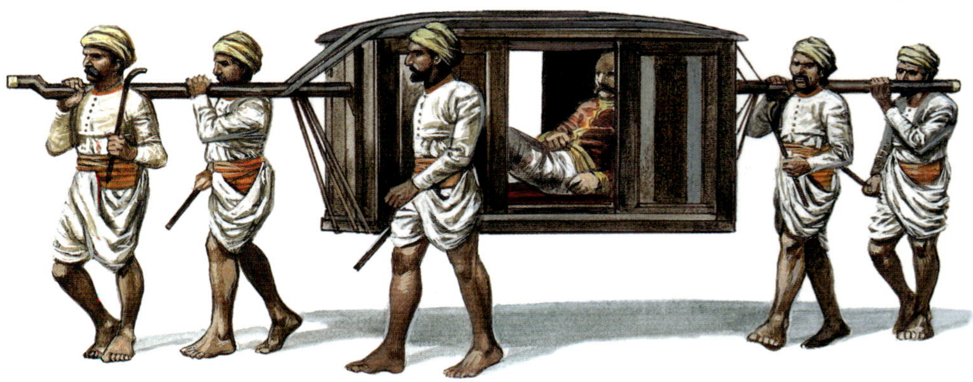

The Dutch concentrated on the islands of Indonesia. The British and French fought over India until 1763, when the British East India Company took control of much of the country.

In the 1830s, the Dutch decided they wanted to control more than just trade with Indonesia, and so they started to oversee agriculture on the islands. They set up plantations to grow crops including coffee and indigo (a plant from which a blue dye is made). Enormous profits were made by Indonesian princes and Dutch colonists at the expense of the ordinary people, who no longer had the time or land to grow the crops they needed for themselves.

As well as controlling India, Britain also began to build up colonies in Southeast Asia. One of the earliest, in 1819, was Singapore on the tip of the Malay peninsula. By 1867, Malacca and Penang had also become British colonies, and, in 1896, the remaining Malay states formed a federation under British advisers. Ruling through the local sultans, the British controlled Malaya, setting up rubber plantations and tin mines. From 1824, Britain also tried to take control of Burma. The Burmese resisted, but were finally defeated in 1885.

THE CRIMEAN WAR

During the Crimean War (1853–56), Turkey, France and Britain fought against Russia. Thousands of British soldiers died from neglect and disease. Florence Nightingale and her team of nurses cleaned up the military hospitals and set up Britain's first training school for nurses.

France, meanwhile, began to take control of Indochina (now Cambodia and Vietnam), and later added Laos.

Much of Britain's wealth came from her colonies. Colonies and trading posts had been established in the 17th and 18th centuries in places as far apart as Canada, India, Australia and the Caribbean. More were added by the Treaty of Vienna at the end of the Napoleonic Wars. During Victoria's reign, still more colonies were added, including New Zealand, many islands in the Pacific and Atlantic oceans, parts of the Far East and large areas of Africa. At its greatest extent, in the late 19th century, the empire contained a quarter of the world's land and a quarter of its people.

The colonies provided raw materials for British factories and a market for their goods. At first, some were run by trading companies, such as the East India Company in India. However, gradually they all came under direct rule from Britain. In many colonies, plantations were set up to produce tea, sugar, coffee, spices, rubber and cotton.

The British empire's influence was worldwide, with other countries adopting British laws, technology and culture. During the 20th century, however, Britain's influence declined and the country was no longer supreme as an industrial power. After World War II, the empire began to break up as countries sought independence.

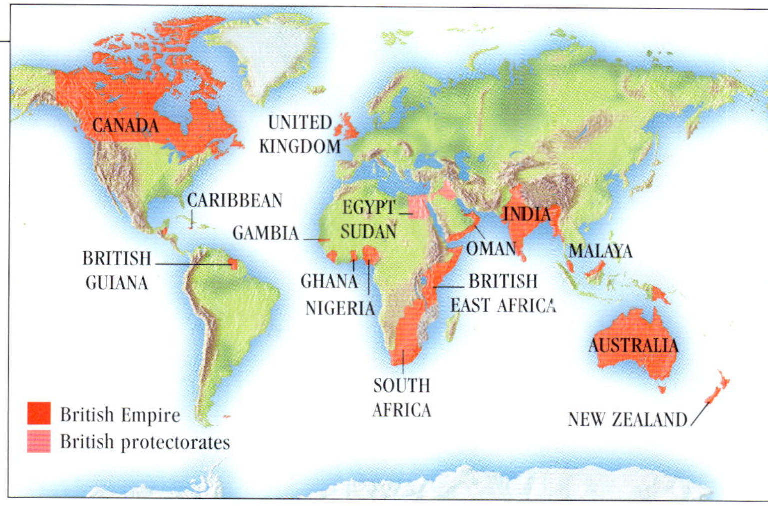

The British Empire *grew throughout the 19th century. The largest empire the world had ever seen was called 'the empire on which the Sun never sets'.*

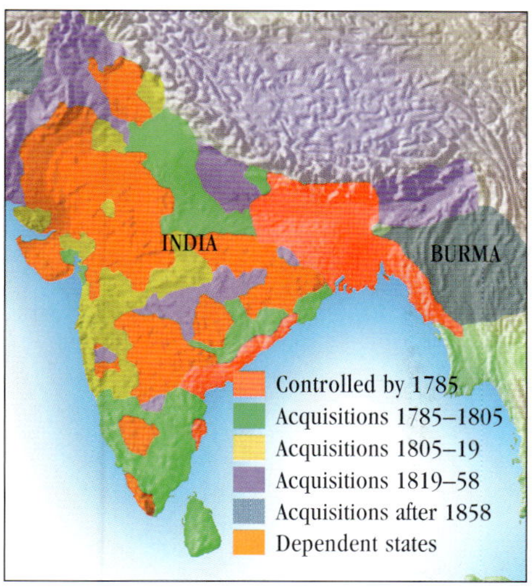

Areas of India under British control *from 1785 to 1858, when India became part of the British empire. Dependent states were ruled by Indian princes, under British 'protection'.*

Indian ports *such as Madras and Calcutta became important centres of imperial trade.*

The American West

1803 The Louisiana Purchase. The US buys the vast area west of the Mississippi from France.
1830 The Indian Removal Act forces all Native Americans to move to reservations.
1835 Texas claims independence from Mexico.
1836 Mexicans defeat the Texans at the Alamo, but are then defeated at San Jacinto.
1842 Border dispute between Canada and the US is settled.
1845 Texas becomes the 28th state of the US.
1846–48 War between the US and Mexico. US gains California, Nevada, Utah and Arizona, plus parts of New Mexico and Texas.
1849 Height of the Gold Rush.
1862 The Homestead Act encourages farmers to move to the Great Plains.
1864 The Navajos are forced to go on 'The Long Walk' to Bosque Redondo.
1867 US buys Alaska from Russia.
1869 The Union Pacific Railroad is completed.
1876 General Custer's cavalry force is trapped and killed by Sioux and Cheyenne warriors at the Battle of Little Bighorn.
1893 The Great Northern Railroad reaches Seattle.

GOLD RUSH
The discovery of gold in California in 1848, and in Nevada and Colorado in 1859, attracted thousands of prospectors. They washed river gravel in large pans, hoping to find gold, but few of them made their fortunes.

After the United States declared independence from Britain in 1776, many more settlers arrived from Europe. Most of the first settlers made their homes in the eastern states, but a few travelled further west towards what are now Ohio, Michigan, Indiana and Illinois.

Many more people moved into the area around the Great Lakes after 1825, when the opening of the Erie Canal made transport much easier. To the west of the Mississippi, explorers and traders set up routes, or trails, to be followed by settlers. In 1848, at the end of the Mexican-American War, people started travelling to the newly acquired land in the West. Known as pioneers, they made the journey in long trains of covered wagons. On reaching their destinations, families chose places to settle. They chopped down trees to build homes and cleared land for farming. If crops failed, families went hungry or gathered food from the wild.

In 1862, the US government passed the Homestead Act, which offered – for a small fee – 65 hectares of land to each family who would settle and farm for at least five years.

Wagon trains took pioneers *westwards. The wagons were pulled by teams of oxen or mules. Water was carried in barrels slung on the side. The pioneers were in constant danger of attack by Native Americans, whose land they were taking.*

***White hunters shot thousands of buffalo** (bison) to feed railway workers. With no buffalo, the Plains Indians starved.*

***The Sioux** were the largest nation of the Great Plains. They lived in tepees – tents made from wooden poles covered in buffalo (bison) hide. Easy to transport, tepees were ideal homes for the hunters as they followed the buffalo herds across the plains.*

Thousands took up the offer, and towns sprang up all over the Great Plains and the West. The land the government was selling so cheaply was taken from the Native Americans, who were forced onto reservations.

The arrival of Europeans soon had a disastrous effect on the Native Americans, who had no resistance to diseases such as measles and smallpox. They died, too, in disputes over land, as more and more Europeans moved west looking for places to settle. The Indian Removal Act of 1830 forced all Native Americans in the eastern states to live on reservations. Their lands were taken over by European settlers.

Native Americans came under more pressure in the 1860s, when the railroads spread westwards. The buffalo (bison), on which many Plains peoples depended, were hunted almost to extinction, partly to feed the construction gangs. In 1876, the Sioux and their allies defeated the US cavalry at the Little Bighorn river. But a final massacre of over 200 Sioux men, women, and children at Wounded Knee Creek in 1890 brought to an end the tragic story of the 'Indian wars'.

GERONIMO

Geronimo (1829–1909) was a leader of the Apaches. When Mexican troops killed his family, he became a guerrilla fighter, feared by both Mexican and American soldiers. He eventually surrendered and in 1905 took part in President Roosevelt's election victory parade.

Civil War

Civil war between the Northern and Southern states split the United States of America and left a legacy of bitterness. The war was fought to prevent the South breaking away from the Union.

***Through his** determination to win, Ulysses S. Grant (1822–85) led the Union armies to victory. He was President of the United States from 1869 to 1877.*

The northern states had the biggest cities and the most factories. Slavery there was banned by 1820, but in the Southern states, which had little industry, plantations relied on large numbers of slave workers. Here slave owning was accepted. In 1861, Abraham Lincoln was elected president. He pledged to end slavery in the United States. Many Southerners saw this as a threat to their way of life and, in 1861, eleven Southern states announced that they were breaking away from the Union to form their own Confederacy. When the government told them they had no right to do this, civil war broke out.

The 23 Union (Northern) states had more soldiers and more money than the Confederacy, as well as railways and the industry to provide weapons and supplies for war. With control of the navy, they were able to blockade Southern ports, cutting off supplies to the South from abroad, and preventing the export of cotton – a major source of wealth to the South.

The early battles were won by the South, but in July 1863 Union troops defeated Confederate forces at Gettysburg, Pennsylvania.

***Before the war,** Robert E. Lee (1807–70) was offered the command of the Federal forces by Lincoln, but turned it down when Virginia (his home state) withdrew from the Union. He became commander in chief of the Confederate army.*

1861 The Civil War starts when Confederate troops attack the Union garrison at Fort Sumter, South Carolina.
1862 Confederate General Lee prevents Union army taking Richmond, Virginia, and defeats another Union army at Fredericksburg, Virginia.
1863 Emancipation Proclamation is signed. Lee is defeated at Gettysburg, Pennsylvania.
1864 Grant's Union forces besiege Lee's forces at Petersburg, Virginia. Union General Sherman captures Atlanta and Savannah, Georgia.
1865 Grant's forces capture Richmond, Virginia. On 9 April, Lee surrenders to Grant at Appomattox, Virginia, bringing the war to an end. On 15 April, Lincoln is shot in a theatre by actor and Confederate sympathizer John Wilkes Booth.

A NEW KIND OF WARFARE

The American Civil War was fought with new weapons, such as quick-loading rifles, ironclad (armoured) ships, submarines and even balloons (for observing enemy movements). Railways and telegraphs speeded up communications. Faced with deadly gunfire, soldiers were killed in large numbers as they tried to attack across open ground.

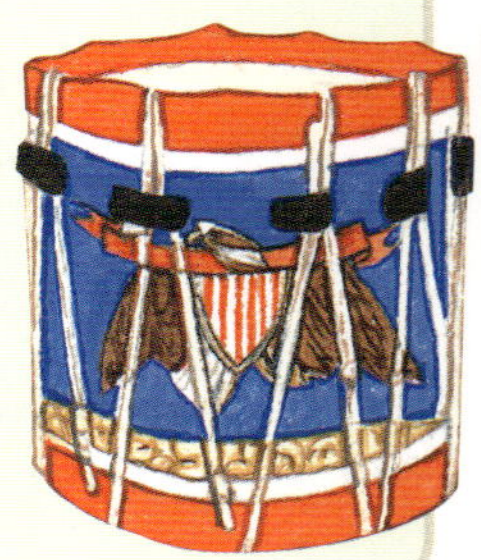

***In 1863, Abraham Lincoln** (1809–65) gave his famous Gettysburg Address and announced the abolition of slavery throughout the United States. This was approved by Congress in 1865.*

Another Union army captured Vicksburg, Mississippi. In April 1865, the Confederate general Robert E. Lee surrendered at Appomattox, Virginia. By this time, much of the South was in ruins. Over 600,000 soldiers had died, more than half from disease. Five days after the surrender, Lincoln was assassinated. Though the war was over and slaves were set free, conditions for them hardly improved.

***Casualties were high** during Civil War battles as large groups of men tried to attack across open ground, under fire from more accurate rifles and cannons.*

1815 The Italian states are given back to their former rulers after the defeat of Napoleon.
From 1820s The Risorgimento – secret societies – are formed to oppose foreign rule.
1847 Austrian troops occupy Papal city of Ferrara, a move which encourages Italian leaders to cooperate against the Austrians.
1848 Unsuccessful revolutions in many states try to bring about unification.
1849 Victor Emmanuel II becomes king of Piedmont-Sardinia.
1852 Count Camillo Cavour unifies northern Italy.
1860 Garibaldi and his Redshirts set out to conquer the Kingdom of the Two Sicilies.
1861 Victor Emmanuel II becomes king of a unified Italy.
1866 Venice becomes part of Italy.
1871 Rome becomes part of Italy.

The Unification of Italy

In the early 1800s, Italy was united under the control of Napoleon. After Napoleon's defeat in 1815, Italy's states were handed back to their former rulers. Only Piedmont-Sardinia stayed independent.

Of the Italian states' foreign rulers, Austria was the most powerful. During the 1820s, opposition to foreign rule grew. The 'Risorgimento' movement encouraged people to campaign for an independent and united Italy. Revolutions broke out in many Italian states in 1848, but were crushed. In 1858, Piedmont-Sardinia allied itself with France and defeated Austria. This was followed in 1860 by a successful revolt led by Giuseppe Garibaldi and his army of 'Redshirts'.

Garibaldi conquered Sicily, then Naples. Meanwhile, the northern states had joined up with Piedmont-Sardinia and accepted Victor Emmanuel II as their new king. Garibaldi handed Naples and Sicily to him in November 1860 and, in 1861, Italy was declared a kingdom.

The unification of Italy took 10 years. *The last region to join was that of the Papal States, which surrounds Rome. Rome became the national capital in 1871.*

Giuseppe Garibaldi *(1807–82), leader of the 'Redshirts', agreeing to hand over the Kingdom of the Two Sicilies to Victor Emmanuel in 1860.*

The Unification of Germany

In 1851 Napoleon III *(1808–73) declared himself emperor of France. He transformed Paris and encouraged industry. After the Franco-Prussian War his empire collapsed and he went into exile.*

Otto von Bismarck *(1815–98) went to war with Austria and France so that he could unite the north German states and make Prussia the ruler of a united Germany.*

Germany, like Italy, was made up of separate states in the early 1800s. In 1815, after Napoleon's defeat, 38 states joined together to form the German Confederation. Austria and Prussia were the two most powerful states to join this group of nations.

From the start, Austria and Prussia competed against each other for leadership of the Confederation, and, in 1866, Prussia declared war on Austria. After Prussia won a battle at Sadowa on the Elbe river, Otto von Bismarck, the chief Prussian minister, set up a separate North German Confederation dominated by Prussia.

The French, threatened by the growing power of Prussia, declared war in 1870. Led by Napoleon III, the French army of 120,000 men was heavily defeated at the Battle of Sedan by a German force of more than 200,000 men. Napoleon III himself was taken prisoner. In response, the people of Paris rose up against him and the French Second Empire was overthrown. The Prussian army then besieged Paris.

When the Franco-Prussian War ended on 10 May, 1871, Germany took control of Alsace and Lorraine from the French, forcing them to pay five billion francs in reparations. The German Second Empire was declared, with William I, the king of Prussia, as emperor and Otto von Bismarck as the chancellor.

This map shows the extent *of the German Confederation in 1815. It included much of the old Holy Roman empire (in red).*

1880 Leopold II, king of Belgium, claims the Congo as his own personal territory.
1882 Britain takes control of Egypt to secure access to the Suez Canal.
1884 Conference of Berlin divides Africa among seven European countries.
1889 The British conquer the Matabele and take their land, calling it Rhodesia.
1890 The Italians take Eritrea and try, but fail, to conquer Abyssinia (now Ethiopia).
1891 Tanganyika (now Tanzania) becomes a German protectorate. The French make northern Algeria part of France.
1893 The French take control of Mali.
1894 Uganda becomes a British protectorate.
1895 Kenya comes under British control and is known as the East African Protectorate.
1899 Start of the Boer Wars between Britain and the Boer people for control of southern Africa.
1910 The Union of South Africa is formed.
1911 The British colony of Rhodesia is divided into Northern Rhodesia (now Zambia) and Southern Rhodesia (now Zimbabwe).
1912 Morocco is divided into Spanish and French protectorates.

Scramble for Africa

In 1880, less than five per cent of the African continent was ruled by European powers. Most European nations had been content with trading colonies around the coast. Only the British and the Boers in South Africa had moved inland and set up new settlements. But within 20 years, the situation changed completely, in what is known as the Scramble for Africa.

Seven European nations took control of the whole of Africa, apart from Liberia and Ethiopia. By 1884, Belgium, Britain, France, Portugal and Spain had started to claim new colonies in Africa or expand their old ones. The newly unified countries of Germany and Italy also wanted shares of the continent. To prevent serious conflict, the European powers met at an international conference on Africa held in Berlin.

***At Isandhlwana** in southern Africa, the Zulus fought the British, killing 1,700 British soldiers at the start of the Zulu War in 1879. Later, the Zulus were themselves defeated.*

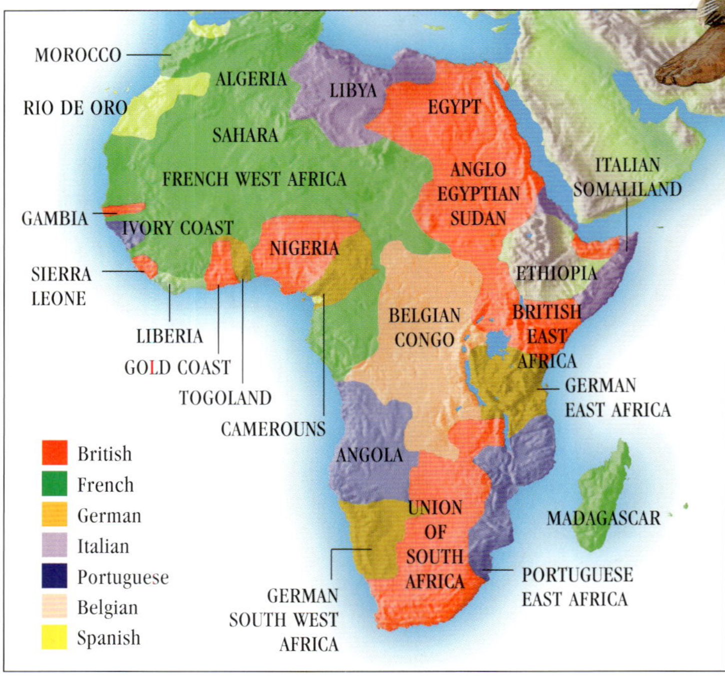

***By 1914,** European powers had control of most of Africa. Only two countries were independent: Ethiopia and Liberia.*

CECIL RHODES

British-born Cecil Rhodes (1853–1902) went to Natal in southern Africa when he was 17 years old. He became a member of the Cape Colony parliament in 1881 and prime minister in 1890. Rhodes helped to bring more territory under British control, but failed in his ambition to give Britain an empire in Africa that extended from the Cape to Egypt.

***Great Britain took control of Egypt** in 1882. Along with control of the country came control of the Suez Canal, which was vital for trade links to India.*

During the conference, the European nations decided to divide Africa among themselves. Little regard was given to the African peoples, their cultures or their natural boundaries. Resistance by black Africans, or indeed by white Boers in southern Africa, was crushed by well-equipped and well-trained European armies. Thousands of Africans died in the fighting, and many thousands more suffered hardship and hunger as their traditional ways of life were destroyed. Some were forced to work as cheap labour in mines and on plantations, growing cotton, tea, coffee and cocoa for export back to Europe. Europeans started farms in suitable areas, and built roads and railways.

In the better-run European colonies, schools and medical centres were set up for local people. In the worst-run colonies, African people were treated little better than slaves. Under European rule, Africans gained access to new ideas, but had no say in how their countries were governed and how their lives were run.

***On the Great Trek** during the 1830s, many Boers left Cape Colony and headed north to escape British rule.*

The Modern World

p156 Emmeline Pankhurst was a women's rights campaigner.

p158 World War I was the first war in which aeroplanes were widely used.

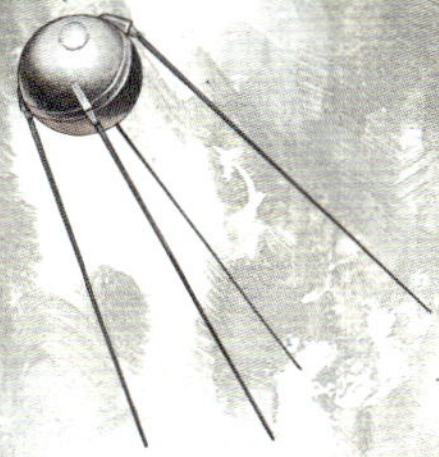

p179 Sputnik 1 was the first craft to go into space.

p198 The study of DNA has opened the door to genetic engineering.

p183 Nelson Mandela became South African president in 1994.

p196 On 11 September, 2001, terrorist attacks on the World Trade Center in New York City and the Pentagon Building in Washington, DC were carried out by al-Qaeda.

From the start of the 20th century, rapid changes in society, in science and technology, and in everyday life occurred. It was the age of aircraft, television, space rockets, computers and genetic engineering. The world's population increased dramatically to over six billion people today. Many of these people were poor and hungry, with others living in comfort and luxury.

In many countries people demanded equal rights and there were many revolutions. The Russian Revolution in 1917 made some people believe that Communism would be the new world order. Anti-Communist revolutions in eastern Europe in the 1980s and 1990s showed this was not so. There were two world wars (1914–18 and 1939–45), and many smaller wars. World War I ended in defeat for Germany and its allies, but the peace that followed did not last long.

World War II was the most costly war of all time, and the most horrific.

By 1950, the United States was the strongest power, for a while challenged by the Communist Soviet Union in what became known as the Cold War. Europe, badly damaged by war, reshaped itself as the European Union. Japan modernized and became an industrial powerhouse. Old empires ended, and new alliances were made. New independent nations joined the United Nations, including India and the new countries of Africa. China emerged from years of isolation.

New developments such as the internet, satellite TV and world tourism made the world seem smaller. Problems in one country often affected others. Global concerns, such as the threat to the tropical rainforests or fast-dwindling oil supplies, could not be contained within national borders. Terrorism became a new threat to peace. So fast is the pace of change that it is hard to predict what the world will be like when the 21st century draws to a close.

p186 Chairman Mao first came to power in China in 1949. Civil war had left the country in financial disorder. Mao's initial reforms, called the Five Year Plan, helped to improve China's economy.

p172 The Allied landings in Normandy began on 6 June, 1944 (D-Day). About 156,000 troops were landed in the largest seaborne attack ever mounted.

Votes for Women

1848 First women's rights convention held in Seneca Falls, New York.

1890 US state of Wyoming allows women to vote in local elections.

1893 New Zealand gives women the vote in national elections.

1897 The National Union of Women's Suffrage Societies is formed in Britain.

1902 Australia gives women the right to vote.

1903 Emmeline Pankhurst forms the Women's Social and Political Union.

1905 The first two suffragettes are sent to prison in Britain.

1906 Finland gives women the vote, and in 1907 the first women MPs are elected to the Finnish parliament.

1913 British suffragette Emily Davison is killed when she throws herself under the king's horse at the Derby horse race. Norway gives women the vote.

1917 Russia gives women the right to vote.

1918 British women over 30 are given the vote. Canadian women are given equal voting rights with men.

1919 Germany, Austria, Poland and Czechoslovakia all give women the right to vote.

1920 Women in the US are given the vote.

Women's right to vote, suggested by British author Mary Wollstonecraft in her book *A Vindication of the Rights of Women* (1792), was a long time coming. Groups campaigning for political reform in the 1830s were only concerned with obtaining the vote for all men. Women were not included.

In the mid-1800s, however, a movement was started in the US that aimed to win voting rights for women across the world. It held its first meeting in Seneca Falls, New York, in 1848. Many other public meetings followed, often fiercely opposed by those who did not want women to have the right to vote. Speakers included Sojourner Truth and Harriet Tubman, both of whom had been born slaves.

The movement grew, and in 1890 Wyoming became the first US state to allow women to vote in local elections. Three years later, New Zealand became the first country to allow women to vote in national elections. In Britain, this triumph encouraged various women's suffrage (right to vote) societies to unite in 1897.

Women's rights campaigner
Emmeline Pankhurst was arrested several times for destroying property. Protesters refused to pay taxes and disrupted political meetings.

Many suffragettes *continued their protests in prison by going on hunger strike. Desperate that they should not die and become martyrs to the suffrage cause, the authorities instructed doctors and prison offices to force-feed the prisoners.*

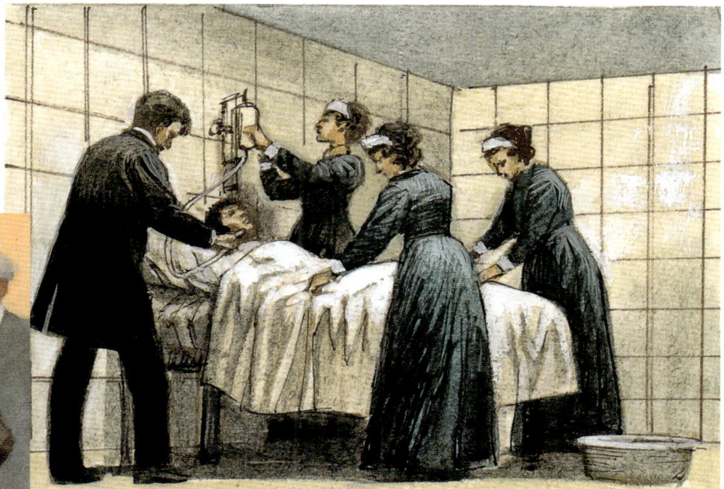

Women's rights campaigners, *or suffragettes, argued their case at elections. These women are speaking during the run-up to the British general election of 1910.*

At first, their campaigns were peaceful, but in 1903 Emmeline Pankhurst set up a new society, the Women's Social and Political Union (WSPU), which advocated action rather than words. The WSPU held demonstrations and attacked property in protest against women's lack of rights. Many members were sent to prison, and went on hunger strike to draw attention to their cause.

With the outbreak of World War I in 1914, many women took on men's jobs, proving that they were just as capable as men. In 1918, the vote was given to all British women over the age of 30 (the voting age for men was only 21). Women in the US were given the right to vote in 1920. In 1928, the voting age for British women was lowered to 21.

Many women campaigned *peacefully for the right to vote. They held rallies to gain support for their cause. However, others became disillusioned with the lack of progress and decided to take part in more direct action which involved destroying property or disrupting major public events.*

1914, 28 June A Serb, Gavrilo Princip, assassinates Archduke Franz Ferdinand in Sarajevo.
1914, 28 July–3 August Austria declares war on Serbia. Russia prepares to defend Serbia. Germany declares war on Russia, then on France.
1914, 4 August German armies march through Belgium to France. Britain declares war on Germany. World War I begins.
1914, 26 August Germany defeats Russian forces at the Battle of Tannenberg.
1914 September At the Battle of the Marne the Allies halt the German advance on Paris.
1914 November At the end of the Battle of Ypres the Germans are prevented from threatening Channel ports.
1915 April–May Germany uses poison gas for first time at second Battle of Ypres.
1915, 22 May Italy joins the Allies.
1916 February Start of Battle for Verdun, lasting for five months.
1916, 1 July Start of the Battle of the Somme; ends in November.
1917 On 6 April the US joins the war on the Allied side.
1917 July Third Battle of Ypres (Passchendaele).
1918, 3 March Ceasefire between Russia and Germany.
1918 November Armistice is signed on 11 November at 11 o'clock. World War I ends.

World War I

World War I began as a European quarrel, caused by rivalry between nations. It spread across the oceans, to the Middle East and to Africa. The war cost the lives of more than 8 million soldiers, many killed in awful trench warfare. The war was so frightful that afterwards people said it had been the Great War and 'the war to end wars'. It was not.

WAR PLANES
World War I (1914–18) was the first war in which aeroplanes were widely used. They were first used to spy on enemy trenches and troop movements. Later, they were used in aerial combat and in bombing raids.

Between 1880 and 1907, the European powers had formed alliances and increased their armies and navies. On one side stood the Allied forces: Britain, France, Russia, Japan and, later, Italy. On the other were the Central Powers: Germany, Austria-Hungary, Turkey and Serbia. The spark that started the war was the assassination in Sarajevo of Austrian Archduke Franz Ferdinand by a Serb in June 1914.

In the trenches *soldiers ate and slept while waiting for orders to go into battle. Dugouts, or underground shelters, offered some protection from enemy shells, but in winter the trenches could be cold, muddy and wet.*

The war in Europe *was fought on the Western Front, between France and Germany, and the Eastern Front, from the Baltic towards the Black Sea. There was also fighting in the Middle East, on the Italy–Austria border, and in Africa.*

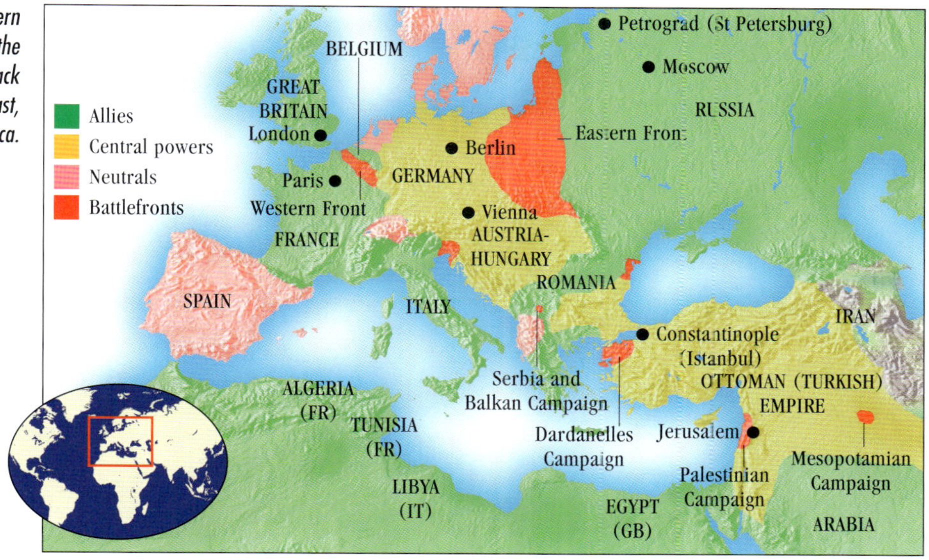

This led to a series of mobilizations (preparations for war), and, on 4 August, German armies invaded Belgium. This drew Britain, Belgium's ally since 1837, into the war.

World War I was fought mostly on land (there was only one big naval battle, at Jutland in 1916). Both sides became bogged down in trench warfare, their armies unable to advance without huge losses. Soldiers had to go 'over the top' (leave the trench), scramble through their own barbed-wire defences, then cross open ground ('no-man's land') to reach the enemy lines. So quick and powerful were the machine guns and heavy artillery guns that soldiers were killed in their thousands. In the Battle of the Somme alone (1916), there were over a million casualties.

By 1917, the Russian army was so weak that it began peace talks with Germany. For a while, Germany had an advantage, but in 1918 the arrival of more than a million soldiers from the United States boosted the Allies, who began to advance. There were food shortages and unrest in Germany, and emperor Wilhelm II abdicated. On 11 November, an armistice was signed between Germany and the Allies, ending the war.

On the Western Front, *most of the fighting took place in northern France and Belgium. Mules and horses were used to bring supplies and heavy guns to the front.*

1887 Lenin becomes a Marxist.

1894 Nicholas II becomes tsar of Russia.

1905 Some 200,000 people march on the Winter Palace in St Petersburg. Lenin is exiled.

1917 Lenin returns. Nicholas II abdicates and a republican government is formed. Revolutionaries attack the Winter Palace and the government falls.

1918 Russia withdraws from World War I. The imperial family is executed. Civil war between the Red Army (Communists) and White Russians (anti-Communists) lasts until 1920.

1922 The Russian empire is renamed the Union of Soviet Socialist Republics (USSR).

The Russian Revolution

Many Russians blamed *Rasputin (1869–1916) for persuading Tsar Nicholas II to ignore the people's complaints. Rasputin, a priest, claimed he had the power to heal the emperor's sick son.*

In the 19th century, efforts to modernize Russia by freeing the serfs (peasants), building factories and introducing democracy came to nothing. Tsar Alexander II made reforms, but, in 1881, he was assassinated. Tsar Alexander III undid most of his father's work, and in desperation some Russians turned to revolution.

Leon Trotsky *(1879–1940), a leader of the Bolshevik revolution, was the most powerful man in Russia after Lenin. When Stalin came to power in 1924, he was exiled and later murdered.*

The first serious rebellion broke out in 1905, after troops fired on striking workers in the Russian capital, St Petersburg. The rebellion was soon crushed and its leaders, including Lenin, were sent into exile. Lenin remained in exile until 1917. The tsar, Nicholas II, who had come to the throne in 1894, promised the people more civil rights, but this promise was soon broken.

The Winter Palace *in St Petersburg which the Bolsheviks stormed and seized in November 1917.*

When World War I started, life for most people in Russia went from bad to worse. The railways no longer carried food, fuel and supplies to the cities. The economy almost collapsed and people went hungry. In March 1917, riots broke out again. This time the troops joined the rioters. Nicholas abdicated and his advisers resigned.

A new government was set up, led by Alexander Kerensky, but unrest continued. The Bolsheviks, led by Lenin, planned a take-over. In November, they attacked the Winter Palace in St Petersburg and seized power (an event known as the October Revolution, because Russia used a different calendar at that time). The Bolsheviks moved the capital to Moscow and made peace with Germany. They broke up large estates and gave the land to the peasants, while workers took control of the factories. In 1918, civil war broke out between the Bolshevik Red Army and anti-Communist White Russians. This ended in victory for the Bolsheviks in 1921. The following year, the Union of Soviet Socialist Republics was formed. Lenin died in 1924, and was succeeded by Joseph Stalin. Stalin's rule was tyrannical. He had millions of people killed or sent to prison camps, where they died.

LENIN

Vladimir Ilyich Ulyanov (1870–1924) used the name Lenin. He led the Bolsheviks from 1898, but was exiled from 1905 to 1917. On his return, the Bolsheviks seized power and he became Russia's new leader.

Armed workers *led by the Bolsheviks stormed St Petersburg's Winter Palace in 1917, starting the revolution. They were joined by Russian soldiers, tired of fighting the Germans in World War I.*

1886–93 Attempts to give Ireland its own parliament are defeated in London.
1905 Sinn Fein, the Irish nationalist party, is founded.
1912 Third Irish Home Rule bill is introduced in the British parliament, but World War I starts in 1914 before it can be enacted.
1916 Easter Rising in Dublin.
1919 Bitter fighting between Irish republicans and British troops.
1921 Anglo-Irish Treaty leads to a split Ireland and civil war until 1923.
1937 The Irish Free State becomes Eire.
1949 Eire becomes the Republic of Ireland.

Irish Home Rule

An uprising in Ireland in 1916 by nationalists, who wanted 'home rule' – an Irish republic independent of Britain – led to decades of argument and violence.

Most people in the north of Ireland, known as Ulster, wanted to stay part of the United Kingdom while the majority of people in the south wanted an independent Ireland. In 1916, republicans in Dublin rose in rebellion on Easter Monday. After four days, they were forced to surrender. In 1918, nationalist Sinn Fein members set up an Irish parliament, the Dáil Eireann. This led to war between the military wing of Sinn Fein (later called the Irish Republican Army, or IRA) and the British. In 1921, Michael Collins agreed a deal with the British. The deal made most of Ireland independent, but left out the six counties of Northern Ireland. This led to more fighting. Collins was assassinated.

In 1949, Ireland became a republic. The IRA continued to fight for a united Ireland, an aim fiercely resisted by Unionists in Northern Ireland. In 1998, a ceasefire (the Good Friday Agreement) brought hope for a peaceful solution to this ancient dispute.

***This map shows Ireland** after the division in 1921. Three of the nine counties of Ulster became part of the Irish Free State; the other six remained part of the United Kingdom.*

***During the Easter rising** of 1916, British soldiers faced Irish Republicans across Dublin's barricades. One hundred British soldiers and 450 Irish republicans were killed.*

1921 Mussolini becomes leader of Italy's Fascists.
1922 The tomb of ancient Egypt's boy-king Tutankhamun is opened.
1923 Lenin resigns as Soviet leader. An earthquake kills 300,000 in Tokyo, Japan.
1926 In Britain, a General Strike (by all trade unions) shuts down buses, trains, mines and many factories.
1927 *The Jazz Singer* is the first film with sound.
1928 Alexander Fleming discovers penicillin.
1929 Seven are shot dead by gangsters in the St Valentine's Day Massacre in Chicago. On 24 October, millions lose money when the New York Stock Market collapses.

The Roaring Twenties

A new dance craze *in 1925 was the Charleston. Young people loved it; many older people were disapproving.*

For people in America and Europe, the 1920s were years of recovery and fun after the horrors of World War I. It was a time of new ideas, jazz music, radio and 'talking pictures' (cinema films with sound). Women enjoyed greater freedom. So did gangsters, in the lawless years that followed the ban in the US on alcoholic drinks.

Spirit of St Louis

In the 'Roaring Twenties' society became more free and easy. For the first time, women cut their hair short and wore short skirts. The heroes of the age included the lone flyer Charles Lindbergh and the film star Rudolf Valentino.

In 1920, the US government brought in Prohibition, a law to ban the making and selling of alcoholic drinks. Many people broke the law by visiting illegal drinking clubs or buying 'bootleg' alcohol made in backstreet workshops. Gangsters fought to control this illegal trade. Prohibition was ended in 1933.

The 1920s brought a false sense that all was well. Problems left by World War I had not been solved. In Germany, the economy collapsed. In Britain, there was the first General Strike by workers. The bubble burst in October 1929, when millions of people lost their savings in the Stock Market Crash. The party of the 'Jazz Age' was over; the Depression was beginning.

In 1927, *US flyer Charles Lindbergh became the first person to fly alone across the Atlantic. It took him 33 hours in his plane* Spirit of St Louis.

1929 In October, the New York Stock Exchange on Wall Street crashes after people panic and sell their shares.

1932 At the height of the Depression there are 12,000,000 unemployed people in the US. Franklin D. Roosevelt is elected president.

1933 Roosevelt introduces the 'New Deal' to protect people's savings and create jobs. In Germany, there are 6,000,000 unemployed.

1935 In Britain, 200 men march from Jarrow to London with a petition drawing attention to unemployment.

1936 The Depression ends in Germany as public works and weapons production bring full employment.

1939 About 15 per cent of the workforce in the US is still unemployed.

1941 Full employment returns to the US as it enters World War II.

The Great Depression

After World War I, the economies of many European countries were in ruins. Defeated Germany had to pay reparations (money as compensation for the war) to Britain and France. German money became worthless because of rampant inflation. By 1929, the world economy seemed to be falling apart. Millions of people lost money, jobs and homes.

On the Jarrow Crusade *(1935) in England, 200 men walked from Jarrow in northern England to London to draw attention to unemployment in their home town.*

In the US, where banks had loaned money to other nations for the war, many people had invested savings in stocks. Buying pushed up prices of company shares beyond their real value. In August 1929, share prices started to fall, and people began to panic. They sold their shares, which made prices fall even faster. Many people lost all their savings in the Stock Market Crash. Banks and businesses closed and many people lost their jobs.

A severe drought in the American Midwest made things even worse. In the 'Dust Bowl', where fertile topsoil was worn away by over-farming, the drought and wind turned the fields to dusty deserts. Many farms were abandoned as families headed west to California.

Soup kitchens *serving free food were set up in many cities to feed the hungry. It was estimated that over a quarter of the population of the US relied on begging, charity and limited public welfare support.*

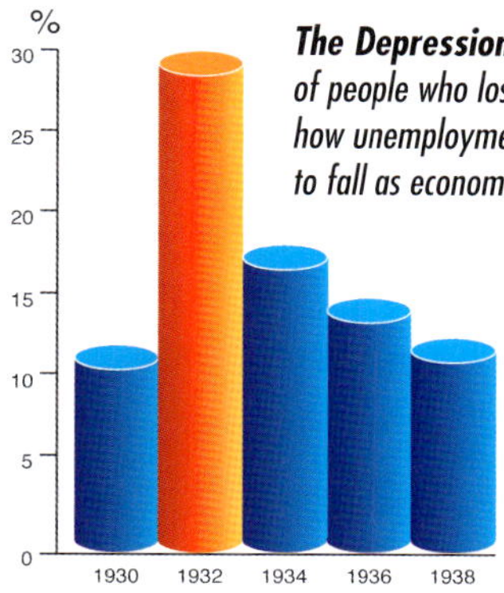

***The Depression** brought misery for millions of people who lost their jobs. This chart shows how unemployment soared in 1932. It started to fall as economies recovered.*

***The New York Stock** Exchange on Wall Street. As share prices fell, many investors rushed to the Exchange to discover that they had lost all their money.*

The crisis in the US affected the world, as money loaned overseas by US banks was called back. Britain and Germany were hit especially hard, and unemployment rose rapidly. Countries tried to protect their industries by taxing foreign goods. By 1932, when the Depression reached its deepest level, world exports of raw materials had fallen by over 70 per cent, ruining the economies of poorer countries that depended on them.

THE NEW DEAL

Part of President Roosevelt's New Deal in 1933 included a programme to create more jobs. Young people were given work in the national forests, and a series of dams were built on the Tennessee river to provide electricity and to prevent soil erosion. New welfare and labour laws improved working conditions.

1922 Fascists led by Mussolini come to power in Italy.
1923–30 Primo de Rivera rules Spain as dictator.
1925 From this date Mussolini rules Italy as dictator.
1931 Spanish monarchy is overthrown as Republican party wins the election.
1932 Sir Oswald Mosley forms the British Union of Fascists.
1933 Nazis led by Adolf Hitler come to power in Germany. In Spain, the Falangist (Fascist) party is created.
1934 Hitler gains total power – his rivals are killed on the 'Night of the Long Knives'.
1935 Italy invades Abyssinia (Ethiopia).
1936–39 Spanish Civil War between Republicans and Nationalists (Falangists). Nationalists win and Franco becomes dictator of Spain.
1937 German aircraft bomb the Spanish town of Guernica in support of the Nationalists.
1938 Hitler unites Germany and Austria. Nazi mobs attack Jews in Germany on 'Kristallnacht'. Munich Agreement is signed.

The Rise of Fascism

Britain's Prime Minister *Neville Chamberlain returned from his meeting with Adolf Hitler in 1938 promising peace. But the Munich Agreement proved worthless.*

Fascism is the right-wing political movement that appeared World War I. In the 1920s, Fascist parties promised strong leadership and a war on Communism. They roused people by promising national glory, more jobs and revenge for past humiliations. The two most prominent Fascist leaders were Italy's Benito Mussolini and Germany's Adolf Hitler.

Italy was the first country to have a Fascist government. Benito Mussolini marched his followers into Rome in October 1922 and threatened to overthrow the government. The king asked him to form a new government. Armed Fascists terrorized and killed members of other political groups, and, by January 1923, Italy had become a one-party state.

Republican fighters *during the Spanish Civil War (1936–39). In this war, the Fascist leader Franco was helped by Italy and Germany. The Republicans were aided by the USSR and by volunteers from other countries, including the US and Britain.*

General Francisco Franco *(1892–1975) led the Falangist (Fascist) party in Spain and won the civil war. Franco kept Spain out of World War II.*

Two years later, Mussolini started ruling as dictator and became known as 'Il Duce' (The Leader).

Spain's Fascist group, the Falangist party, was founded in 1933. In 1936, under the leadership of General Franco, the Falangist party overthrew the elected government in Spain. A terrible civil war lasted until 1939, when Franco became dictator of Spain.

In Germany, the Nazi party and its leader Adolf Hitler won power in 1933. Hitler set up a programme to create jobs and built up munitions and the armed forces. He banned other political parties, introduced a secret police and persecuted the Jews. In 1936, Hitler sent troops into the Rhineland, a region of Germany that bordered France and had been declared a military-free zone by the Treaty of Versailles at the end of World War I. Two years later, Austria and Germany were unified, a move known as the 'Anschluss'. Hitler also threatened to take over the Sudetenland in Czechoslovakia. To try to keep the peace, the Munich Agreement, signed by Germany and various European powers, gave the Sudetenland to Germany. The following March, however, Hitler's troops took over the whole of Czechoslovakia and threatened to invade Poland.

***Benito Mussolini** (1883–1945) at first impressed many Italians with his 'modernizing' government. He became a tyrant, however, and led Italy into World War II, with disastrous results. In the end, Mussolini was overthrown and killed by his own people.*

***Adolf Hitler** (1889–1945) saluting to a rally of Nazis at Nuremberg in 1938. The Nazis made Germany a police state, jailing or murdering opponents, and controlling radio, films and newspapers.*

Revolution in China

1905 Sun Yat-sen founds the Kuomintang (Chinese Nationalist party).
1911 Collapse of the Manchu empire. Sun Yat-sen becomes president.
1921 Foundation of the Chinese Communist party.
1925 Death of Sun Yat-sen. Chiang Kai-shek succeeds him as leader of China.
1926 With help from Communists, Chiang Kai-shek defeats the northern warlords.
1927 Civil war between the Communists and the Kuomintang. Communists are forced out of Shanghai and into the Jiangxi hills.
1931 Communists set up a rival government in the south.
1933 Chiang Kai-shek attacks the Communists in Jiangxi.
1934 Mao leads Communists on the 'Long March'.
1935 Mao becomes leader of the Communist party.
1937–45 The Kuomintang and Communists unite to fight against Japan.
1938 Japan controls most of the east. Mao's Communists control the northwest.
1939 The Soviet army stops the Japanese from advancing further west in China.
1945 Civil war breaks out again.
1949 The People's Republic of China is proclaimed. Chiang escapes to Taiwan.

***The Empress Dowager Cixi** (1832–1908) was mother to one emperor and aunt to another. Acting regent, she refused to allow change in China, which helped bring about the fall of the Manchu empire.*

By 1900, large parts of China were dominated by foreign powers. The Chinese Nationalist party, the Kuomintang, was founded by Sun Yat-sen. He tried to unify China under a democratic government. In 1911, China became a republic and, in 1912, the last emperor abdicated.

However, Sun died in 1925 and Chiang Kai-shek succeeded him as president and leader of the Kuomintang. The Chinese Communist party first met in Shanghai in 1921. Mao Zedong was an early member.

During the 1920s, warlords in northern China tried to gain control. To fight them, the Kuomintang and the Communists united in 1926.

Mao Zedong *(1893–1976) was born into a land-owning family in Hunan province. While fighting in the revolutionary army of 1911, he became interested in politics. In 1923, he joined the Chinese Communist party, eventually becoming China's leader.*

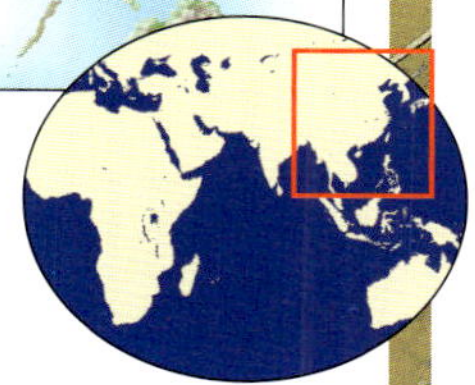

This map shows *the route taken on the Long March from 1934 to 1935. It covered about 9,700 km. At the end of the march, Mao Zedong said: 'It proclaims to the world that the Red Army is an army of heroes.'*

The Long March *from Jiangxi in the south to Shaanxi in the north took 568 days. Of the 100,000 who set out, about 80,000 died on the journey. The Communist marchers were pursued by the Kuomintang.*

But in 1927 civil war broke out between the Kuomintang and the Communists. The Communists took refuge in the province of Jiangxi. There, in 1931, they set up a rival government. In 1933, Chiang Kai-shek sent his army to Jiangxi to wipe them out. To escape, Mao led 100,000 Communists on the 'Long March' from Jiangxi in the south to Shaanxi in the north. Mao was then confirmed as leader of the Communists.

In 1937, Japan invaded China and the Communists and Nationalists united to fight the Japanese. When World War II ended in 1945, civil war broke out again in China. This time the Communists waged a successful war against the Kuomintang, who then fled to Taiwan to establish a separate state. On 1 October, 1949, mainland China became the People's Republic of China with Mao as its first president.

1939 Germany annexes Czechoslovakia. Italy annexes Albania. Italy and Germany form an alliance.
1939, 23 August Germany and the USSR sign a non-aggression pact.
1939, 25 August Britain, France and Poland form an alliance.
1939, 1 September Germany invades Poland.
1939, 3 September Britain and France declare war on Germany.
1939, 17 September The USSR invades Poland.
1940 March The USSR takes Finland.
1940 April–May Germany occupies Norway, Denmark, Belgium and the Netherlands.
1940 June Germany occupies France. Allies evacuate from Dunkirk.
1940 August–October Battle of Britain.
1940 November Italy tries to invade Greece. Hungary, Romania and Slovakia join the Axis powers.
1941 February Allies capture 113,000 Italian soldiers in North Africa.
1941 April Yugoslavia and Greece fall to Germany.
1941 May German invasion of USSR begins.
1941, 7 December Japan attacks Pearl Harbor. The US declares war on Japan. Italy and Germany declare war on the US.

World War II

World War II began on 3 September, 1939, two days after German armies invaded Poland. When Germany's leader, Adolf Hitler, refused to withdraw his troops, Britain and France declared war. The war was fought between the Axis powers (chiefly Germany, Italy and Japan) and the Allies (who included Britain and its Commonwealth partners, France, the Soviet Union and the United States).

Many children from British cities *were sent to live with families in the country, away from the bombs. They were evacuees.*

On 17 September, the Soviet Union invaded Poland from the east. By the end of 1939, Soviet troops had also invaded Estonia, Latvia, Lithuania and Finland. In the spring of 1940, German troops invaded Denmark, Norway, Belgium, the Netherlands and France. Using vast numbers of tanks and bomber planes, they swiftly overwhelmed defences – a tactic known as Blitzkrieg (German for 'lightning war'). Infantry completed the take-overs.

The Battle of Britain *raged above southern England from August to October 1940. RAF planes (below) fought off German planes (left). Over 2,600 aircraft were shot down.*

By June 1940, most of Europe had fallen. Britain stood alone. In August and September, Hitler's air force, the Luftwaffe, attacked southeast England and London in daylight raids. Despite having fewer planes, the British air force managed to fight off the Germans and so prevent an invasion. Even so, many British towns and cities were damaged in these bombing raids.

In September 1940, Italian troops moved into Egypt, where Britain had part of its army stationed to defend the Suez Canal. By February 1941, the Italians had been defeated, but German troops forced the British back to the Egyptian border.

Encouraged by his successes, Hitler launched an attack on his former ally, the Soviet Union. In June 1941, Germany invaded the vast country with the help of Finland, Hungary and Romania. By the end of 1941, however, Allied fortunes were about to change as the US joined the war, following the unprovoked attack on Pearl Harbor in Hawaii by the Japanese.

After bombing raids, *rescuers battled fires and pulled out survivors. German planes bombed Britain during the Blitz. Later, Allied bombers destroyed homes and industrial plants in Germany and Japan. An Allied raid on the German city of Dresden in 1945 killed about 80,000 people.*

By the end of 1941, *Germany controlled most of Europe and North Africa and part of Russia. In Europe, only neutral countries and Britain were still free.*

1941 December Japan invades Malaya and Hong Kong.
1942 February to May Singapore, the Dutch East Indies, the Philippines and Burma fall to Japan.
1942 August US victory at Guadalcanal ends Japanese expansion. The siege of Stalingrad begins.
1942 October Allies defeat Axis forces at the Battle of El Alamein, Egypt.
1943 February Germans defeated at Stalingrad.
1943 May Axis troops in North Africa surrender.
1943 July Allied troops invade Sicily. Mussolini is overthrown and Italy declares war on Germany.
1944 June Allied forces land in Normandy, France.
1944 December Start of Battle of the Bulge, last German offensive in Europe.
1945 February At the Yalta Conference, Allies agree to divide Germany into four zones after the war.
1945 March US troops capture Iwo Jima, in the Pacific.
1945 April Adolf Hitler kills himself.
1945 May Soviet troops enter Berlin. Germany surrenders.
1945 June US forces capture Okinawa island, close to Japan.
1945 August Atomic bombs dropped on Hiroshima and Nagasaki. Japan surrenders.
1945 October The United Nations is formed.

World at War

The Japanese attack on the US naval base at Pearl Harbor brought the United States, with its industrial and military might, into the war. Before this, many Americans had supported Britain in its fight against Nazi Germany, but had been reluctant to get involved in a European war. Now it was different.

German and Finnish forces *besieged Leningrad (now St Petersburg) from 1941 to 1944. About one million people died of cold, hunger, disease and injury.*

Millions of US troops were soon on their way to fight in Europe and the Pacific, and the US threw its airforce and navy into the battles against both Germany and Japan. US guns, tanks and planes were shipped across the Atlantic Ocean to Britain, which was still suffering from German air raids and from shortages caused by German submarine attacks on supply ships. The Allies began to bomb German cities, the British bombing by night while the Americans raided by day. They used ships and planes to hunt enemy submarines or U-boats.

By August 1941, the US forces in the Pacific had defeated the Japanese at the battles of the Coral Sea, Midway and Guadalcanal. These victories halted the Japanese advance through Southeast Asia and the Pacific.

The Allied invasion *of Normandy began on 6 June, 1944 (D-Day). About 156,000 troops landed in the largest seaborne attack ever.*

The US used aircraft carriers against Japanese ships, and from captured island bases sent planes on bombing raids against Japan itself.

In Africa, British and Commonwealth troops won a decisive battle at El Alamein, Egypt, in late 1942. As the British advanced west across the desert, they trapped the enemy between more Allied forces advancing from Algeria and Morocco. The North African battles were over by May 1943, and the Allies began plans to invade Italy and France.

In Russia, German armies got to within sight of Moscow by November 1941, but were forced back. The Germans were beaten at Stalingrad (now Volgograd) in 1943, and retreated from Russia as the Soviet Red Army moved steadily west. The long-awaited 'second front' in western Europe opened on 6 June, 1944, when Allied armies landed in Normandy, France.

***Allied soldiers rescued** thousands of sick and starved survivors from Nazi death camps such as Belsen and Auschwitz. Millions of people had been killed in the camps.*

By 2 July, one million Allied troops had landed in France. In March 1945, Allied troops crossed the river Rhine and in April they reached the Ruhr, the heartland of German industry. Realizing he was facing defeat, Hitler committed suicide on 30 April. Soviet troops captured Berlin two days later. On 9 May, Germany officially surrendered.

***US B-17 'Flying Fortress' bombers** raided targets in Europe and Asia during daylight raids.*

The Allies planned to invade Japan in late 1945, but feared heavy losses. On 6 August, 1945, an atomic bomb was dropped on the Japanese city of Hiroshima, and three days later a second bomb fell on Nagasaki. The Japanese surrendered, and, on 14 August, World War II was over.

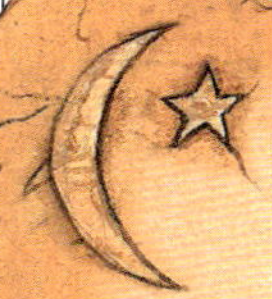

1885 Indian National Congress (INC) founded.
1887 Gandhi goes to London to study law. He works in South Africa from 1893.
1905 Foundation of the Muslim League in India.
1919 Government of India Act passed. Massacre at Amritsar.
1920 Gandhi, now leader of the INC, urges non-cooperation with British.
1934 Mohammed Ali Jinnah becomes president of the Indian Muslim League.
1945 British government agrees to grant independence to India.
1947, 14 August Northeast and northwest India become Pakistan.
1947, 15 August The rest of India becomes independent.

India and Pakistan

***Jawaharlal Nehru** (left) was India's first prime minister (died 1964). Mohammed Ali Jinnah (right) was the first leader of independent Pakistan.*

At the start of the 20th century, India was the largest colonial territory in the world. It included Pakistan and Bangladesh, as well as India, and had been ruled directly from Britain since 1858.

However, the people of India wanted independence and, in 1917, the Indian National Congress began a campaign for Home Rule. Britain was reluctant to give up its rule. Instead, mainly in gratitude for India's support during World War I, the British government passed the Government of India Act (1919). This gave some independence, but most power remained with Britain. In the same year, British soldiers in Amritsar opened fire on a crowd protesting against British rule. Almost 400 people were killed. The campaign for Indian independence grew.

By 1920, Mahatma Gandhi had become leader of the Indian National Congress. He launched a policy of non-cooperation with the British and was himself arrested several times. In prison, he continued his campaign by going on hunger strike.

***The flag of Pakistan.** The country was established on 14 August, 1947. The region that was known as East Pakistan later changed its name to Bangladesh.*

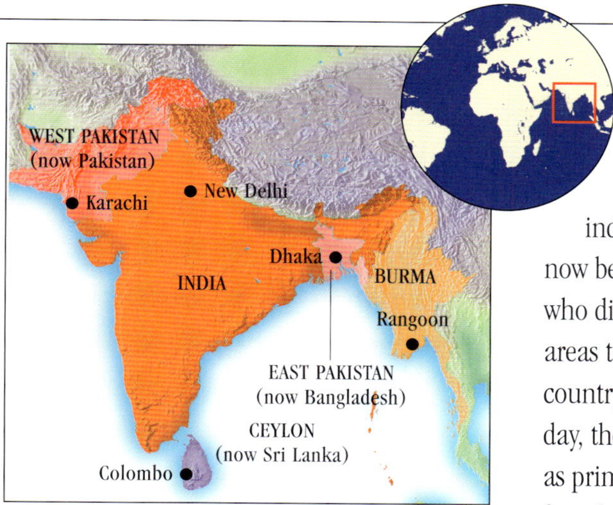

This map shows how India was divided. *East Pakistan broke away to become Bangladesh in 1971. Burma and Ceylon (now Sri Lanka) gained their independence in 1948.*

In 1930, Gandhi led thousands to the coast on a 'Salt March', in protest against having to buy heavily taxed salt. In 1945, the British government finally agreed to India's independence. The majority of Indians were Hindus, but other people now began to campaign for a separate state for India's many Muslims, who did not want to live under Hindu rule. On 14 August, 1947, two areas to the northeast and northwest of India became the independent country of Pakistan, with Jinnah as its first governor general. The next day, the rest of India gained its independence, led by Jawaharlal Nehru as prime minister. Immediately, violence broke out. Millions of people found themselves living in the 'wrong' country – Muslims in India and Hindus in Pakistan. Mass migrations began. As people fled, hundreds of thousands were killed.

The partition of India *was followed by a mass migration of Muslims from India to Pakistan and of Hindus from Pakistan to India. Over one million people were killed as violence flared up between the two groups.*

1840 After brief rule by Egypt, Palestine becomes part of the Ottoman empire again.
1882 First Zionist settlement established in Palestine.
1917 The Balfour Declaration supports a Jewish homeland in Palestine.
1920 The Treaty of Sèvres ends the Ottoman empire.
1922 Britain is given the mandate to govern Palestine.
1929 First major conflict between Jews and Arabs.
1933 Persecution of the Jews begins in Germany.
1939 Britain agrees to restrict the number of Jews emigrating to Palestine.
1947 The United Nations votes to divide Palestine.
1948 On 14 May, the state of Israel is founded and the Arab League declares war.
1949 A United Nations negotiated ceasefire leaves Israel with the territory given to it in 1947.

Israel and Palestine

Polish-born David Ben-Gurion *(1886–1973) emigrated to Palestine in 1906. Known as the 'Father of the Nation', he was Israel's first prime minister.*

The ancient homeland of the Jews was the land around Jerusalem. The Jews were expelled from Israel during the diaspora in AD 70 and settled in other parts of the world. The land, now called Palestine, had for many years been part of the Ottoman empire. The Jews' desire to return to their homeland led to a long conflict with the people living there.

Most Palestinians were Arabs. Small numbers of Jews, known as Zionists, began to settle in Palestine during the 1880s. In 1917, Britain declared its support for a Jewish homeland in Palestine. The Ottoman empire was breaking up following Turkey's defeat in World War I. The new League of Nations gave Britain its mandate (permission) to rule Palestine in the short term.

Jews continued to settle in Palestine, especially during the 1930s when the Nazis in Germany began to persecute German Jews. To escape imprisonment or murder, those Jews who could began to leave Germany. Some moved to Palestine.

Tel Aviv-Jaffa on the Mediterranean coast *is Israel's largest city. It was formed in 1950 with the merger of the ancient port of Jaffa and its suburb of Tel Aviv.*

T. E. Lawrence *(1888–1935), known as Lawrence of Arabia, was a British soldier who helped to lead an Arab revolt against the Ottoman empire during World War I. After that war, many Arabs hoped to see a new Arab nation, including Palestine. This did not happen.*

***The Wailing Wall in Jerusalem** is a Jewish place of prayer. After 1948, the Wall was in the part of the city held by Jordan. Israel regained it in 1967 and claimed all Jerusalem as its capital. Finding a future for Jerusalem that satisfies all has proved very difficult.*

The growing numbers of immigrants led to fighting between Jews and Arabs, and Britain tried to restrict the numbers of settlers allowed in.

After World War II, many more Jews wanted to move to Palestine. Britain took the matter to the United Nations and, in 1947, it was decided to split Palestine into two states, one Jewish and the other Arab. Jerusalem would become an international city, because it was sacred to Jews, Muslims and Christians. The Jews agreed to this, but the Arabs did not. Britain gave up its mandate on 14 May, 1948 and, on the same day, the Jewish leader David Ben-Gurion announced the founding of the state of Israel. The Arab League (Syria, Lebanon, Iraq, Iran, Jordan and Egypt) declared war on Israel and attacked. Israel quickly defeated them, gaining even more territory.

***Golda Meir** (1898–1978) was Israel's prime minister from 1969 to 1974. Born in Russia, she lived in the US as a child and moved to Palestine in 1921.*

The Cold War

1947 The US-backed Marshall Plan gives financial aid to European countries.
1948 Blockade of West Berlin for five months by the Soviet Union.
1949 North Atlantic Treaty Organization (NATO) is formed. Communists come to power in mainland China.
1950–53 The Korean War. North Korea, supported by China, invades South Korea, supported by the US.
1953 Death of Joseph Stalin.
1955 Warsaw Pact formed among countries of Eastern Europe.
1956 Soviets invade Hungary to preserve Communist rule.
1958 Fidel Castro comes to power in Cuba and allies Cuba with the Soviet Union.
1960 A split develops between the Soviet Union and China.
1961 The Berlin Wall is built.
1962 Cuban missile crisis.
1963 The US and the Soviet Union sign a Nuclear Test-Ban Treaty.
1964 The US becomes involved in the Vietnam War.
1968 Invasion of Czechoslovakia by the Soviet Union to preserve Communist rule.

***In 1968, Soviet tanks** invaded Prague, the Czech capital. A new Czech government had brought in reforms that were feared by the Soviet Communist leaders.*

The United States and the Soviet Union emerged from World War II as the world's dominant superpowers. Former allies, they soon became enemies in what was known as the Cold War.

***This map shows how Europe** was divided after World War II. The boundary between democratic (pink) and Communist (orange) Europe was first named the 'iron curtain' by Winston Churchill.*

The Cold War started when the Soviet Union set up Communist governments in the countries of Eastern Europe liberated by the Red Army. This effectively divided Europe by an 'iron curtain'.

After the war, Germany was divided between the Allies. The US, Britain and France controlled the west of the country, while the east was controlled by the Soviet Union. The capital, Berlin, lay within Soviet-controlled territory, but was also divided by a concrete wall.

Both sides built up huge stocks of nuclear weapons. This led to another crisis in 1962, when Cuban dictator Fidel Castro allowed the Soviet Union to build missile bases in Cuba. US President John F. Kennedy ordered a blockade of Cuba. The missiles were eventually removed, preventing a nuclear war.

Both sides spent vast sums on weapons. Although they never fought directly, they did get involved in the Korean War and the Vietnam War. They also carried on a spying and propaganda campaign against one another for many years.

ALLIANCES

The North Atlantic Treaty Organization (whose symbol is shown here) was set up on 4 April, 1949, with its headquarters in Brussels, Belgium. It was a military alliance between several Western European countries, Canada and the United States against aggression from any outside nation. In 1955, the Soviet Union formed an alliance of Communist states – the Warsaw Pact.

1957 The Soviet Union launches the first artificial satellite, *Sputnik 1*. Laika the dog is the first animal in space on *Sputnik 2*.
1958 The US launches its first satellite, *Explorer 1*.
1959 The Soviet space probe *Luna 2* reaches the Moon.
1961 Soviets launch first manned spacecraft, *Vostok I*. A month later, the US launches its first manned spacecraft, *Mercury*.
1963 Russian cosmonaut Valentina Tereshkova is the first woman in space.
1965 Russian cosmonaut Alexi Leonov becomes the first person to walk in space.
1969 US astronaut Neil Armstrong is the first person to land on the Moon.
1970 A Soviet spacecraft lands on Venus.
1972 The US makes its last *Apollo* Moon landing.
1975 Soviet and US spacecraft link up in space.
1977 US *Viking* craft land on Mars.
1990 *Hubble* space telescope is launched by a US shuttle.
1995 Russia's Valeriy Polyiakov stays in space for 437 days on the *Mir* space station.

The Space Race

***John F Kennedy** (1917–63) became president of the US in 1960. He promised to send Americans to the Moon by 1970.*

Scientists in Germany in the 1940s had developed the first guided missiles, using technology that might make it possible for people to travel into space. This prompted the US and the Soviet Union to embark on a 'space race'.

***Sputnik 1**, launched on October 4, 1957, was the first craft to go into space. It travelled at 28,000 km/h, transmitting a radio bleep that was picked up around the world.*

In 1957, the Soviet Union launched *Sputnik 1*, the first artificial Earth satellite. It took 96 minutes to orbit the Earth. In the following year, the US launched its first satellite, *Explorer 1*. Both countries spent vast amounts of money on space science.

The first person to orbit the Earth was Yuri Gagarin of the Soviet Union in 1961. The US set out to land a man on the Moon by 1970. This ambition was achieved when Neil Armstrong became the first person to walk on the Moon in 1969.

During the 1970s, Britain, China, France, India and Japan sent small spacecraft into orbit. Many of these were satellites, used for weather forecasting and for communications. The US and the Soviet Union sent craft deeper into space, sending back pictures and scientific information from the planets.

Since the 1990s and the easing of the Cold War, US and Russian scientists have worked together on space projects such as building the *International Space Station*.

***Yuri Gagarin** aboard* Vostok 1 *orbited Earth for 89 minutes on 12 April 1961, at about 300 km above Earth's surface.*

***Buzz Aldrin** became the second person, after Neil Armstrong, to walk on the Moon, on 21 July, 1969. The third crew member, Michael Collins, remained on board Apollo 11, orbiting the Moon.*

1951 Libya is the first African country to gain independence (from Italy).
1952 Kenyan Mau Mau terrorists campaign for independence from Britain.
1957 Ghana is first British colony to gain independence.
1956 Morocco and Tunisia gain independence from France.
1960 Zaire (now Congo) gains independence from Belgium; Nigeria and Somalia from Britain; Chad and Mali from France.
1961 Sierra Leone and Tanzania independent from Britain.
1962 Uganda independent from Britain; Algeria from France; Burundi and Rwanda from Belgium.
1963 Kenya independent from Britain.
1964 Malawi and Zambia independent from Britain.
1965 Gambia independent; white colonists in Rhodesia declare independence.
1966 Botswana and Lesotho independent from Britain.
1969 War as Biafra seeks independence from Nigeria.
1975 Angola and Mozambique independent from Portugal.
1976 Civil war in Angola.
1977 Djibouti independent from France.
1980 Zimbabwe (Rhodesia) has black-majority government.
1993 Eritrea, part of Ethiopia since 1962, declares itself independent.

New Africa

From the 1950s, most African countries gained independence from colonial rule. They developed their own systems of government and built up new economies. However, famine, poverty and civil wars have caused major hardships.

Kwame Nkrumah *(1909–72) led Ghana, formerly the Gold Coast, to independence in 1957, and was president from 1960 to 1966. He believed in a united Africa.*

The borders of many countries in the new Africa were the same as those that had been fixed by the European colonizers in the late 1800s. These borders often ignored traditional tribal groupings, and independence was sometimes followed by civil war as peoples within one country tried to set up new states of their own. This happened in the Congo (formerly Belgian) and in Nigeria (formerly British-ruled), where a breakaway state named itself Biafra. In Ethiopia, which had never been a colony, a revolution overthrew the king, Haile Selassie. In Angola, nationalists fought against the Portuguese, who were reluctant to give up control of their colony. In the nations of Rwanda and Burundi in central Africa, there was fighting between rival ethnic groups, each wanting control of the country.

***Local rulers**, such as these tribal chiefs in Ghana, continued to wield power in many African countries after they had gained independence.*

1 Algeria 1962
2 Angola 1975
3 Botswana 1966
4 Burundi 1962
5 Cameroon 1960
6 Chad 1960
7 Djibouti 1977
8 Egypt 1922
9 Eritrea 1993
10 Ethiopia
11 Gabon 1960
12 Gambia 1965
13 Ghana 1957
14 Ivory Coast 1960
15 Kenya 1963
16 Lesotho 1966
17 Liberia
18 Libya 1951
19 Malawi 1964
20 Mali 1960
21 Morocco 1956
22 Mozambique 1975
23 Namibia 1990
24 Niger 1960
25 Nigeria 1960
26 Rwanda 1962
27 Senegal 1960
28 Sierra Leone 1961
29 Somalia 1960
30 South Africa 1931
31 Sudan 1956
32 Swaziland 1968
33 Tanzania 1961
34 Tunisia 1956
35 Uganda 1962
36 Zaire (Congo) 1960
37 Zambia 1964
38 Zimbabwe 1980
39 Mauritania 1960
40 Madagascar 1960

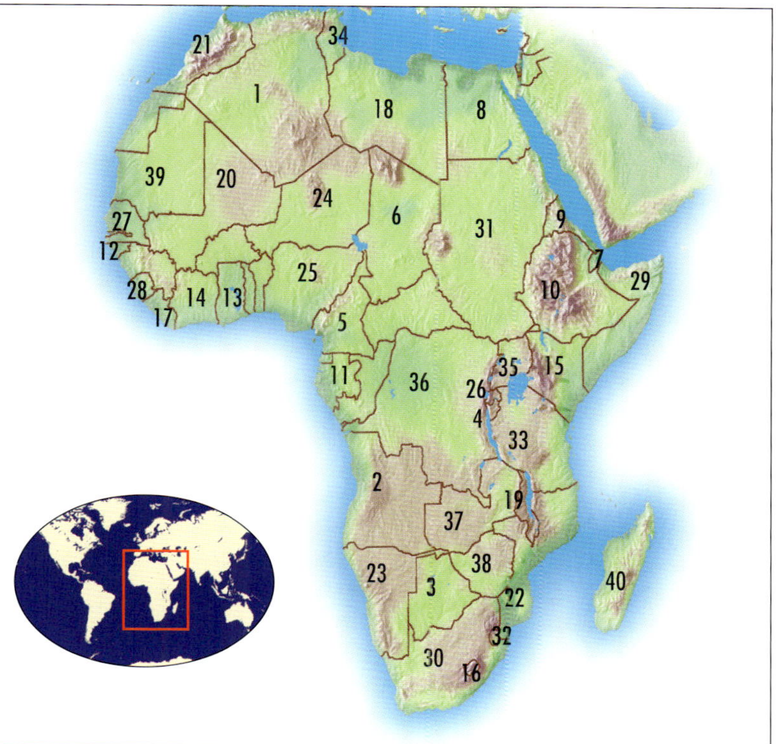

This map shows *many of the independent nations of Africa, with the date they achieved nationhood. Only Ethiopia and Liberia were never colonized.*

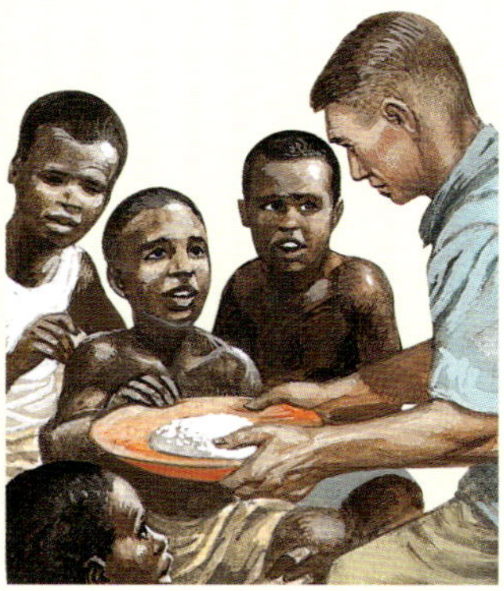

FAMINE

African nations frequently suffer famine on a massive scale when drought hits areas with poor soil and the crops fail. People caught in the disaster have to rely on aid or face starvation and disease.

In Uganda, a brutal dictator, Idi Amin, expelled Ugandan Asians in the 1970s. Problems also occurred in countries where white settlers wanted to stay in control, as in Algeria, Rhodesia (now Zimbabwe) and South Africa. In South Africa, from 1948 to 1990, the whites-only government used a system known as apartheid to keep blacks out of power. Once apartheid was abolished, free elections were held and, in 1994, Nelson Mandela became the first black president of South Africa.

The ruins of Great Zimbabwe *after which the country is named. As Rhodesia, the country declared itself independent from Great Britain in 1965 but it did not achieve international recognition for its independence until 1980, when it changed its name to Zimbabwe.*

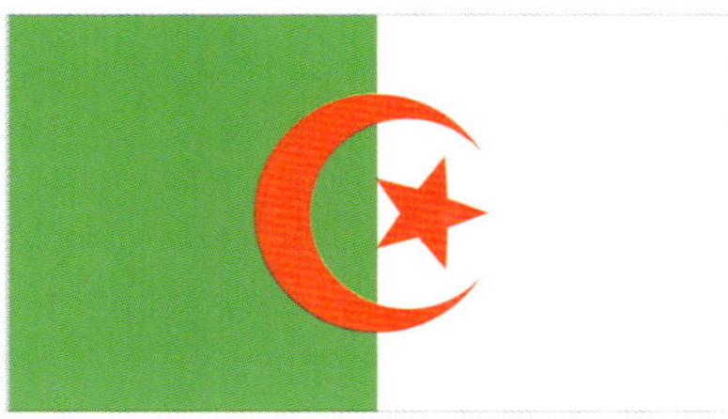

The flag of Algeria. *After several years of armed struggle against France in the years following World War II, Algeria finally won independence in 1962.*

1955 Rosa Parks is arrested in Alabama for refusing to give up her seat on a bus.
1957 In the US, Martin Luther King brings many civil rights groups together.
1960 South African police fire on anti-Apartheid demonstrators at Sharpeville, killing 69.
1962 Nelson Mandela is imprisoned for political activities.
1963 Martin Luther King organizes a march to Washington, DC, asking for equal rights for all.
1964 The Civil Rights Act is passed in the US to end all discrimination because of race, colour, religion or national origin.
1966 American feminists found the National Organization for Women.
1971 Swiss women are given the right to vote.
1980 Solidarity, an independent trade union, is set up in Poland (banned until 1989).
1985 Marriage between blacks and whites is made legal in South Africa.
1986 Fighting in black townships in South Africa by civil rights protesters.
1989 In Beijing, China, government troops crush a student demonstration for greater democracy.
1993 Nelson Mandela and F. W. de Klerk win the Nobel peace prize for their work to end apartheid.

Fight for Rights

During the second half of the 20th century, people all over the world fought for civil rights. Many were being treated unfairly because of their race, skin colour, religion or gender. Others were being denied the vote, barred from forming free trade unions, or prevented from choosing the political leaders they wanted.

The civil rights movement came to the fore in the US in the 1960s. In the southern states, blacks were discriminated against in schools, jobs, transport, health care and public life. Protests began in 1955, after Rosa Parks, a black American, was arrested for refusing to give up her seat to a white man on a bus in Alabama. Non-violent protests were inspired by the words of civil rights leader Dr Martin Luther King.

***Martin Luther King** (1929–68) was an outstanding speaker. His belief in non-violent resistance to oppression won him the Nobel peace prize in 1964. His most famous speech included the words: 'I have a dream'. In 1968, King was shot dead in Memphis, Tennessee.*

***Martin Luther King** made his famous 'I have a dream' speech in front of the Lincoln Memorial, Washington, DC in 1963. The speech was made as part of the March on Washington, when 200,000 people campaigned for jobs and civil rights.*

The shipyards of Gdansk, Poland, *saw the rise of the Solidarity organization. Under the leadership of Lech Walesa, Solidarity campaigned for greater democracy in communist Poland.*

APARTHEID

Apartheid means 'apartness'. It was a policy used in South Africa from 1948 to 1990 to divide the country into separate areas for whites and blacks. There was segregated education, employment, housing and health care. Most whites had good jobs and lived in comfort; blacks did the heavy work and lived in crowded townships.

King led a march to Washington, DC, in 1963. Over 250,000 people took part, and in 1964 the US government passed a Civil Rights Act that made racial discrimination illegal.

There was a similar struggle in South Africa, where the white minority government's policy of apartheid (separating the races) was oppressive and cruel. After 69 African protesters were shot dead at Sharpeville in 1960, the campaign became more violent. Black leader Nelson Mandela was jailed from 1962 until 1990. After a long international campaign of protest and sanctions against South Africa, Mandela was released from prison and apartheid ended in 1990.

In Communist countries, people demanded the right to form free trade unions and to vote for whatever kind of government they wanted. Women campaigned for equal pay and job opportunities. New laws in some countries banned sex and age discrimination in employment.

Nelson Mandela *(born 1918) was imprisoned in 1962 for his political views, and only released in 1990. In April 1994, he was able to vote for the first time in the country's first free elections. Mandela's party, the African National Congress (ANC), won and he became president.*

1946 Start of the war between Ho Chi Minh's Vietnamese nationalists and French colonial troops.
1954 Vietnamese Communists defeat the French at Dien Bien Phu. The country is divided into North Vietnam and South Vietnam.
1961 South Vietnamese ask for military advice from the US to combat Communist Viet Cong guerrillas.
1964 War between North Vietnam (backed by the USSR) and South Vietnam (backed by the US).
1965 US sends combat troops to South Vietnam.
1966 Australian troops arrive in Vietnam to fight with US troops. The first anti-war demonstrations take place in the US.
1968 North Vietnamese and Viet Cong launch an attack known as the Tet offensive against the South.
1969 The USA withdraws 25,000 of its 540,000 troops. The fighting – and the anti-war protests – continue.
1971 Fighting spreads to Laos.
1973 Ceasefire. US troops withdraw. Vietnamese continue to fight.
1975 Communists take control of South Vietnam.
1976 Vietnam is reunited under a Communist government.

The Vietnam War

***Ho Chi Minh** (1892–1969) led Vietnam's struggle for independence from France. As president of North Vietnam from 1954 he fought for a united Vietnam, achieved after his death.*

Vietnam, together with Cambodia and Laos, was part of the French colony of Indochina. It was occupied by the Japanese in World War II. During this time, the Viet Minh league, led by the Communist Ho Chi Minh, declared Vietnam independent from France.

After the war, France refused to recognize Ho Chi Minh's government and war broke out between the French and the Vietnamese. This war ended in defeat for the French at the Battle of Dien Bien Phu in 1954. An international agreement then divided Vietnam into Communist North and non-Communist South.

Almost immediately, civil war broke out. From 1959, Communist guerrillas in the south, known as the Viet Cong, were helped by North Vietnam. The US, anxious to prevent the spread of Communism, sent military aid to the South Vietnamese. However, the Viet Cong's guerrilla tactics were hard to combat. In an attempt to cut off supply lines, US planes bombed North Vietnam. Vast areas of forest were sprayed with chemicals to destroy any vegetation that may have been concealing Viet Cong bases.

***Much of Vietnam** is covered in dense rainforest which made it easy for Viet Cong forces to hide. US aircraft dropped thousands of tonnes of defoliants, such as Agent Orange, in an attempt to destroy the tree cover and reduce the number of places where the Viet Cong could hide.*

ANTI-WAR DEMONSTRATIONS
The Vietnam War was the first to be widely covered on television. People were able to see events as they happened. As growing numbers of US troops were killed or injured, people took to America's streets in protest. By 1967, the protests had spread beyond the US. The strength of anti-war feeling helped persuade President Richard Nixon to withdraw from the war.

***A ruined American tank** abandoned in Vietnam. The conflict involved troops from the US, North and South Korea, Thailand, Australia, New Zealand, China and the Philippines.*

***Most of the war** was fought in the jungles of South Vietnam. The Ho Chi Minh trail was the Viet Cong's supply line from the North. It ran from China through Laos and into South Vietnam.*

In 1968, the Viet Cong's Tet offensive in the South convinced most Americans that the war could not be won. In 1969, the US began to withdraw its troops and a ceasefire was agreed in 1973. Fighting continued until 1975, when North Vietnamese troops took over the south. Vietnam was united.

***The majority of Vietnamese lived by farming,** mostly growing rice in the fields around their villages. Many suffered greatly in the war as crops and villages were destroyed.*

China's New Power

When the Communists, led by Mao Zedong, won power in China, they set out to modernize the country. Their aim was to provide food, schools, hospitals and work for China's millions. These plans were blown off course in the 1960s by Mao's 'Cultural Revolution'. Later leaders were less radical, but refused to allow the people more freedom or democracy.

Deng Xiaoping *(1904–95) ruled China from 1977 until his death. He reopened contacts with the outside world and encouraged China's economy to grow by setting up privately owned factories.*

1949 Mao Zedong's Communist party takes power in China.
1953 In the Five Year Plan, peasants are encouraged to set up collective (cooperative) farms.
1958–60 The Great Leap Forward. It is abandoned when its policies result in widespread famine.
1959 Mao Zedong retires as Chairman of the Chinese Communist party.
1966 Mao sweeps back to power and starts the Cultural Revolution. By 1968, factory productivity is 12 per cent lower than it was in 1966.
1973 Rivalry grows between Mao's supporters, known as the 'Gang of Four', and Deng Xiaoping over who will succeed Mao.
1974 China tests its first nuclear weapons.
1976 Death of Mao. He is briefly succeeded by the Gang of Four, who want to continue the Cultural Revolution.
1977 Deng Xiaoping comes to power. He visits the US.
1989 Tiananmen Square demonstration by pro-democracy students.
1995 Death of Deng Xiaoping. China's next leader, Jiang Zemin (to 2002), modernizes the Chinese economy.

The Communists gave women the same rights as men and shared out land among the peasants. They built roads and railways, factories and power stations. In the 'Great Leap Forward', every village was meant to be self-sufficient, growing its own food and producing clothes and tools in small factories. But these policies failed, and after several bad harvests and mass starvation, Mao retired.

The little red book *containing the 'thoughts of Chairman Mao' was carried by many Chinese citizens during the turmoil of the Cultural Revolution in China.*

Mao first came to power *in 1949. Civil war had left the country in financial disorder. Mao's initial reforms, called the Five Year Plan, helped to improve China's economy.*

Tiananmen Square, Beijing, *was the site of a pro-democracy demonstration in May 1989. The Chinese government sent in troops and tanks to clear the protesters and many people were killed.*

Mao returned to power in 1966, determined that China should not lose its revolutionary spirit. He set in progress the Cultural Revolution, with the aim of overthrowing the old China. All his youthful followers carried his little red book for inspiration. Traditional customs and thinking were prohibited. Foreigners and old people were insulted. College professors and teachers were turned out of their jobs to work in the fields. Hospitals and factories, left without doctors and managers, closed.

When Mao died in 1976, his revolution ended. His successor was Deng Xiaoping, who re-established trade links with the outside world and encouraged Chinese businesses to grow. This policy continued under the next leader, Jiang Zemin. China began to prosper again, but the government was still hesitant to allow political freedom and showed little regard for human rights. Student protests in 1989 were brutally crushed.

During the Cultural Revolution, *schools and colleges were closed and teachers and students were forced to work on the land. Opposition was brutally put down by the Red Guards.*

Middle East in Crisis

1956 Egypt takes control of the Suez Canal.
1964 Formation of the Palestinian Liberation Organization (PLO).
1967 Six-Day War, between Israel and Egypt, Jordan and Syria, is won by Israel.
1973 The Yom Kippur War. Israel fights Egypt and Syria.
1976 Fighting breaks out in Lebanon.
1979 Peace treaty between Israel and Egypt. Shah of Iran is overthrown and Islamic republican government is set up.
1980–88 Iran-Iraq War.
1982 Israel invades Lebanon.
1987 Fighting between Palestinians and Israeli troops in the West Bank and Gaza Strip.
1990–91 In the Gulf War, Iraq invades Kuwait, but is repulsed by UN troops.
1993 Israeli and Palestinian leaders hold talks in the US.
1994 Israel and Jordan sign a peace agreement.
1995 Israel signs an agreement to extend self-rule to the Palestinians.
2003 Short war in Iraq removes Saddam Hussein.
2006 Saddam Hussein is executed for crimes against humanity.

__Ayatollah Khomeini__ (1900–89) was a revolutionary religious leader of Iran. He came to power in 1979 after the Shah of Iran was overthrown. Under Khomeini, Iran became a strict Muslim state.

The Middle East has been a world troublespot since 1948, when an uneasy peace followed the Arab-Israeli war. Israel fought three more wars against its Arab neighbours, and the Palestinians remained without a homeland of their own. Terrorism became a terrible weapon in this conflict, which was bound up with two other issues: the world's thirst for oil, much of which comes from Middle East states, and the rise of Islamic fundamentalism.

Israel's population increased during the 1950s as Jews emigrated from Europe, Russia and the US. The Palestinian Arabs, pushed into separate communities within Israel, began a campaign for their own state. Wars were fought in 1956, 1967 and 1973. The first war began after Egypt took control of the Suez Canal. Britain and France invaded Egypt, but later withdrew. Israel also attacked Egypt. In the Six-Day War in 1967, Israel won control of Jerusalem and the West Bank of the Jordan river.

__In order to protect itself from attacks__ by Palestinian fighters, Israel has built a huge concrete wall between its territories and Palestinian lands.

It fought off Egyptian and Syrian attacks in the Yom Kippur War of 1973.

Israel also became involved in the civil war in Lebanon, where many Palestinians lived in refugee camps. By the 1990s, Israel had signed peace agreements with Egypt, Jordan and Syria, and the Palestinians had attained limited self-government. Yet terrorist attacks by extremist groups opposed to new Israeli settlements, and even Israel's very existence, continued.

In 1979, the Shah of Iran was overthrown and an Islamic regime took over. Iran went to war with Iraq in 1980. Neither side won a costly conflict. In 1990, Iraq invaded its tiny neighbour Kuwait, but was defeated in the brief Gulf War by a UN coalition force led by the US. Iraq's ruler Saddam Hussein was finally deposed in 2003, when US-led forces invaded Iraq.

***Saddam Hussein** (shown here on an Iraqi banknote) ruled oil-rich Iraq from 1979 to 2003. A brutal dictator, he was tried by the Iraq Special Tribunal in 2006 and sentenced to death by hanging. He was executed on 30 December, 2006.*

***The US has tried to mediate in the Middle East,** though many Arabs see America as Israel's ally. In 1993, President Bill Clinton (centre) welcomed a deal between Israeli Prime Minister Yitzhak Rabin (left) and Yasser Arafat, leader of the Palestinians, to establish Palestinian self-rule. Rabin was assassinated in 1995.*

1949 Chinese Nationalists set up a republic on the island of Taiwan, which though not recognized by the United Nations, builds a thriving economy.
1953 Korean War ends. South Korea grows rapidly as an industrial nation.
1960s Japan starts selling cars on the world market.
1970s Taiwan starts to develop high-technology industries.
1975 Vietnam War ends. Vietnam emerges from isolation to become an active trading nation. Japan launches the first VHS (Video Home System) on to the market.
1976 From this date, Japan has a balance of trade surplus, which means its exports are more valuable than its imports.
1979 Vietnam and China fight a short war. Compact discs are co-developed by Dutch and Japanese companies.
1980s Japan becomes a world leader in motor vehicle manufacture.
1995 By this date, over half of China's industrial output is from privately owned businesses.
1997 Britain returns Hong Kong to Chinese control.

Asian Industry

After World War II, Asia made a spectacular economic recovery. Japan, Singapore, South Korea, Malaysia and Taiwan all became 'tiger economies', with rising living standards and modern factories. These produce goods that are sold all over the world.

Japan, whose factories had been bombed during World War II by the Allies, was aided by the US throughout the 1940s and 1950s. New factories, with the latest machinery, began turning out cars, radios, office equipment and gadgets for the home. In the 1980s, the factories began using automated robots to make electronic and other goods, including televisions and computers, and Japan became the world's biggest maker of cars and trucks.

Japan was reluctant to play a big part in world affairs, other than in trade. It had given up its large military forces at the end of World War II, and no Japanese troops took part in any of the post-war conflicts, such as the Korean and Vietnam wars. South Korea emerged from its war with its Communist neighbour, North Korea, to undergo an economic transformation similar to Japan's. It too had a well-trained and organized work force, and invested money in new machinery and computers. North Korea, under Communist rule, lagged far behind the South in terms of wealth.

***Tokyo is the centre of** the Japanese business world. With the port of Yokohama and the industrial area of Kawasaki, it is one of the world's largest cities.*

***In the 1980s,** automated robots became widely used in Japan for making cars and computers. The Japanese were among the first to use modern assembly methods.*

In India many women and children *are employed making shoes and clothes for export.*

Singapore and Hong Kong, both small, grew rich on trade and banking. Hong Kong was under British rule until 1997, when it was returned to China by agreement. It retained its special status as a trading area for China, which in the 1990s relaxed its restrictions on private businesses. Vietnam has also turned to a 'free market' economy. India, Malaysia, Indonesia and the Philippines have prospered from industries employing many people who are paid low wages to make shoes and clothes, or to assemble electronic equipment for export. India, still mainly an agricultural country, has expanded its industrial production by over six times since 1950. The biggest employers are the clothing and textile industries.

Hong Kong, whose name means 'good harbour', *is a major centre for banking, finance and industry in China.*

1967 The US, Britain and the Soviet Union sign a treaty banning the use of nuclear weapons in outer space.
1969 US President Lyndon B. Johnson starts the Strategic Arms Limitation Talks (SALT).
1972 The first SALT agreement is signed by US President Richard Nixon and Leonid Brezhnev of the Soviet Union.
1979 Second SALT agreement is signed by US President Carter and Brezhnev. Soviet troops invade Afghanistan. Margaret Thatcher becomes British prime minister.
1981 Ronald Reagan becomes US President. He increases military spending.
1985 Mikhail Gorbachev comes to power in the Soviet Union and starts to make reforms.
1989 Free elections are held in Poland. Communism collapses in Hungary, East Germany, Czechoslovakia and Romania. The Berlin Wall is demolished.
1990 East and West Germany are reunited. Free elections are held in Bulgaria.
1991 A multi-party government is set up in Albania. The Soviet Union is abolished and replaced by 15 independent nations.

The Cold War Ends

The Cold War, a time of suspicion, spies and super-missiles, began to look less dangerous in the 1970s. The United States and the Soviet Union found they could agree on some things, such as cutting their arms bills, and signed agreements. The pressure on the Soviet leader was intense; his Communist empire was cracking apart.

In 1972, the US and USSR signed the first SALT (missile disarmament) agreement. By 1980, the Russians had become involved in a long and costly war in Afghanistan, and their economy was in a bad way. In 1985, a new leader, Mikhail Gorbachev, set about introducing political and economic reforms. He also sought friendship with the West. The US president was Ronald Reagan, elected in 1980 on an anti-Communist stand. He was ready to spend billions of dollars on a defensive missile shield in space. But in 1987, Reagan and his British ally, Margaret Thatcher, signed an important agreement with the USSR to ban medium-range nuclear missiles.

***The Berlin Wall** was demolished in 1989. It had divided the city since 1961. People took pieces as souvenirs. A few pieces remain standing as a reminder of the once divided city.*

***Many symbols of Communism** were destroyed after the Soviet Union broke up. Statues of past leaders such as Lenin were pulled down and used as scrap metal. The Communists had dealt similarly with symbols of tsarist rule in 1917.*

Gorbachev's reforms in the Soviet Union led to demands for free elections in Eastern Europe. By the end of 1989, Communism had collapsed in Poland, Hungary, East Germany, Czechoslovakia and Romania. In 1990, East and West Germany were reunited and free elections were held in Bulgaria. In August 1991, an attempted coup in the Soviet Union led to the downfall of Gorbachev's government. Boris Yeltsin took over as Russian president until 1999, when he was succeeded by Vladimir Putin. The Soviet Union broke up as more former Soviet states became independent from Russia. In some cases, such as Chechnya, claims for independence were violently opposed by the Russian government who sent in the army to put down any rebellion. With the collapse of the Soviet Union, the Cold War came to an end. There was just one superpower left in the world, the United States of America.

McDonald's' first restaurant in Moscow. *Gorbachev began opening up Russia to Western enterprise. Long queues for new Western fastfood soon built up.*

Prague, the Czech capital, was the scene of major demonstrations in 1989. *Throughout that year, people across Eastern Europe began to demand democracy and an end to repression.*

One World

The 20th century brought startling changes in the speed at which information moved around the world. Countries came together in new groups, some with their own parliaments and laws, like the European Union. Multinational corporations, doing business in many countries, became richer than all but a few countries.

These changes have made people more aware of global events. They feel they are citizens not just of a country, but of a planet – and a small planet, with limited resources. Local ways of life are rapidly vanishing, replaced by a 'mono-culture'. In many countries, people wear Western-style clothes instead of traditional dress, eat the same fast foods, and watch the same TV shows, beamed to them by satellite or down cables.

The world's wealth is not distributed equally. Many people go hungry and have no clean water. Rich countries use too big a share of Earth's resources to support their high living standards.

1962 Rachel Carson's book *Silent Spring* alerts people to the dangers of pollution.

1971 Founding of Greenpeace, the international organization concerned with protecting the environment.

1972 Government concern for the environment starts when the US bans DDT, a powerful pesticide.

1976 US scientists voice fears about damage to the ozone layer in the atmosphere.

1985 In New Zealand, French agents blow up the Greenpeace ship *Rainbow Warrior*, which is protesting against nuclear testing in the Pacific. 'Live Aid' concerts in Britain and the USA raise money for Ethiopia's famine victims.

1986 An explosion and fire at the nuclear power station at Chernobyl, Ukraine (then part of the Soviet Union), releases large amounts of radioactivity.

1987 Scientists discover a hole in the ozone layer above the Antarctic.

1992 All nations send representatives to the first Earth summit in Rio de Janeiro, Brazil, organized by the UN to discuss the future of the planet.

1998 UN environment summit at Kyoto, Japan, targets a 5 per cent cut in carbon dioxide emissions by 2012. 178 countries (but not the US) agree.

2000 122 governments agree to stop using a number of dangerous chemicals in paints and pesticides.

THE UNITED NATIONS

The United Nations Organization came into operation after World War II, on 24 October, 1945. Taking over from the failed League of Nations, its aim was to keep world peace and to solve international problems by cooperation rather than fighting. This is reflected in its symbol, which shows a map of the world surrounded by olive branches.

***Recycling helps conserve Earth's** resources. Paper, glass, metal and some plastics can all be reused again and again. Too much rubbish is burned in incinerators or buried in landfill sites.*

Burning fossil fuels releases carbon dioxide *into the atmosphere, where it dissolves in rainwater, making acid rain that can destroy trees and kill fish.*

During the 1970s, pressure groups such as Greenpeace began to campaign on environmental issues. There is much that can be done to safeguard resources for future generations, such as stopping the dumping of nuclear waste, protecting endangered wildlife, saving what remains of tropical rainforests, recycling more, and turning to alternative energy sources (such as as wind, wave and solar power) before we burn up all Earth's fossil fuels (coal, oil and gas).

Governments meet at international conferences to discuss environmental problems and set targets, but in the end the answers lie with us all.

FAMINE IN AFRICA

TV pictures of people starving in Africa frequently shock the world. Money donated to charities to help provide food and medicine tackles the problem in the short term. But long-term projects are essential to prevent future famines.

11 September, 2001 Terrorists fly airliners into the World Trade Center and Pentagon in the US. More than 2,500 people are killed in the attack.

October 2001 US-led forces invade Afghanistan to topple the Taliban regime there and find members of al-Qaeda.

20 March, 2003 US-led forces invade Iraq.

9 April, 2003 Iraqi forces are defeated and Baghdad is captured.

13 December, 2003 Saddam Hussein is captured.

11 March, 2004 Bombs explode on commuter trains in Madrid, Spain, killing 192 people. Many people blame al-Qaeda for the attack.

7 July, 2005 Four bombs explode on the London underground and a bus, killing 56 people.

New York City's World Trade Center *towers fell to horrifying terrorist attacks in 2001.*

The War Against Terror

The events of 11 September, 2001 changed the political landscape. Almost immediately, the US started a war against terrorism, determined to stop terrorists from using certain countries as bases to launch attacks. This led to invasions of Afghanistan and Iraq.

Afghanistan, under the Taliban regime, was seen as the hiding place of Osama bin Laden, head of the al-Qaeda terrorist organization which carried out the attacks on New York City and Washington, DC. American forces, with support from other nations, attacked Afghanistan, toppling the Taliban regime.

The defeat of Iraqi forces in 2003 *did not see the end of military involvement in Iraq. Suicide bombings and booby-trap attacks have kept foreign troops occupied long after the official end of hostilities.*

***The remains of a London bus** destroyed by an explosion during the terrorist attacks of 7 July, 2005. Three suicide bombers attacked the underground system and a fourth blew himself up on this bus. In total, 56 people were killed in the attacks.*

***US-led forces** can rely on the latest weaponry in the fight against terrorism, such as the B-2 Stealth Bomber.*

The next target was Iraq, which the US president, George W. Bush, accused of helping terrorists and of having weapons of mass destruction, including biological and chemical weapons. Many people disagreed with this idea, including the United Nations. The United Nations relies on debate and agreement before taking action against a nation. It sent weapons inspectors into Iraq to seek out any weapons of mass destruction. UN members disagreed about whether war against Iraq, or any 'rogue state', was justified.

Nevertheless, the US, along with a small coalition of other countries, invaded Iraq in March 2003, and overthrew its leader, Saddam Hussein, less than a month later.

However, terrorist attacks did not finish. Suicide bombings continued in Iraq and Afghanistan long after the fall of the Taliban and Saddam Hussein, and there were even attacks on European capital cities. On 11 March, 2004, several bombs exploded on commuter trains in Madrid at rush hour, killing 192 people and wounding many others. Just over a year later, on 7 July, 2005, four suicide bombers attacked London at rush hour on busy tube trains and a double-decker bus. Fifty-six people were killed in these attacks.

***In modern wars,** air power and hi-tech weapons may be used alongside the guns and rocket launchers of local fighters, as in Afghanistan in 2001.*

1999 Vladimir Putin becomes leader of Russia.

1999 World population reaches 6 billion.

2000 Hispanic Americans are the largest minority group in the US.

2000 Data from the US Global Surveyor suggests that Mars may have water – vital for any future manned exploration.

2000 The US presidential election ends in a legal row over ballots. George W. Bush wins.

2000 Scientists have almost completed the map of the human genome.

2002 The European Union starts to use its new currency, the euro, in coins and notes, though Britain is not yet using the euro.

2002 The African Union sets up its own parliament.

2002 Queen Elizabeth II celebrates 50 years as Britain's queen. The Queen Mother dies aged 101.

2002 Former Communist Warsaw Pact members are allowed to join NATO.

The Future

When the 21st century began, people looked forward to a new millennium (the next 1,000 years). No one could say what kind of new world would take shape. Would computers take over more jobs from people? Scientists have made amazing advances in understanding how the human body works by identifying genes. Could science create new plants or even animals?

The world is rich enough to support even today's population of over 6 billion. But never before in human history has it seemed so small and under such pressure. Humans may visit Mars in the next 100 years, but there is no nearby planet like Earth to move to. *Homo sapiens* has to live in, and conserve, the world our prehistoric ancestors first explored. This must also happen under increasing pressure from an expanding population – it is predicted to reach 7 billion by 2012.

***The Internet** has opened up a whole world of information for millions of people. It has allowed the spread of ideas to happen much faster and, with email, has let people communicate with each other quickly and easily. However, some people see the internet as a problem, where dangerous ideas can be spread.*

SECRETS OF THE GENE

The study of the DNA molecule (above) opened the door to genetic engineering – changing living things by altering their genetic makeup.

Many people believe that resources are being used at an unsustainable rate and that, before too long, we will not be able to create enough energy to provide food, clothing, heating and shelter for everyone. Others point to the impact that energy production today is having on the planet. They feel that pollution from the burning of fossil fuels is pushing the world's temperatures up, causing global warming, and this will have disastrous consequences on the natural world as well as the towns and cities we live in.

There is also a great inequality as to how energy production and wealth are distributed around the planet. A small minority of people have the vast majority of the wealth and use the most energy, while huge numbers of people live in poverty.

***We must keep a balance** between development (which too often means recklessly cutting down rainforests) and conservation, preserving Earth's natural riches for all to share.*

***People living in a slum** sort through rubbish on a dump in order to find materials they can reuse or sell.*

	10,000–2000 BC	2000–1000 BC	1000–500 BC	500–200 BC	200 BC–AD 0
POLITICS	c. 3500 BC Sumerians set up city-states in Mesopotamia c. 3100 BC King Menes unites Upper and Lower Egypt c. 2500 BC Indus Valley civilization in ancient India is at its height	c. 1800 BC Babylon begins to build new empire in Mesopotamia c. 1600–1100 BC The Mycenaeans dominate ancient Greece c. 1200 BC Beginning of Olmec rule in western Mexico	c. 1000–960 BC David rules united kingdom of Judah and Israel 883–859 BC Ashurnasirpal II rules kingdom of Assyria in Mesopotamia 753 BC Traditional date of the foundation of the city of Rome	479–431 BC Athens dominates ancient Greece 336–323 BC Alexander the Great of Macedonia rules Greece, Persia and Egypt 221 BC Qin Shi Huangdi unites China, calling himself the First Emperor	147–146 BC Romans invade and conquer Greece 49–44 BC Julius Caesar rules Rome as dictator 27 BC Octavian becomes Rome's first emperor, taking the title Augustus
EXPLORATION	c. 3000 BC Phoenician ships are sailing around the Mediterranean Sea c. 2300 BC Egyptian explorer Harkhuf sails south along the river Nile	c. 1492 BC Egyptians travel to the Land of Punt (possibly Ethiopia) c. 1001 BC People from Southeast Asia begin colonizing Polynesia	c. 650 BC Greek sailors discover the Strait of Gibraltar c. 600 BC Phoenicians sail into Atlantic and may have sailed round Africa c. 515 BC Greek geographer Scylax explores the river Indus	c. 470 BC Carthaginian navigator Hanno founds settlement in West Africa 449–444 BC Greek historian Herodotus explores the Near East c. 330 BC Pytheas of Marseille sails around the British Isles	138–125 BC Chang Ch'ien of China explores central Asia and India 120 BC Eudoxus of Greece travels from Egypt to India 55–54 BC Roman general Julius Caesar twice invades Britain
TECHNOLOGY	c. 4000 BC Boats on the river Nile are the first to use sails c. 3500 BC Sumerians in Mesopotamia invent writing and the wheel c. 3000 BC Egyptians build irrigation system to water their fields	c. 2000 BC Tobacco is grown in Mexico and South America c. 2000 BC Babylonians begin counting in 60s – hence 360° in a circle c. 1450 BC Ancient Greeks begin using shadow clocks	c. 1000 BC Phoenicians introduce purple dye made from murex snails 876 BC First known use of a symbol for zero on an inscription in India c. 700 BC Assyrians begin using water clocks	c. 500 BC Indian surgeon Susrata performs eye operations for cataracts c. 500 BC Steel is made in India 406 BC Dionysius of Syracuse, Greece, makes the first war catapult	c. 200 BC Gear wheels are invented c. 110 BC The Chinese invent the horse collar, which is still in use
ARTS	c. 2800 BC Building begins at Stonehenge in England c. 2600 BC Work begins on the Great Pyramid in Egypt c. 2000 BC In Sumeria the *Epic of Gilgamesh* is written down	c. 1500 BC Tapestries are made in Egypt, China and Babylonia 1339 BC In Egypt, king Tutankhamun is buried with hoard of treasure c. 1100 BC First Chinese dictionary is compiled	At this period: Music flourishes in Babylonia, Greece and Israel c. 950 BC Solomon's temple is built in Jerusalem c. 850 BC Chavin people of Peru make many clay pots and sculptures	c. 450–387 BC Greek playwright Aristophanes is at work 447–438 BC Greeks build the Parthenon temple in Athens 351 BC Tomb of Mausolus, one of the Seven Wonders of the World, is built	c. 140 BC The Venus of Milo is carved in Greece c. 112 BC Pharisees sect develops in Palestine 47 BC The great library at Alexandria, Egypt, is destroyed by fire
RELIGION	c. 3000 BC During this period: Sumerians worship mother-goddess Tammuz c. 3000 BC During this period: Egyptians worship their pharaoh as a god-king	c. 2000 BC Babylonians begin worship of the god Marduk c. 1500 BC Probable date of origin of the Hindu religion c. 1364–1347 BC New religion based on worship of one god, Aten, in Egypt	700s BC The Hebrew prophet Isaiah is active c. 563 BC Birth of the Buddha (Siddhartha Gautama in Nepal) c. 551 BC Birth of the Chinese philosopher Confucius (Kong Qiu)	c. 400 BC The first five books of the Bible reach their final form 260 BC Emperor Ashoka Maurya makes Buddhism India's state religion c. 255 BC Greek version of the Old Testament is compiled	168 BC Antiochus IV of Syria persecutes the Jews and sacks Jerusalem c. 165 BC The *Book of Daniel* in the Old Testament is written 4 BC Probable birth date of Jesus of Nazareth
DAILY LIFE	c. 8000 BC Farming first practised in Near East and in Southeast Asia c. 5000 BC Aboriginal Australians begin using boomerangs During this period: copper is first used in Asia and North America	c. 1500 BC First glass vessels used in Egypt and Mesopotamia c. 1450 BC Explosion of Thera volcano in Mediterranean wipes out Cretan civilization	c. 950 BC Poppies are grown in Egypt c. 900 BC Noble Egyptians and Assyrians begin wearing wigs 776 BC The first Olympic Games are held in Greece	430–423 BC Plague breaks out in Athens c. 250 BC Parchment is first made in Pergamum (now Bergama, Turkey) 214 BC The building of the Great Wall of China is started	c. 170 BC Rome has its first paved streets 46 BC Romans adopt the Julian Calendar and the idea of leap years c. 50 BC Basic Hindu medical book, the *Ayurveda*, is compiled

AD 0–600	AD 600–700	AD 700–800	AD 800–900	AD 900–1000	
AD 100s Kingdom of Axum rises to power in what is now Ethiopia AD 350–550 The Gupta empire dominates India AD 476 Collapse of Western Roman empire; Byzantine empire survives in the East	c. AD 600 Huari empire begins to develop in Peru AD 655–698 Arabs dominate North Africa and spread Islam AD 687 Pepin of Herstal becomes leader of the Franks in Gaul	AD 732 Charles Martel of France defeats Muslims at Battle of Poitiers AD 786 Harun al-Rashid becomes Caliph of Baghdad AD 800 Frankish king Charlemagne is crowned Emperor of the West	AD 800s Ife kingdom rises to power in Nigeria AD 802 Khmer empire is founded in Cambodia AD 878 Alfred the Great defeats Vikings and divides England with them	AD 926 Welsh, Picts and Scots submit to King Athelstan of England AD 936 Otto I of Germany is crowned Holy Roman emperor AD 968 Toltecs in Mexico build their capital city, Tula	POLITICS
AD 14–37 Hippalus of Rome sails from the Red Sea to the Indus river c. AD 50 Greek scientist Ptolemy publishes *Guide to Geography* AD 399 Chinese monk Fu-Hsien begins journey to India, Sri Lanka and Java	AD 629–645 Chinese monk Hsüan-Tang goes to India to obtain Buddhist texts AD 698 Willibrord of Utrecht (Netherlands) discovers Heligoland	AD 787 First Viking raid on Britain c. AD 800 Vikings colonize Shetland Islands, Orkneys, Hebrides and Faeroes	c. AD 850 Arab merchant Soleiman sails to Melaka, now in Malaysia c. AD 860 Irish saint Brendan of Clonfert is said to have sailed to America and back	c. AD 982 Viking Erik the Red explores Greenland coast c. AD 986 Viking Bjarni Herjolfson lands in North America c. AD 1000 Viking Leif Eriksson sails to Vinland, North America	EXPLORATION
c. AD 100 Scientist Hero of Alexandria makes the first steam engine c. AD 150 The Chinese make the first paper AD 271 Chinese invent the first form of compass; it points south	c. AD 600 Earliest known windmills are built in Persia (now Iran) c. AD 650 Greek fire, which burns in water, is invented in Egypt c. AD 670 Hindu works on mathematics are translated into Arabic	c. AD 725 Native Americans build Casa Grande fort, Arizona AD 765 Japanese print first pictorial books AD 782 In England, Offa's Dyke (a barrier against the Welsh) is started	c. AD 850 Earliest reference in China to gunpowder	c. AD 940 Astronomers in China produce a star map c. AD 960 French priest Gerbert introduces Arabic numerals to Europe AD 984 Canal locks are invented in China	TECHNOLOGY
c. AD 164 The oldest Maya monuments are built AD 386 Ambrose, bishop of Milan, introduces hymn singing AD 478 First Shinto shrines erected in Japan	AD 650 Art of weaving develops in Byzantium AD 650 Neumes, early form of music notation, are developed AD 700 Rock-cut temples are begun at Ellora, India	c. AD 750 Wind organs begin to replace water (hydraulic) organs	c. AD 850 Building of Great Zimbabwe, now in modern Zimbabwe	AD 942 Arabs introduce trumpets and kettledrums into Europe AD 961 Emperor Li Yü of China establishes an academy of painting at Nanking	ARTS
AD 30 Probable date of the crucifixion of Jesus of Nazareth AD 45 St Paul begins his mission to the Gentiles AD 313 Roman Emperor Constantine decrees toleration of Christians	AD 700 Rock-cut temples are begun at Ellora, India AD 632 Abu Bakr, the first Caliph, begins to spread Islam through Arabia c. AD 680 St Wilfrid converts people of Sussex to Christianity	AD 730 Venerable Bede works on his *History of the English Church* AD 782 Alcuin of York goes to Aachen to teach in Charlemagne's school	AD 845 Persecution of Buddhists in China is rife AD 879 The oldest mosque in Cairo, Ibn Tulun, is built	AD 959 In England, St Dunstan becomes Archbishop of Canterbury AD 963 First monastery is established at Mount Athos, Greece AD 966 The Poles are converted to Christianity	RELIGION
AD 79 Vesuvius erupts, destroying Pompeii and Herculaneum c. AD 200 The Chinese invent porcelain c. AD 300 Maya of Central America invent a calendar		AD 750 Hops are first used to make beer in Bavaria, Germany AD 789 Charlemagne introduces his foot as a unit of measurement	AD 812 China issues the earliest paper money AD 851 The crossbow first comes into use in France AD 870 Calibrated candles are used in England to measure time	AD 942 Weaving of linen and wool is established in Flanders (Belgium) AD 962 Hospice is established at St Bernard's Pass, Switzerland AD 1000 The Danegeld (a tax to buy off Viking raiders) levied in England	DAILY LIFE

	1000–1050	1050–1100	1100–1150	1150–1200	1200–1250
POLITICS	1016 Canute II of Denmark becomes King of England 1040 Macbeth murders Duncan of Scotland and becomes king 1042 Saxon Edward the Confessor becomes King of England	1066 Harold II becomes King of England; he defeats an invasion from Norway, but is killed at the Battle of Hastings and William of Normandy becomes king 1076 Pope Gregory VII excommunicates German emperor Henry IV	1120 Heir of Henry I of England is drowned in the White Ship disaster 1135 Henry I dies; his nephew Stephen takes the throne; he is challenged by Henry's daughter Matilda and civil war breaks out	1154 Henry Plantagenet becomes King of England as Henry II 1155 Pope Adrian IV 'gives' Ireland to Henry II of England 1187 Muslim leader Saladin captures Jerusalem	1206 Tribal chief Temujin is proclaimed Genghis Khan, ruler of Mongolia 1215 King John of England is forced to agree to Magna Carta 1228 Emperor Frederick II of Germany leads the Sixth Crusade to Palestine
EXPLORATION	1004–13 Vikings try unsuccessfully to settle in Vinland, North America	1096–99 Members of the First Crusade travel to Turkey and Palestine	c. 1150 Rabbi Benjamin of Tudela, Spain, travels to Mesopotamia and Iran	c. 1154 Al-Idrisi's map muddles the Nile and the Niger rivers 1183–87 Ibn Jubayr, a Spanish Moor, travels to Mecca, Baghdad and Damascus	1245–47 Franciscan friar John of Pian del Carpine visits Mongolia
TECHNOLOGY	1035 Spinning wheels are in use in China c. 1050 Arabs introduce the decimal system into Spain c. 1050 Chinese begin printing books from movable type	1066 Halley's Comet is seen, and is feared in Europe to portend evil 1100 Italians find out how to distil brandy from wine	1129 Flying buttresses are first used in building churches throughout Europe 1142–1154 Books on algebra and optics are translated from Arabic	1150 The Chinese make the first rockets 1189 First European paper mill is built in Hérault, France	1202 Italian Leonardo Fibonacci introduces zero to Europe 1221 Chinese use bombs containing shrapnel
ARTS	c. 1050 Polyphonic (many voiced) singing is introduced in the Christian Church	1067 Monte Cassino Monastery, Italy, is rebuilt 1078 Work begins to build the Tower of London	1110 Earliest known miracle play is performed in England 1147 Geoffrey of Monmouth writes his *History of Britain*	1151 Golden age of Buddhist art in Burma (now Myanmar) 1174 Bell tower of Pisa, Italy, is built and at once begins to lean	c. 1220 Italian poets develop the form of the sonnet 1225 *Sumer is icumin in* is the earliest known English round song
RELIGION	1012 Persecution of heretics begins in Germany 1030 Norway is converted to Christianity 1042 Edward the Confessor begins to build Westminster Abbey	1084 Carthusian order of monks is founded 1098 First Cistercian monastery is founded at Cîteaux, France	1119 Military Order of Knights Templars is founded	1154 Adrian IV becomes the only English pope (Nicholas Breakspear) 1155 Carmelite Order of monks is founded in Palestine 1170 Archbishop Thomas à Becket is murdered in Canterbury Cathedral	1215 Spanish priest Dominic founds the Dominican Order 1229 The Inquisition in Toulouse, France, forbids laymen to read the Bible 1233 Pope Gregory IX asks the Dominicans to carry out the Inquisition
DAILY LIFE	c. 1009 Persians introduce seven-day week to China, which had 10-day weeks	1086 Domesday Book is first complete survey of England 1094 Gondolas come into use in Venice	1119 Military Order of Knights Templars is founded 1133 St Bartholomew's Hospital, London, founded 1133 St Bartholomew's Fair begins in London (closed 1855)	1151 Game of chess is introduced into England 1189 Silver florins are first minted at Florence, Italy	1230 Returning Crusaders bring disease of leprosy to Europe 1233 Coal mining at Newcastle, England, begins 1244 First competition for the Dunmow Flitch for married couples is held

	1250–1300	1300–1350	1350–1400	1400–1450	1450–1500
POLITICS	1272 Edward I becomes King of England 1274 Kublai Khan, emperor of China, tries to conquer Japan, but fails 1286 Margaret, the Maid of Norway, becomes Queen of Scotland, aged three; she dies in 1290	1301 Edward I of England creates his son Prince of Wales 1306 Robert Bruce is crowned King of Scotland 1337 Hundred Years' War between England and France begins	1363 Mongol ruler Tamerlane begins the conquest of Asia 1368 Ming dynasty in China ousts the Mongol Yuan dynasty 1375 Truce halts Hundred Years' War (until 1378)	1413 Henry V becomes King of England and claims large areas of France 1428–30 Joan of Arc leads the French armies against England 1438 Inca rule begins in Peru	1453 Hundred Years' War ends 1453 Turks capture Constantinople; end of the Byzantine empire 1455 Wars of the Roses break out in England; end with accession of Henry VII (Tudor) in 1485
EXPLORATION	1253–54 Guillaume of Rubruquis, a French friar, travels to Mongolia 1271–95 Venetian trader Marco Polo spends 24 years at the court of Kublai Khan in China	1325–49 Moroccan explorer Ibn Battuta visits Mecca, India and China	c. 1352 Ibn Battuta explores African empires of Songhai and Mali 1391 Venetian brothers Niccolo and Antonio Zeno set off to Iceland and the Faeroe Islands	1420 João Zarco of Portugal discovers Madeira	1488 Bartolomeu Dias rounds Cape of Good Hope, at the southern tip of Africa 1492 Christopher Columbus explores the Caribbean 1498 Vasco da Gama makes the first sea voyage to India
TECHNOLOGY	1267 English scientist Roger Bacon proposes the use of spectacles for poor eyesight c. 1290 Cable bridges are built over deep valleys in the Andes 1299 Florence, Italy, bans the use of Arabic numerals	c. 1310 First mechanical clocks are made in Europe 1327 Grand Canal in China, begun AD 70, is completed 1336 University of Paris insists that students study mathematics	c. 1380 Cast iron becomes generally used in Europe 1391 Geoffrey Chaucer of England writes on how to make and use an astrolabe c. 1400 Ethiopians start making a drink from wild coffee	1408 The Dutch use a windmill for pumping water c. 1440 Johannes Gutenberg of Germany begins printing with type	1454 Gutenberg produces the first printed Bible 1476 William Caxton prints the first book in English 1480 Italian artist Leonardo da Vinci designs a parachute
ARTS	1257 Persian poet Saadi writes *The Fruit Garden* 1285 French composer Adam de la Halle writes comic opera *Le Jeu de Robin et de Marion*	1325 Aztecs of Mexico build their capital city, Tenochtitlan 1341 Italian poet Petrarch is crowned as poet laureate in Rome 1348 Italian poet Giovanni Boccaccio begins writing *The Decameron* (to 1353)	1369 Geoffrey Chaucer writes *The Book of the Duchesse* 1375 First appearance of Robin Hood in English legends 1387–1400 Chaucer writes *The Canterbury Tales*	1414 German monk Thomas à Kempis writes *The Imitation of Christ* 1426 Netherlands becomes the centre of music in Europe 1444 Cosimo de Medici founds a library in Florence, Italy	1463 French poet François Villon sentenced to death for brawling, but escapes 1473 Sheet music printed from wood blocks is produced in Germany
RELIGION	1256 Order of Augustine Hermits, or Austin Friars, is founded 1268–71 Quarrels keep the papacy vacant until Gregory X is elected 1276 Popes Gregory X, Innocent V and Adrian V die in turn; John XXI succeeds them	1309 Pope Clement V moves his office from Rome to Avignon, France 1322 Pope John XXII bans the singing of counterpoint in churches 1349 Persecution of Jews breaks out in Germany	1377 Gregory XI returns the papacy to Rome 1378 Gregory dies: Great Schism begins when two popes are elected, one in Rome, one in France	1415 Bohemian reformer Jan Hus is burned at the stake for heresy 1417 End of the Great Schism: Martin V is elected pope in Rome	1453 St Sophia Basilica, Constantinople, becomes a mosque 1484 Papal bull is issued against witchcraft and sorcery 1492 Roderigo Borgia becomes pope as Alexander VI
DAILY LIFE	1278 In London, 278 Jews are hanged for clipping coins 1284 Legend of the Pied Piper of Hamelin begins; it may be founded on fact	1332 Bubonic plague is first heard of in India 1347–51 The Black Death (bubonic plague) kills 75 million Europeans 1348 Edward III of England founds the Order of the Garter	1360 France issues its first francs 1373 English merchants are made to pay tunnage and poundage taxes	1416 Dutch fishermen begin using drift nets 1433 Holy Roman emperors adopt the double eagle as an emblem c. 1450 Mocha in southern Arabia (now in Yemen) begins exporting coffee	467 Scots parliament bans football and golf 1485 Yeomen of the Guard formed in England 1489 The symbols '+' and '–' come into general use

	1500–1520	1520–1540	1540–1560	1560–1580	1580–1600
POLITICS	1509 Henry VIII becomes King of England, marries Catherine of Aragon 1517 Ottoman Turks conquer Egypt 1519 Charles I of Spain becomes Holy Roman emperor, uniting Austria and Spain	1531 Protestants in the Holy Roman empire form a defensive alliance 1533 Henry VIII divorces his wife and marries Anne Boleyn 1536 England and Wales are united by the Act of Union	1541 Ottoman Turks conquer Hungary 1553 Mary I, a Roman Catholic, becomes Queen of England 1558 Elizabeth I, a Protestant, succeeds Mary as Queen of England	1562 Huguenots (French Protestants) begin emigrating to England 1567 Mary, Queen of Scots, abdicates after her husband's murder 1571 Christian fleet defeats a Turkish fleet at Battle of Lepanto	1581–82 Livonian War: Poles take Livonia and cut Russian access to sea 1587 Mary, Queen of Scots, imprisoned in England, is executed 1588 The Spanish Armada, an attempt to invade England, fails
EXPLORATION	1502–08 Ludovico de Varthema is the first Christian to visit Mecca 1519–21 Hernando Cortés conquers Aztec empire in Mexico 1519–22 Sebastian del Cano is the first captain to sail round the world	1527–36 Cabeza de Vaca explores southern North America 1531–32 Francisco Pizarro explores Peru and conquers the Incas 1535 Jacques Cartier explores the St Lawrence River for France	1541 Spanish soldier Hernando de Soto discovers the Mississippi 1553–54 Richard Chancellor opens up trade between England and Moscow, which he reaches by way of the White Sea	1577–80 Francis Drake of England sails round the world	1584 Sir Walter Raleigh begins colonization of Virginia 1596–97 Dutch navigator Willem Barents dies trying to find the Northeast Passage
TECHNOLOGY	1502 Peter Henlein of Germany makes the first pocket watch 1507 The name America is used on maps for the first time 1520 First turkeys are imported to Europe from America	1523 Anthony Fitzherbert writes the first English manual on agriculture 1528 Michelangelo designs fortifications for the city of Florence, Italy 1530 Swiss physician Paracelsus writes book on medicine	1543 Nicolas Copernicus declares that the Earth travels around the Sun 1551 Leonard Digges invents the theodolite, used for surveying 1557 Julius Scaliger of Italy discovers the metal platinum	1569 Gerhardus Mercator invents his projection for maps 1570 The camera obscura, or pinhole camera, is invented 1573 Danish astronomer Tycho Brahe proves that stars are more distant than the Moon	1589 William Lee in England invents a knitting machine 1592 Galileo of Italy invents a primitive thermometer 1600 William Gilbert of England proposes that the Earth is a giant magnet
ARTS	1503 Leonardo da Vinci paints the *Mona Lisa*	1532 François Rabelais of France writes the comic book *Pantagruel* 1538 The first five-part madrigals are published	1543 Benvenuto Cellini makes golden salt cellars for the King of France 1545 First ever book fair is held in Leipzig, Germany 1548 Building of the Pitti Palace, Florence, begins	1570 Andrea Palladio writes influential work on architecture 1572 Luis de Camöens of Portugal writes his epic poem *Os Lusíados* 1576 First theatre in England opens in London	1587 Christopher Marlowe of England writes play *Tamburlaine the Great* 1590–94 William Shakespeare of England begins writing plays
RELIGION	1507 Church begins selling indulgences to pay for St Peter's Basilica, Rome 1517 Martin Luther begins the Reformation in Europe 1519 Ulrich Zwingli reforms the Church in Switzerland	1526 Sweden converts to Protestantism 1534 English Church breaks from Rome, with the monarch as its head 1534 Ignatius Loyola of Spain founds the Jesuit order	1545 Council of Trent begins the Counter Reformation 1549 Jesuit missions are sent to Brazil and Japan 1555 In England, persecution of Protestants begins; many are burned	1560 Scotland breaks with the Roman Catholic Church 1570 Pope Pius V excommunicates Queen Elizabeth of England 1572 Massacre of St Bartholomew: French Protestants are killed	1590–92 Three popes die in a period of three months 1593 Attendance in church on Sundays is made compulsory in England
DAILY LIFE	1504 First shillings are minted in England 1517 The first coffee is imported into Europe 1519 Hernando Cortés reintroduces horses to North America	1525 Hops are introduced to England from France 1528 Severe outbreak of bubonic plague hits England 1531 Halley's Comet returns, causing great alarm	1547 Fire destroys Moscow 1550 People begin playing billiards in Italy 1555 Tobacco is imported to Spain from America	1560 Madrid becomes the capital of Spain 1565 The first potatoes arrive in Spain from America 1568 Bottled beer is first produced in London	1582 Most Roman Catholic countries adopt new Gregorian calendar 1596 Tomatoes are introduced into Europe from America 1596 Sir John Harington of England invents the first water closet (lavatory)

	1600–1620	1620–1640	1640–1660	1660–1680	1680–1700
POLITICS	1603 James VI of Scotland becomes King of England as James I, uniting crowns 1614 French Estates General (parliament) suspended until 1789 1618–48 Thirty Years' War engulfs most of Europe	1624 Cardinal Richelieu becomes all-powerful in France 1629 Charles I of England quarrels with Parliament, rules without it until 1640 1637 Manchu rulers of China turn Korea into a vassal state	1642 Civil War breaks out in England between King Charles I and Parliament 1649 Charles I is beheaded and England becomes a republic under Cromwell 1660 England's monarchy is restored under Charles II	1662 England sells its last French possession, Dunkirk, to France 1664 England seizes New Netherland (now New York) from the Dutch 1665–74 England is at war with the Dutch Republic	1686 France annexes the island of Madagascar 1688–89 Peaceful revolution in England drives the Catholic James II off the throne; Protestants William III and Mary II are offered the throne
EXPLORATION	1605 Samuel de Champlain of France explores Nova Scotia coast 1615 Luis Vaez de Torres discovers strait between Australia and New Guinea 1620 Pilgrim Fathers sail to America in *Mayflower* and found Plymouth Colony	1613 Pedro Paez of Spain discovers source of the Blue Nile in Ethiopia 1627 Thomas Herbert of England explores Persia (now Iran) 1637–39 Pedro Teixeira of Portugal explores the river Amazon	1642 Abel Tasman of the Netherlands discovers New Zealand and Tasmania 1650 Franciscan missionaries explore the upper river Amazon 1651 Dutch pioneers begin to settle at the Cape of Good Hope	1673 Jacques Marquette and Louis Joliet of France explore the Mississippi 1679 Louis de Hennepin and René Cavalier of France reach the Niagara Falls	1686 William Dampier of England explores northern coast of Australia 1689 Louis de Lahontain of France reaches the Great Salt Lake in Utah
TECHNOLOGY	1608 Hans Lippershey of the Netherlands invents the microscope 1610 Using a telescope, Galileo of Italy discovers Jupiter's moons 1613 Galileo agrees with the theory that the Earth goes round the Sun	1622 William Oughtred, English mathematician, invents the slide-rule 1624 Flemish chemist Jan van Helmont invents the word 'gas' 1637 Pierre Fermat and René Descartes of France develop analytic geometry	1642 Blaise Pascal of France designs an adding machine 1642 Evangelista Torricelli of Italy invents the barometer 1650 Otto von Guericke of Germany invents an air pump	1665 Isaac Newton of England develops calculus 1675 Greenwich Royal Observatory is founded in England 1679 Denis Papin of France invents the pressure cooker	1682 Edmund Halley of England observes comet now named after him 1684 Robert Hooke of England invents the heliograph 1698 Thomas Savery of England invents the first steam pump
ARTS	1605 Miguel de Cervantes of Spain writes the first part of *Don Quixote* 1607 Composer Claudio Monteverdi is working in Mantua, Italy 1611 Royal mosque at Isfahan, Persia (Iran) is built	1623 The First Folio prints most of Shakespeare's plays 1624 Frans Hals of the Netherlands paints *The Laughing Cavalier* 1633 John Milton of England writes poems *L'Allegro* and *Il Penseroso*	1642 Rembrandt van Rijn of the Netherlands paints *The Night Watch* 1652 Vienna opens its first opera house 1660 Samuel Pepys, English civil servant, begins his diary	1662 Work begins on Louis XIV's Palace of Versailles in France 1667 The colonnaded square of St Peter's, Rome, is completed 1677 John Dryden is England's leading poet	1688 Aphra Behn is the first professional woman writer in English 1692 Henry Purcell of England composes opera *The Fairy Queen*
RELIGION	1604 James I of England clamps down on Roman Catholics and Puritans 1611 *The Authorized Version of the Bible* is published in Britain 1616 Protestants in Bohemia are oppressed	1633 The Catholic Church forces Galileo to say Sun travels around Earth 1634 First Oberammergau Passion Play is put on as thanks for avoiding the plague 1637 Japan bans Christian missionaries	1645 Presbyterianism is made England's official religion 1648 George Fox founds the Society of Friends (Quakers) 1650 Archbishop James Ussher of Ireland says the Creation was in 4004 BC	1662 England forbids Nonconformist priests to preach 1678–84 John Bunyan of England writes *The Pilgrim's Progress*	1684 Increase Mather becomes a leading preacher in Massachusetts 1692 After witch trials in Salem, Massachusetts, 19 people are hanged 1699 Roman Catholic priests face life in jail in England
DAILY LIFE	1607 Table forks come into use in England and France 1610 The first China tea is imported into Europe by the Dutch 1619 First black slaves are used in Virginia	1625 England has its first fire engines and hackney coaches 1626 The Dutch buy Manhattan Island from Native Americans for $24 1630 The card game cribbage is invented	1650 England has its first coffee house (in Oxford) and starts drinking tea 1654 Paris has its first letter-boxes 1658 Sweden's state bank issues the first banknotes in Europe	1665 Plague ravages London, killing 68,596 people 1666 Fire destroys most of London and ends the plague there 1677 Ice cream becomes popular in Paris	1683 Wild boars become extinct in Britain 1692 Lloyd's Coffee House, London, becomes marine insurance office 1697 Fire destroys most of the Palace of Whitehall, London

	1700–1720	1720–1740	1740–1760	1760–1780	1780–1800
POLITICS	1702 Anne, daughter of James II, succeeds to the English throne 1707 England and Scotland are united as Great Britain 1715 Jacobite (Stuart) rebellion in Britain against new king, George I, fails	1721 Robert Walpole is Britain's first prime minister (to 1742) 1727–28 War between Britain and Spain over Gibraltar	1745–46 Second Jacobite rebellion, led by Bonnie Prince Charlie, fails 1756 Seven Years' War begins in Europe 1760 George III becomes British king (to 1820)	1763 Seven Years' War ends: Britain gains French lands in India and America 1775–83 American War of Independence against Britain 1776 The 13 American Colonies declare independence from Britain	1789 The French Revolution begins 1789 George Washington is elected US president 1800 Napoleon Bonaparte assumes power in France
EXPLORATION	1708 Alexander Selkirk, the original 'Robinson Crusoe', is rescued from an island off the coast of Chile 1719 Bernard de la Harpe of France explores North American rivers	1722 Jacob Roggeveen of the Netherlands discovers Easter Island and Samoa 1736 Anders Celsius leads French expedition to Lapland 1740 George Anson of Britain begins round-the-world voyage (to 1744)	1741 Vitus Bering explores Alaskan coast for Russia 1748 American Pioneers cross the Cumberland Gap in the Appalachian Mountains	1766 Louis de Bougainville of France discovers Tahiti and New Guinea 1768–71 James Cook of Britain makes his first round-the-world voyage	1790 George Vancouver (British) explores north-west coast of America 1793 Alexander Mackenzie (British) explores northwest Canada 1795 In Africa, Scots explorer Mungo Park travels along river Niger
TECHNOLOGY	1707 Johann Böttger of Germany discovers how to make hard porcelain 1709 Abraham Darby of England begins using coke to smelt iron 1714 Gabriel Fahrenheit of Germany makes a mercury thermometer	1733 John Kay of Britain invents the flying shuttle 1735 John Harrison of Britain builds first accurate chronometer 1737 Georg Brandt of Sweden discovers cobalt	1742 Anders Celsius of Sweden invents the centigrade thermometer 1751 Carl Linnaeus of Sweden publishes his landmark book on botany 1752 American Benjamin Franklin invents the lightning conductor	1769 James Watt of Scotland invents the steam condenser 1769 Nicolas Cugnot of France builds first steam road carriage 1773 First cast-iron bridge built at Coalbrookdale, England	1783 Montgolfier brothers of France make first hot-air balloon ascent 1792 Claude Chappe of France invents the mechanical semaphore 1793 Eli Whitney of the United States invents the cotton gin
ARTS	1709 Bartolommeo Cristofori of Italy invents the piano 1710 Building of St Paul's Cathedral in London is completed 1719 Daniel Defoe writes first part of *Robinson Crusoe*	1721 J. S. Bach of Germany composes the *Brandenburg Concertos* 1735 Imperial ballet school in St Petersburg, Russia, opens 1737 England begins censorship of plays	1741 German George Frederick Handel composes *Messiah* in England 1747 Samuel Johnson of Britain begins work on his dictionary 1751–72 French scholars compile the *Encyclopédie*	1768 The Royal Academy of Arts is founded in London 1773 Johann von Goethe of Germany writes first version of *Faust* 1778 In Milan, Italy, La Scala Opera House opens	1786 In Scotland, Robert Burns publishes his first book of poems 1790 In Austria, Mozart composes the opera *Cosé Fan Tutte* 1793 Building of the Capitol in Washington, DC, begins
RELIGION	1716 Chinese emperor bans the teaching of Christianity 1719 Dunkards, German Baptist Brethren, settle in Pennsylvania	1730 John and Charles Wesley establish the Methodist movement 1734 The Koran is translated into English 1737 Alexander Cruden of Britain compiles his *Concordance to the Bible*	1759 Jesuits are expelled from Portugal and its colonies	1766 Catherine the Great of Russia grants her people freedom of worship 1767 Jesuits are expelled from Spain 1776 Mystic Ann Lee forms the first Shaker colony in America	1781 Religious tolerance is proclaimed in Austria 1785 State of Virginia passes a statute of religious freedom 1790 Jews in France are granted civil liberties
DAILY LIFE	1711 South Sea Company takes over £9 million of Britain's National Debt 1712 The last execution of a witch in England takes place 1720 South Sea Company crashes; thousands of people are ruined	1722 Thomas Guy, British bookseller, helps found Guy's Hospital, London 1725 New York City gets its first newspaper, the *New York Gazette* 1727 Brazil sets up its first coffee plantation	1744 First official cricket match in Britain (Kent versus All England) 1752 Britain adopts the Gregorian calendar, dropping 11 days 1755 Earthquake kills 30,000 people in Lisbon	1768 Publication of the *Encyclopaedia Britannica* in weekly parts begins 1770 Paris has its first public restaurant 1779 First running of the Derby horse race at Epsom, England	1787 United States adopts the Stars and Stripes flag 1792 Denmark abolishes the slave trade 1792 Scot William Murdoch is first person to light his home with gas

	1800–1820	1820–1840	1840–1860	1860–1880	1880–1900
POLITICS	1801 Act of Union unites Great Britain and Ireland 1803 USA buys Louisiana from France 1804 Napoleon becomes Emperor of France and is finally defeated in 1815	1821 Simón Bolívar liberates Venezuela from Spain 1822 Brazil becomes independent of Portugal 1837 Queen Victoria comes to the British throne, aged 18	1845 The United States annexes Texas 1848 Year of revolts in Austria, France, Germany, Italy and Hungary 1853–56 The Crimean War: Britain, France and Turkey against Russia	1861–65 American Civil War: 11 states secede from the Union 1865 President Abraham Lincoln is assassinated; Civil War ends 1867 The United States buys Alaska from Russia for $7,200,000	1881 President James Garfield of the US is assassinated 1883 The scramble for European colonies in Africa starts 1899 The Boer War in South Africa starts (to 1902)
EXPLORATION	1803–06 Lewis and Clark expedition crosses North America from east to west 1812 William Moorcroft (British) explores Tibet 1822–25 Denham Dixon and other Britons cross the Sahara	1829 Charles Sturt finds the Murray River in Australia 1831 James Clark Ross of Britain reaches the North Magnetic Pole 1840–41 Edward Eyre crosses the Nullarbor Plain of Australia	1852–56 David Livingstone (British) explores the Zambesi river 1854 Richard Burton (British) explores East Africa, including Ethiopia 1858 John Speke and Richard Burton discover Lake Tanganyika	1871 Henry Stanley is sent to look for Livingstone and finds him at Ujiji 1872 *HMS Challenger* begins a world survey of the oceans 1879 Nils Nordenskiöld of Sweden sails through the Northeast Passage	1882 Adolphus Greely (US) explores Greenland and the Arctic 1888–92 Emin Pasha of Germany explores central Africa 1893 Fritjof Nansen of Norway tries to reach the North Pole, but fails
TECHNOLOGY	1814 George Stephenson (British) builds first successful steam locomotive 1815 Humphry Davy (British) invents the miners' safety lamp 1816 Réné Laennec of France invents the stethoscope	1825 First passenger railway opens in northern England 1827 Joseph Niépce of France takes the world's first photograph 1834 Cyrus McCormick of the United States invents a reaping machine	1844 Artist Samuel Morse of the US demonstrates the use of the Morse Code 1847 James Simpson of Britain uses chloroform as an anaesthetic 1860 Christopher Scholes of the US invents a practical typewriter	1873 Joseph Glidden of the US invents barbed wire 1876 Alexander Graham Bell (British/American) invents the telephone 1879 Electric lamp bulbs are invented	1885 Karl Benz of Germany builds the first motor-car 1895 Guglielmo Marconi of Italy invents wireless telegraphy 1900 Graf von Zeppelin (Germany) invents the rigid airship
ARTS	1801 Joseph Haydn of Austria composes oratorio *The Seasons* 1813 Franz Schubert of Austria writes his first symphony 1814 Walter Scott writes his first novel, *Waverley*	1822 Royal Academy of Music is founded in London 1835 Hans Christian Andersen publishes his first fairy tales in Denmark	1843 Richard Wagner of Germany writes opera *The Flying Dutchman* 1846 Adolphe Sax of Belgium invents the saxophone 1860 George Eliot (Mary Anne Evans) of Britain writes *The Mill on the Floss*	1868 Louisa M. Alcott writes *Little Women* 1874 Impressionist movement in painting starts in Paris 1875 Gilbert and Sullivan produce their first light opera, *Trial by Jury*	1883 Royal College of Music in London founded 1884 Mark Twain writes *Huckleberry Finn* 1895 Promenade Concerts begin in London
RELIGION	1804 British and Foreign Bible Society is formed in London 1808 Napoleon abolishes the Inquisition in Italy and Spain 1812 Restrictions on Nonconformists in England are relaxed	1826 Jesuits are allowed to return to France 1827 John Nelson Darby founds the Plymouth Brethren 1830 Joseph Smith founds the Church of Latter-Day Saints (Mormons)	1846 Mormons in the US begin migrating to the Great Salt Lake, Utah 1854 Pope Pius IX proclaims Immaculate Conception as dogma	1865 William Booth founds the Salvation Army in Britain 1871 Charles Russell founds the Jehovah's Witnesses 1879 Mary Baker Eddy founds the Christian Science Church	1890 James Frazer of Britain writes *The Golden Bough: A Study in Magic and Religion* 1896 Theodor Herzl of Austria proposes a Jewish state in Palestine
DAILY LIFE	1807 Britain ends the slave trade 1815 Tambora Volcano in Indonesia erupts: 50,000 people are killed 1819 Freedom of the press is guaranteed in France	1829 First Oxford and Cambridge Boat Race on river Thames in London 1834 Fire destroys Britain's Houses of Parliament 1840 Penny Postage and adhesive stamps are introduced in Britain	1844 First cooperative society is formed in Rochdale, England 1851 The Great Exhibition is held in Hyde Park, London 1855 Britain abolishes stamp duty on newspapers	1864 Louis Pasteur of France invents pasteurization 1868 The first Trades Union Congress meets in Britain 1874 Walter Wingfield invents Sphairistiké – now called lawn tennis	1887 Victoria celebrates her Golden Jubilee as Britain's queen 1900 The Labour Party is founded in Britain

	1900–1910	1910–1920	1920–1930	1930–1940	1940–1950
POLITICS	1901 Edward VII succeeds Victoria as British monarch 1902 The Boer War ends 1904–05 Russo-Japanese War; Japan wins	1911 China becomes a republic after 2,000 years under emperors 1914–18 World War I: nearly 10 million soldiers die 1917 October Revolution in Russia: Lenin and the Bolsheviks seize power	1922 Benito Mussolini forms a Fascist government in Italy 1924 Joseph Stalin becomes ruler of the Soviet Union 1924 Britain has its first Labour government	1933 The Nazi leader Adolf Hitler becomes dictator of Germany 1936–39 Spanish Civil War 1939 World War II begins as Germany and the Soviet Union invade Poland	1941 The US enters World War II, following Japan's attack on Pearl Harbor 1945 World War II ends with German and Japanese surrender 1945–51 Labour returns to power in Britain; many industries nationalized
EXPLORATION	1901–03 Erich von Drygalski of Germany explores Antarctica 1907–09 Ernest Shackleton of Britain nearly reaches the South Pole 1909 Robert Peary of the US reaches the North Pole	1911 Roald Amundsen of Norway leads first party to reach the South Pole 1912 Briton Robert Falcon Scott also reaches the South Pole, but dies on the way back 1919 Alcock and Brown make first non-stop flight across the Atlantic	1926 Richard Byrd and Floyd Bennett of the US fly over the North Pole 1926 Umberto Nobile of Norway makes airship flight over North Pole 1929 Richard Byrd flies over the South Pole	1931 First submarine ventures under the Arctic Ocean ice 1932 Auguste Piccard climbs to an altitude of 28 km in a stratospheric balloon	1946–47 Operation Highjump maps coast of Antarctica from the air 1947 Thor Heyerdahl of Norway sails the raft Kon Tiki across the Pacific from Peru to the Tuamoto Islands
TECHNOLOGY	1903 In the US, the Wright Brothers make the first powered flights 1907 Louis Lumière of France develops colour photography 1909 Louis Blériot of France flies across the English Channel	1917 Ernest Rutherford of Britain splits the atom 1919 First mass spectrograph machine is built 1920 First public broadcasting station in Britain opens	1922 Insulin is first given to diabetics 1925 John Logie Baird invents a primitive form of television 1928 Alexander Fleming accidentally discovers penicillin	1935 Radar is developed for use in detecting aircraft 1937 Frank Whittle builds the first jet engine 1940 Howard Florey develops penicillin as a working antibiotic	1942 Magnetic recording tape is invented 1946 ENIAC, first fully electronic digital computer, is built 1948 Peter Goldmar invents the long-playing record
ARTS	1901 Ragtime music becomes popular in America 1905 First regular cinema opens in Pittsburgh, Pennsylvania 1909 Sergei Diaghilev's Ballets Russes starts performing in Paris	1914 Charlie Chaplin creates his film character in *The Tramp* 1916 Artists and poets start the Dadaist movement in Switzerland 1917 The Original Dixieland Jazz Band is formed in New York	1926 A. A. Milne writes *Winnie the Pooh* 1927 Theremin, the first electronic musical instrument, is invented	1935 American George Gershwin writes *Porgy and Bess* 1937 First full-length cartoon film, *Snow White and the Seven Dwarfs* 1938 Radio play *War of the Worlds* causes panic in the United States	1947 *The Diary of Anne Frank* is published 1949 George Orwell writes the satire *Nineteen Eighty-Four* 1950 United Nations building in New York City is completed
RELIGION	1904 Germany partly lifts its ban on Jesuits 1909 First Jewish kibbutz is founded in Palestine	1912 Church of Scotland issues a revised prayer book 1917 Balfour Declaration: Britain backs homeland for Jews in Palestine 1920 Joan of Arc is canonized (declared to be a saint)	1924 Mahatma Gandhi fasts in protest at religious feuding in India 1929 Presbyterian Churches in Scotland unite	1932 Methodist Churches in Britain reunite (split since 1797) 1933 All Protestant Churches in Germany unite 1937 Protestant parson Martin Niemöller is interned by Hitler	1946 Pope Pius XII creates 32 new cardinals 1947 The Dead Sea Scrolls are discovered in caves at Qumran, Jordan 1948 The World Council of Churches is established
DAILY LIFE	1902 Eruption of Mount Pelée in Martinique kills 38,000 people 1903 The first teddy bears are made in Germany 1906 An earthquake destroys most of San Francisco; 3,000 people die	1912 Liner *Titanic* sinks on her maiden voyage; more than 1,500 people drowned 1918 British women over the age of 30 gain the vote 1918 First airmail service is established in the US	1920 Women in the US gain the right to vote 1929 Wall Street crash: biggest world economic crisis begins 1930 The Youth Hostels Association is founded	1932–34 Pontine Marshes in Italy are drained 1934 Dionne Quintuplets are born in Canada 1936 King Edward VIII abdicates to marry divorcee Wallis Simpson	1941–49 Clothes rationing in force in Britain 1945 Bebop form of jazz comes into fashion 1947 First microwave ovens go on sale

	1950–1960	1960–1970	1970–1980	1980–1990	1990–2000s
POLITICS	1956 Egypt's ruler Gamel Nasser seizes Suez Canal 1960 Seventeen African colonies gain independence from European powers	1961 Communists build the Berlin Wall 1963 US President John F. Kennedy is assassinated 1965–73 The Vietnam War 1967 Six-Day War between Israel and Arab nations	1974 US President Nixon resigns over Watergate scandal 1979 Margaret Thatcher becomes Britain's first woman prime minister 1980 Marshal Tito, leader of Yugoslavia since 1953, dies	1982 Argentina's invasion of the Falkland Islands fails 1989 Communist rule ends in East Germany; Berlin Wall is demolished	1991 Collapse of the Soviet Union: republics become independent 1991 Breakup of Yugoslavia: civil war leads to NATO involvement 2001 Terrorist attacks on New York and Washingyon DC, begin the 'War on Terror'.
EXPLORATION	1957–58 Vivien Fuchs of Britain makes first crossing of Antarctica 1958 US nuclear submarine *Nautilus* travels under the North Polar ice 1960 The Bathyscaphe *Trieste* descends 10,910 m into the Mariana Trench	1961 Yuri Gagarin of the Soviet Union makes the first manned space flight 1968 US space craft *Apollo 8* first to orbit the Moon 1969 Neil Armstrong of the US is the first person to walk on the Moon	1971 Space probes orbit Mars and send back photographs 1979–89 Space probe *Voyager 2* flies past and photographs Jupiter, Saturn, Uranus and Neptune	1981 The first space shuttle, *Columbia*, orbits the Earth 1982 Soviet space probes land on Venus and send back colour pictures 1984 Two US astronauts fly in space untethered to their spacecraft	1993 Two Britons complete the first foot crossing of Antarctica 1997 US robot, controlled from Earth, explores surface of Mars 2000 *Global Surveyor* finds evidence of water on Mars
TECHNOLOGY	1951 Heart-lung machine is invented 1956 Albert Sabin invents oral vaccine against polio 1957 Soviet Union launches the first Earth satellites, *Sputnik 1* and *Sputnik 2*	1967 Christiaan Barnard from South Africa performs first human heart transplant 1963 Theory of continental drift is proved by two British geophysicists 1969 First flight of the supersonic airliner Concorde	1972 *Apollo 17* crew make last manned visit to the Moon 1978 Louise Brown, the first 'test-tube baby', is born 1980 Smallpox is eradicated worldwide	1984 The first Apple Macintosh microcomputer goes on sale 1986 The Dutch complete their flood protection scheme after 33 years 1988 Undersea tunnel linking Honshu and Hokkaido, Japan, opens	1993 Astronauts repair the Hubble Space Telescope (launched 1990) 1994 Channel Tunnel is completed, linking Britain and France 2001 Mapping of human genetic code nears completion
ARTS	1950s Rock and Roll develops 1951 John Osborne's *Look Back in Anger* is staged in London 1960 New buildings completed in Brasilia, capital of Brazil	1965 Op Art, based on optical illusions, becomes popular 1966 New Metropolitan Opera House opens in New York City 1968 Four Soviet writers are jailed for 'dissidence'	1971 *Fiddler on the Roof* closes after record New York run of 3,242 performances 1980 Former Beatle John Lennon is murdered in New York	1983 Symphony written by Mozart aged nine is discovered 1985 Live Aid rock concert raises $60 million for African famine relief 1986 Wole Soyinka is the first black African to win the Nobel Prize for Literature	1993 Missing treasure from Troy found in 1873 is rediscovered in Russia 2001 *Harry Potter* and *Lord of the Rings* are worldwide favourites in books and films
RELIGION	1958 John XXIII becomes pope 1958 Supreme Religious Centre for World Jewry is opened in Jerusalem 1960 Swedish Lutheran Church admits women ministers	1968 In Northern Ireland, Catholics and Protestants clash over civil rights 1969 Pope Paul VI removes 200 saints from the liturgical calendar 1970 Jewish and Roman Catholic leaders confer in Rome	1978 Deaths of Pope Paul VI and his successor Pope John Paul I; succeeded by Pope John II, a Pole and fist non-Italian pope for 456 years	1981 John Paul II becomes the first pope to visit Britain 1986 Desmond Tutu becomes the first black archbishop of Cape Town 1990 First Anglican women priests are ordained in Northern Ireland	1992 Ten women become Anglican priests in Australia 1996–2001 Strict Islamic law is imposed in Afghanistan before removal of Taliban regime 2005 Death of Pope John Paul II. Succeeded by Pope Benedict XVI
DAILY LIFE	1953 Mount Everest is climbed for the first time 1954 Roger Bannister from Britain runs the mile in under four minutes 1958 First life peerages are created in Britain	1966 Miniskirts come into fashion 1967 Francis Chichester completes single-handed voyage around the world 1970 Storms and floods kill 500,000 people in East Pakistan (Bangladesh)	1976 Earthquakes shake China, Guatemala, Indonesia, Italy, the Philippines and Turkey: 780,000 people die 1978–79 Union troubles close London's *The Times* newspaper for nearly a year	1982 Disease kills 20 million elm trees in Britain 1987 World stock market crash on 'Black Monday' 1989 World ban on ivory trading is imposed	1997 Hong Kong is returned to China 2002 Euro currency is introduced in European Union 2005 Hurricane Katrina hits US, killing more than 1,800 people

Glossary

AD (ANNO DOMINI) Indicates dates after the birth of Christ. It means 'in the year of our Lord'.

AIRCRAFT CARRIER A large warship with an open, flat-topped deck designed so that planes can take off and land on it.

AGRICULTURAL REVOLUTION The changing of farming methods during the 18th and 19th centuries which saw a large increase in the amount of food produced.

ANGLO-SAXON A person or object that originally came from what is today western Germany and settled in Britain during the fifth century AD.

ASSASSINATION The killing of a person for political reasons.

ASTROLABE A device used to measure the angle of stars above the horizon. From this, a person can work out his or her position.

ASTRONOMER A person who studies stars.

BC (BEFORE CHRIST) Indicates dates before the birth of Christ.

BOLSHEVIKS A group of Russian Communists who seized power in a revolution in 1917 under the leadership of Lenin.

BLACK DEATH Another name for the bubonic plague.

BLITZ Short for 'blitzkrieg' which is German for 'lightning war', it describes the German aerial bombardment of British cities in 1940.

BOERS Descendants of Dutch farmers who settled in South Africa.

CELT A person who lived in Britain, Gaul (France) and Spain before the arrival of the Romans.

CHIVALRY The code that described how a knight should behave. It demanded courage, fighting skill, loyalty, generosity and courtesy, especially towards women.

CHOLERA A disease which affects the intestines, causing cramps, vomiting and diarrhoea. It is caused by eating and drinking infected food and water and it can be fatal if untreated.

CIVIL WAR A war that is fought between two groups of people who live in the same country.

COAT OF ARMS A system of symbols used to show to which family a noble man or woman belonged.

COLD WAR The period during the last half of the 20th century when there was a stand-off between western countries and Communist countries.

COMMONWEALTH The countries that used to make up the British empire that have now joined together to form an economic organization.

CROP ROTATION Alternating which crops grow in fields to keep the soil rich and fertile.

CRUSADES A series of campaigns by Christian armies to capture and control the Holy Land in the Middle East.

DEPRESSION An economic downturn when businesses become bankrupt and many people become unemployed.

DYNASTY A long line of rulers who inherit a throne from their ancestors.

EMIGRANT A person who leaves one country to go to live in another.

ENLIGHTENMENT A period during the 17th and 18th centuries that saw great advances in science, the arts and philosophy.

EUROPEAN UNION The economic organization formed by countries throughout Europe. Many of these countries replaced their old currencies with a single currency – the euro.

EVACUATE To withdraw or pull out of a place.

EXCOMMUNICATE To exclude someone from the Roman Catholic Church.

FAMINE A period with very little food and when a great many people starve and die.

FEUDALISM The system under which medieval society was structured, with kings and lords granting land in return for military service or rent.

FORUM The central part of a Roman town which acted as its marketplace and the centre for business.

GARRISON A group of soldiers who guard a military base.

GAUL A part of Europe that is now modern-day France.

GENES The biological information stored within our cells that dictates our looks and behaviour.

GRAVE GOODS Items placed inside a tomb that were intended for the dead person to use in the afterlife.

GUERILLA A fighter who uses sabotage and surprise tactics to fight a more powerful enemy.

HENGE A circular structure that was built out of standing stones or wooden posts.

ICE AGE A period in Earth's history when temperatures were cooler and large ice sheets covered much of Europe, Asia and North America.

INDEPENDENCE Freedom of a country from the rule of another country, to govern itself.

INDUSTRIAL REVOLUTION A period during the 18th and 19th centuries when industry expanded greatly and people moved in large numbers to live and work in towns.

MACHINE GUN A type of gun that can fire a large number of bullets with a single squeeze of the trigger.

MARTYR A person who is killed because of his or her religious beliefs.

MIDDLE AGES A historical period lasting from the fall of the Roman empire in 476 AD to 1453 and the start of the Renaissance.

MIDDLE EAST The region of the world that lies between Africa and Asia.

MILITANT Someone who holds extreme views and promotes them vigorously.

MISSIONARY A person who teaches a religion in a different area or country.

MOAT A large lake surrounding a castle.

MONASTERY A place where monks live and worship.

MOURNING To grieve for the death of someone.

MOVABLE TYPE Individual letters carved from wood or metal which can be laid out to spell words and used for printing leaflets or books.

NORMANS People who came from Normandy in what is modern France.

NEANDERTHALS A primitive form of human that evolved between 200,000 and 100,000 years ago.

OBSOLETE Out of date.

OTTOMAN EMPIRE The Turkish empire which lasted from the 13th century until 1918 and the end of World War I.

PILGRIMS People who travel to sacred places. Also, a term used to describe a group of settlers who moved from Britain to North America in 1620.

PLANTAGENET The royal family of England from Henry II (1154) until Richard III (died 1485).

RECYCLING To reuse a product or a material in order to save on resources and energy.

REFORMATION A movement to reform the Catholic Church during the 16th century which led to the creation of the Protestant Church.

REGENT A person who governs a country while the king or queen is away, sick or too young to govern.

RENAISSANCE Literally 'rebirth'. A period during the 15th and 16th centuries which saw an outburst of creative ideas in art, music and architecture.

REPEAL To cancel a law or decision.

SACRIFICE To kill an animal or a human and offer it to a leader or god.

SATELLITE An object which orbits another, larger object. Natural satellites include the Moon. Artificial satellites are used to predict the weather and to study other planets.

SEED DRILL A machine invented in 1701 that automated the process of sowing seeds.

SELECTIVE BREEDING Choosing the best animals to breed and have young in order to gradually improve the quality and quantity of meat, milk or wool.

SHOGUNS Military leaders in Japan who acted as the country's rulers.

SOUP KITCHEN A place where free food is given to the poor.

STOCKADE A protective fence.

STUART The royal family of Scotland from 1371 to 1714, that also ruled England from 1603 to 1714.

SUFFRAGE The right to cast a vote in an election.

SUFFRAGETTES Women who campaigned to get the vote at the start of the 20th century.

TAPESTRY A large piece of cloth with a woven picture showing a scene or event.

TARTAN A type of checked, woven material. In Scotland, the checked pattern of the tartan told people to which family you belonged.

TRADE UNION An organization that campaigns to improve workers' rights and conditions.

TRANSPORTATION Sending criminals overseas to carry out their sentences.

TRILITHON A stone structure that is made up of two standing stones with a third stone placed across them.

TUDOR The royal family of England from Henry VII (1485) to the death of Elizabeth I (1603).

VIKING A person who came from Scandinavia (Denmark, Norway and Sweden) between the 8th and 11th centuries.

WELFARE STATE A system where the government gives money and support to the poor, elderly and sick.

WEBSITES

http://www.bbc.co.uk/history

http://www.channel4.com/history

http://www.royal.gov.uk

http://www.spartacus.schoolnet.co.uk/REVhistory.htm

http://www.historyonthenet.com

http://www.activehistory.co.uk

http://www.nationalarchives.gov.uk/museum

http://www.thehistorychannel.co.uk/site/home

http://americanhistory.si.edu/kids/index.cfm

http://www.history.com

http://www.worldalmanacforkids.com/explore/timeline.html

* Parragon does not accept responsibility for the content of any websites mentioned in this publication. If you have any queries about their content, please refer to the organization that produced the website. If you are under 18, the websites should only be used with the involvement of a parent or guardian.

Important
Battles and Wars

Marathon (490 BC) The armies of Athens crushed an attempt by Persian forces to conquer Greece

Salamis (480 BC) Greek ships defeated a much larger Persian fleet and thwarted an invasion

Syracuse (414–413 BC) During a long war between the city states of Athens and Sparta the Athenians besieged Syracuse but lost power after a heavy defeat

Gaugamela (331 BC) Alexander the Great of Macedonia defeated the Persians and conquered the Persian Empire

Metaurus (207 BC) A Roman army defeated a Carthaginian attempt to invade Italy

Actium (30 BC) A Roman fleet destroyed the Egyptian fleet of Mark Antony and Cleopatra, ending Egypt's threat to Rome

Teutoburg Forest (AD 9) German tribes led by Arminius ambushed and destroyed three Roman legions

Châlons (451) Roman legions and their Visigoth allies defeated the Huns, led by Attila the Hun

Poitiers (732) The Franks led by Charles Martel defeated a Muslim attempt to conquer western Europe

Hastings (1066) Duke William of Normandy defeated the Saxons under King Harold II and conquered England

Crécy (1346) Edward III of England defeated Philip VI of France, using archers to shoot his opponents

Agincourt (1415) Henry V of England defeated a much larger French army and captured Normandy

Orléans (1429) The French under Joan of Arc raised the siege of Orléans and began liberating France from England

Constantinople (1453) Ottoman Turks captured the city and ended the Byzantine (Eastern Roman) empire

Lepanto (1571) A Christian fleet defeated a Turkish fleet in the Mediterranean and halted Muslim advance on Europe

Spanish Armada (1588) England's navy fought off a Spanish attempt to invade and conquer

Naseby (1645) Parliamentary forces defeated Charles I during the English Civil War

Blenheim (1704) During the War of the Spanish Succession, British and Austrian forces stopped a French and Bavarian attempt to capture Vienna

Poltava (1709) Peter the Great of Russia fought off an invasion by Swedish forces led by Charles XII

Plassey (1757) An Anglo-Indian army defeated the Nawab of Bengal, beginning Britain's domination of India

Quebec (1759) British troops under James Wolfe defeated the French and secured Canada for Britain

Bunker Hill (1775) In the American War of Independence, British troops drove the Americans from hills near Boston

Brandywine Creek (1777) British troops forced American forces to retreat

Saratoga (1777) American troops surrounded a British army and forced it to surrender

Savannah (1778) Britain captured the port of Savannah from the Americans and gained control of Georgia

King's Mountain (1780) Americans surrounded and captured part of a British army

Yorktown (1781) A British army surrendered to a larger American force, ending the American War of Independence

The Nile (1798) British defeat the French in Abu Kir Bay, ending Napoleon's attempt to conquer Egypt

Trafalgar (1805) A British fleet defeated a Franco-Spanish fleet, ending Napoleon I's hopes of invading England

Austerlitz (1805) Napoleon I defeated a combined force of Austrian and Russian troops

Leipzig (1813) Austrian, Prussian, Russian and Swedish armies defeated Napoleon I, leading to his abdication the following year

Waterloo (1815) A British, Belgian and Dutch army supported by the Prussians defeated Napoleon I, ending his brief return to power in France

Fort Sumter (1861) In the opening battle of the American Civil War, Confederate forces captured this fort in the harbour of Charleston, South Carolina

Merrimack and *Monitor* (1862) This US Civil War battle was the first between two ironclad warships

Gettysburg (1863) Union forces defeated the Confederates, marking a turning point in the American Civil War

Vicksburg (1863) After a long siege, Union forces captured this key city on the Mississippi

Chickamauga (1863) At this town in Georgia, the Confederates won their last major battle

Chattanooga (1863) A few weeks after Chickamauga, Union forces won a decisive victory over the Confederates

Sedan (1870) Germany defeated France during a decisive battle in the Franco-Prussian War

Tsushima (1905) A Japanese fleet overwhelmed a Russian one, ending the Russo-Japanese War

Tannenberg (1914) At the start of World War I, two Russian armies invaded East Prussia, but were defeated by a German force

Marne (1914) The French and British halted a German invasion of France at the start of World War I

Ypres (1914–15) A series of German attacks on this Belgian town were beaten back with heavy losses on each side in two fierce battles

Verdun (1916) French forces under Philippe Pétain fought off a German attempt to take this stronghold

Jutland (1916) This was the major naval battle of World War I; neither Germans nor British won

Brusilov Offensive (1916) A Russian attack led by General Alexei Brusilov nearly knocked Germany's Austrian allies out of the war

Somme (1916) A British and French attack was beaten back by German machine-gunners; total casualties for both sides were more than 1 million

Third Battle of Ypres (1917) British and Canadian troops attacked German positions in order to drive the Germans back. Fighting took place in heavy rain and mud

Passchendaele (1917) This village was the furthest advance of the Third Battle of Ypres; casualties of both sides totalled 500,000

Fourth Battle of Ypres (1918) This was part of a general German offensive, which died down after heavy fighting

Marne (1918) French, US and British forces halted the last German attack of World War I

Britain (1940–41) In World War II, German attempt to eliminate Britain's airforce failed

The Atlantic (1940–44) Germany narrowly lost the submarine war against Allied shipping

Pearl Harbor (1941) In a surprise air attack Japan knocked out the United States fleet at Hawaii

Coral Sea (1942) In the first all-air naval battle, Americans thwarted a Japanese attack on New Guinea

Stalingrad (1942–43) The German siege of Stalingrad (now Volgograd, Russia) ended with the surrender of a German army of 100,000 men

El Alamein (1942) The British Eighth Army finally drove German and Italian forces out of Egypt

Midway (1942) An American fleet defeated a Japanese attempt to capture Midway Island

Normandy (1944) American and British troops landed in occupied France to begin the defeat of Germany; the largest-ever seaborne attack

Leyte Gulf (1944) In the biggest naval battle of World War II, an American fleet thwarted a Japanese attempt to hold on to the Philippines

Ardennes Bulge (1944–45) A final German attempt to counter the Allied invasion failed

Hiroshima and Nagasaki (1945) Two US atomic bombs dropped on these Japanese cities ended World War II

Inchon (1950) US forces defeated North Koreans during the Korean War

Dien Bien Phu (1954) Vietnamese defeated French in Indochina

Tet Offensive (1968) North Vietnamese and Viet Cong forces launched an attack against South Vietnam

Falklands (1982) A British seaborne assault recaptured the Falkland Islands following an Argentine invasion

Desert Storm (1991) A UN force including American, British and Arab units ended Iraq's invasion of Kuwait

Invasion of Afghanistan (2001) NATO forces led by the US invaded Afghanistan and overthrew the Taliban regime

Invasion of Iraq (2003) Forces led by the US invaded Iraq and overthrew Saddam Hussein

Index

C

D

E

F

G

H

I

J

K

L

M

N

O

P

Spirit
St Louis

Acknowledgements

The publishers wish to thank the following artists who have contributed to this book:

Martin Camm, Richard Hook, Rob Jakeway, John James, Shane Marsh, Roger Payne, Mark Peppé, Eric Rowe, Peter Sarson, Roger Smith, Ross Watton, Michael Welply, Michael White, Linden Artists, Maltings Partnership and Temple Rogers Agency.

The publishers wish to thank the following for supplying photographs for this book:
19br istockphoto.com, 23tl Dreamstime.com/Alessandro Bolis, 25b Dreamstime.com/Bryan Buovicki, 28bl istockphoto.com, 32bl stock.xchng.com, 39b istockphoto.com, 42b Dreamstime.com/Jenny Solomon, 51t Dreamstime.com/Gustavo Fadel, 54b Dreamstime.com, 55t Dreamstime.com, 57t Tall Tree Ltd, 61t Dreamstime.com/Marcus Brown, 67tr istockphoto.com, 68b Dreamstime.com, 70b Dreamstime.com/David McKee, 72b Dreamstime.com/Andrew Kazmierski, 82-83 Dreamstime.com/Michal Wozniak, 83tr Dreamstime.com/Craig Ruaux, 86b Dreamstime.com, 87 Tall Tree Ltd, 93bl Dreamstime.com, 98b Dreamstime.com/Hazlan Abdul Hakim, 100b Dreamstime.com, 107b Dreamstime.com/Chris McCooey, 111t istockphoto.com, 116b Dreamstime.com, 117t Dreamstime.com/Jorge Felix Costa, 127t Dreamstime.com, 128t istockphoto.com, 131tl Dreamstime.com/Gautier Willaume, 132-133t Dreamstime.com/Steve Lovegrove, 136b Digital Vision, 142t Dreamstime.com, 143t Dreamstime.com/Francois Etienne Du Plessis, 147t Dreamstime.com, 149t Dreamstime.com/Svetlana Larina, 153tr Dreamstime.com, 159br Dreamstime.com, 160b Dreamstime.com/Dainis Derics, 165 Dreamstime.com, 166c, b and 167tr ITN archive, 169tl Dreamstime.com, 174 Dreamstime.com/Paul Cowan, 176bl Dreamstime.com, 177t Dreamstime.com, 179br NASA, 181br Dreamstime.com, 182b Dreamstime.com/Svetlana Larina, 183t Dreamstime.com/Jakub Niezabitowski, 184b Dreamstime.com/Sitha Suppalertpisit, 185t Dreamstime.com, 187t istockphoto.com, 188b Dreamstime.com, 189tr Dreamstime.com, 190tr Dreamstime.com/Jenny Solomon, 191b Dreamstime.com/Bartlomiej Kwieciszewski, 192tr Dreamstime.com/Gabriele Sochor, 193b Dreamstime.com, 194b Dreamstime.com/Norman Chan, 195t Dreamstime.com, 197cr Digital Vision, 198cr Tall Tree Ltd, 199b Digital Vision.

Cover images:
Front: br Paul Almasy/CORBIS, bc Pete Turner/GETTY IMAGES, bl Ellen Rooney/Robert Harding World Imagery/CORBIS, c Paul Souders/CORBIS, tr David Turnley/CORBIS, tc Archivo Iconografico, S.A./CORBIS, tl Leif Milling/GETTY IMAGES.
Back: bl José Nicolas/Hemis/CORBIS, bc JJamArt/JJamArt/CORBIS, tl Gustavo Tomsich/CORBIS, tr Parallax Photography/CORBIS.
Spine: Charles & Josette Lenars/CORBIS.